T0339788

THE MAKING OF THE SLAVE CLASS

THE MAKING OF THE SLAVE CLASS

Jerry Carrier

Algora Publishing
New York

Library of Congress Cataloging-in-Publication Data —

Carrier, Jerry, 1948-
    The making of the slave class / Jerry Carrier.
        p. cm.
    Includes bibliographical references and index.
    ISBN 978-0-87586-768-7 (trade paper : alk. paper) — ISBN 978-0-87586-769-4 (case
laminate: alk. paper) 1. Social classes—United States. 2. Social stratification—United
States. 3. Poor—United States. 4. United States—Economic conditions. I. Title.
    HN90.S6C36 2010
    305.5'690973—dc22
                                2009054259

Printed in the United States

To my mother, who said I should, and my wife, who said I could

Glossary of Terms

Anomie: The state of an individual or society characterized by the breakdown of social norms, habits and values, as in the case of uprooted people. In this text it is used to describe the feeling of displacement and not belonging by people who move up in class.

Capture Theory: An economics theory that states that regulators one way or another become captured and work to promote the special interests of the people and institutions they are meant to regulate. In banking, for example, regulators will spend significant time learning the regulations as public employees and when they have mastered their craft they will cash in by becoming bankers and advising the bank how to avoid the regulations. (See Rational Ignorance.)

Charter Borrowing: Charging high rates on loans and financial services by lending in the name of an out-of-state bank to avoid state usury laws.

Community Action Agencies: These are nonprofit local corporations created by Congress during the 1960s War on Poverty. They deliver a variety of programs and services to the poor. They are also called CAP Agencies.

Community Development Corporations, CDCs: See nonprofits corporations.

Community Development Financial Institutions (CDFI): A program created and operated by the U.S. Treasury to fund community development activities and lending.

Community Reinvestment Act of 1977(CRA): An act of Congress forbidding banks and financial institutions from discriminating and withholding services from low income areas. (See redlining and the Home Mortgage Disclosure Act.)

Creation Theory: It is not really a theory but a belief. It is the Christian concept that god created the earth in seven days, and is contrasted to the rational, science-based Theory of Evolution.

Credit Union: Non-profit member owned democratic financial institutions which are allowed as co-ops under Section 501 (c) (4) of the U.S. Tax Code. They are regulated and insured by the federal government under the National Credit Union Administration. Community Development Credit Unions are special entities serving primarily low income people.

Cultural Universal: A widespread fundamental belief, true or not, that is unquestioned by the dominant culture.

Divine Right of Kings: A European Christian assertion that essentially said, "I am King because god chose me to be and you are a peasant because god chose you to be, and who are we to question god?" This then trickles down to a generalized belief that a person's status and wealth are god-given.

Fringe Banks: A variety of high interest, low service, under-regulated financial institutions that thrive in low income areas. These include payday lenders, loan sharks, car and household goods loans, rent-to own, pawn shops, etc., some of which are sometimes illegal.

Gentrification: The buying and renovation of houses and stores in low-income deteriorated neighborhoods by members of wealthier classes, thus raising property values but displacing low-income people.

GINI Index or Coefficient: A statistical measurement used to measure the inequality of wealth between the rich and poor in nations. The Index measures the wealth of the top 10% of a nation compared to the lowest 10% of a nation. The Index shows the unequal distribution of wealth in the United States lags behind all developed nations and is comparable to some third world nations.

Government Sponsored Enterprises (GSE): These are mostly nonprofit and some for profit corporations created by Congress. The most notable are the mortgage giants Fannie Mae and Freddie Mac.

Home Mortgage Disclosure Act (HMDA): A law passed by Congress to prohibit the discrimination of mortgage lending in low income areas and to people of color and ethnic minorities.

Housing Rehabilitation or Housing Rehab: The renovation of housing which is usually occupied by low income people.

Judicial Activist: A title given by Christian conservatives to a jurist who makes decisions not in keeping with Christian conservative beliefs.

Liar Loans or Income Stated Loans: A low-document mortgage loan granted based upon a statement of income by the borrower where no proof of actual income is given.

Matthew Effect: from the Bible verse Matthew 25:29, "For unto everyone that hath shall be given, and he shall have abundance. But from him that hath not shall be taken away even that which he hath." The term is sometimes used by sociologists to describe the fate of the poor in America.

Monetarists: Those economists who believe that controlling the nation's money supply will determine the direction of the economy. They are usually devotees of Adam Smith who believe in natural laws of economics and markets and dislike financial regulation.

Neighborworks: A nonprofit corporation created by Congress (See GSEs) to implement the CRA Act of 1977 (See CRA) The national corporation charters local housing, homeownership counseling and business lending nonprofits throughout the nation.

New Urbanism: Also known as Neo-Classical. It is a mixed-income 19th century style of urban development with multiple stories of mixed-use zoning including housing, office and commercial sharing building space. It is promoted as less land intensive and pedestrian friendly. It is frequently promoted as "green development" and anti-urban sprawl.

Nonprofit Corporation: A corporate charity set up under 501 (c) (3) of the U.S. Tax Code. These corporations when working in housing and community economic development are also called Community Development Corporations or CDCs.

Okies: A large group of Midwestern farmers who lost their farms in the 1930s' Dust Bowl drought and migrated en masse to California. The first group was from Oklahoma and thus, regardless of origination, they were all called Okies by the California locals. The word has become a derisive term in California to describe the working class.

Plunge Protection Team (PPT): Formally named the President's Working Group on Financial Markets, it was created by Executive Order 12631 in 1988 by President Reagan in the wake of "Black Monday" and the stock market collapse of 1987. The group's actions are secret and classified and they can take extraordinary methods in ordering the private market to covertly buy stocks, real estate and financial instruments on the government's behalf to shore up the financial markets when they are in crisis.

Poverty Pimp: A nonprofit or charity manager or director who is more interested in his salary and career than his client's needs.

Predestination: The belief that your destiny or fate is beyond your control or is controlled by others. In religious terms it is the belief that god controls fate and not the individual.

Pro-Family: Christian conservative label meaning to be against abortion, women's and gay rights and for a conservative Christian agenda.

Puritan Work Ethic: An American Christian and Puritan cultural universal that asserts that gain and wealth are deserved and come from hard work. "If any shouldn't work neither should he eat." It is part of the Christian ethic that induces the working class to "know their place and serve their masters well."

Rational Ignorance: A theory dear to some economists that holds that it is not realistic or rational to expect that the public can know or has the time to understand the complications of regulations governing industry and individuals that protect the public. Therefore the public will assume that the regulators are acting on their behalf, which frequently is not true. (See Capture Theory.)

Redlining: The act of banks and financial institutions of forbidding and withholding lending and financial services into low income areas by drawing red lines on loan officers' maps. (See self-cleaning ovens.) In 1977, Congress made this illegal by passing the Community Reinvestment Act. (See CRA.) The term has been also applied to grocery stores, drug stores and insurance companies for their refusal to serve low income areas.

Right-brained thinking: The ability to create and use inductive versus deductive reasoning. It is frequently associated with "big picture" thinking.

Schadenfreude: A word borrowed from German meaning to take a quiet and satisfied delight in the deserved misery of another.

Secondary markets: Financial institutions buy mortgages made by banks and mortgage companies which allows for greatly fluidity in the financial markets. The largest secondary markets are Fannie Mae and Freddie Mac (See GSEs)

Self-cleaning oven: A term thought to originate with the banking community whereby the withholding of all credit and money from a poor area would make the area so bad that the poor would be eventually forced to leave allowing for gentrification and profits by the bank. Forcing the poor out was described as "turning up the heat and cooking out the dirt," like a self-cleaning oven.

Southern Strategy: The Republican strategy first implemented by Richard Nixon to attract voters from the South and conservative Catholics who had been traditionally Democratic voters by changing the Republican Party philosophy to be against civil rights like the right to abortions and the rights of women, minorities and gays, and to promote the Christian conservative social agenda, including prayer and the teaching of "creation theory" in schools. Nixon called them the "Silent Majority." The Evangelist Pat Robertson would later change it to the "Moral Majority."

Social Darwinism: Based upon the work of an American sociologist Herbert Spencer who coined the term "survival of the fittest" (which is frequently misattributed to Charles Darwin's theory of natural selection) and the Theory of Evolution. Spencer argued that superior people and races achieve success because they are the "fittest." This theory has been adopted by Christian conservatives, many whom reject Darwin in favor of "creation theory" but have ironically accepted Social Darwinism to say why some people are wealthy and others are poor and to justify "free markets."

Telecommuting: Working from home or other remote locations away from the company workplace by means of computers and other electronic devices.

Upward Mobility: The false notion that anyone and everyone can rise in class and income in the United States.

U.S. 67 or McNamara's Hundred Thousand: These were the soldiers that were of marginal intelligence or were illiterates. The U.S. Army drafted them during the Vietnam War because so many middle and upper class young men had received exemptions from the draft that there was a shortage of soldiers. The character in the movie *Forest Gump* was based upon these men.

Values Voters: Mostly working-class voters who vote against their own economic interests by choosing candidates who advocate Christian Conservative social policies such as anti-abortion, anti-gay rights, prayer and creation theory in the schools. These candidates also advocate for policies such as no regulation of business and low taxes on the rich, policies which hurt working class voters. They are sometimes called the "Moral Majority." See *Southern Strategy*.

Voluntary Poor: Usually a middle-class or upper-class young person who has just completed college and is low income because of doing volunteer work or entry-level work while starting a career.

FOREWORD

Perhaps you may be offended by the premise of this book: that there is an American slave class, and that it is caused by our culture, particularly by our Christian culture, and by government policies that insure its continued existence. As the author, all I ask is that you read this book before making any judgment.

In addition there are some who may be outraged by the use of the word "slave" and the phrase "slave class," believing that these somehow belittle the brutality of pre-Civil War slavery. This book makes no such comparison. Slavery has many forms, some more brutal than others. And while some of the most brutal acts of American slavery occurred before the Civil War, these acts do not excuse or lessen the brutality committed on the current slave class, which includes but is not limited to many of the heirs of those pre-Civil War slaves.

TABLE OF CONTENTS

Chapter 1. The Not So Free Market

> The distribution of wealth "Is a matter of human institution solely. The things once there, mankind, individually or collectively, can do with them as they like."
> — John Stuart Mill

Adam Smith is said to be the founder of the free market economy and was arguably the father of American capitalism, so much so that it has been reported that during the inaugural functions of the "free market President," Ronald Regan, a large number of guests wore ties with Smith's likeness on them. What these followers of Smith, especially the Monetarists who currently are in economic favor, fail to realize is that the "free market" isn't free if the powerful and the wealthy own it and manipulate the market as they please, particularly to enrich themselves at the expense of many others.

Ironically, this was the conundrum that vexed their hero, Adam Smith. In developing his free market theories, Smith greatly feared that the wealthy and powerful would always restrict liberty and manipulate the free market if unchecked, and he could never wholly reconcile these fears or account for their power in a "free market." Mathematical theories and rationalization couldn't solve Smith's dilemma so he brought in a higher power for support. In this regard, Smith said that man "neither intends to promote the public interest, nor knows how much he is promoting it....He intends only his own gain and in this, as in many other cases, is led by an invisible hand."

Smith's rationalization was that the "invisible hand," which he defined as both natural law and divine intervention, would check their power. So far, this it hasn't seemed to work. Apparently neither god nor Herbert Spencer, the creator of social Darwinism and who coined the phrase "survival of the fittest," are economists. Despite this failure, capitalism and Christianity are married to each other in American culture.

The Archer Daniels Midland price-fixing scandal of the 1990s was one of the largest examples of corporate greed, power and corruption in history. The scandal was superbly documented by investigative reporter Kurt Eichenwald in his award winning book, *The Informant*. In the aftermath of the ADM scandal, Eichenwald summarized, "It has become evident that a free market left to its own devices would not be free at all, but enslaved to the whims of the powerful."

The American economy is, unfortunately, subject to the whims of the powerful, and as a result many are enslaved by its consequences.

In the US many see Adam Smith's invisible hand as divine intervention by the Christian god. In anthropological terms, it is thought that there is a cultural universal in America which leads Americans to believe that god has chosen which citizens deserve to be rich and powerful and which deserve to be poor and miserable. Americans inherited this cultural universal from their European ancestors. They called it the Divine Right of Kings. The Divine Right states that the King is the King because god chose him to be, and the peasants are the peasants, because god chose them to be, and who are we to question the wisdom of god? In America this concept was summed up very explicitly by the leader of the Mormon Church who not that long ago said, "There is a reason why one man is born white, rich and with many blessings, and another born black with very few, god has determined each man's proper reward."

And while he was condemned by many for his remarks, it wasn't because the majority don't believe his views, but rather they deemed him politically incorrect for bringing race into the question and for saying aloud what many quietly think and many more subconsciously believe. In his book *Blink*, Malcolm Gladwell calls this process "priming." It means that as people are exposed to certain negative words which we are culturally conditioned to respond to, we will then act to fulfill these self defeating prophesies. An example he gave was that African-Americans when asked to list their race on college testing would do more poorly on these tests than when they are not asked this question. They underperform because they are culturally conditioned to believe that they will perform worse than whites on these tests. Culture is a primary factor in determining an individual's success, much more so than intelligence or ability.

In 2006 the *Time* cover story was *Does God Want You to Be Rich?* The article highlighted the growing "prosperity" movement in American Christian churches which promote the philosophy that if you give the church money and are deserving, god will make you rich. The article reported that sixty-one percent of American Christians believed god could make you rich. Religion after all is the ability to see the folly of all other's beliefs but see none in your own.

In America, we believe that if you are rich it is because you deserve it, and if you are poor it is your fault. Our Puritan forbears made sure the American culture kept the Divine right of Kings, and also passed on another cultural universal; the Puritan Work Ethic, which states that all good comes from hard work. The great sociologist Max Weber in his work *The Protestant Ethic and the Spirit of Capitalism* stated that Protestantism and the "work ethic" gave birth to capitalism.

The "work ethic" is very entrenched in the American psyche. "If any shouldn't work, neither should he eat." The amusing thing about this quote is that it is has now become the backbone of American welfare policies, whereas it was originally intended to make the more wealthy, ambitious and greedy colonists quit searching for gold and help with the mundane labor of food production before they too starved. It had nothing to do with "lazy" common people, who were at the time trying to produce enough for everyone to eat, including the merchant class and aristocrats who were spending every waking hour searching for gold for their own gain.

Because of the "work ethic" Americans believe that hard work will result in success despite all evidence to the contrary. "Work your way to the top," we are told. But these phrases are as hollow as the gateway sign to Auschwitz which proclaimed, "Work will set you free."

The truth is that the hardest workers in the US are frequently the poorest and most miserable. Farm workers, a job no one would argue is easy, are born into poverty and almost all die in poverty or near poverty despite a long life of brutally hard work.

US service industry workers work very hard for very little compensation and are also not generally rewarded by either job satisfaction or significant promotion. Most don't even receive basic necessities like health insurance. Many work extra hours for no pay as is evidenced by the legal actions against, and the subsequent settlements, from large corporations like Wal-Mart whose workers reportedly were required to work "off the clock" before or after their shifts and during required lunch and rest breaks.

Many well-compensated managers will burden you with details of how hard their "pressure filled" jobs are and why they should be very well compensated for their work. Do you think that Larry Ellison, the former CEO of Oracle, whose annual compensation was well over $100 million, would trade places with a farm worker hoeing a sugar beet field twelve to sixteen hours a day even for his same Oracle pay? He would not.

The hardest workers in the US are generally paid the lowest wages and have the least benefits, few or no advancement possibilities, and little if any job satisfaction. They are required to work at inconvenient times of the day, and some are required to work extra hours sometimes for no pay to keep their jobs. Why do they do this work? They are slaves because they have no other economic choices. This is the American Slave Class.

Under the Divine Right of Kings it is propagandized that the hard work of the peasants generally goes unrewarded, therefore, it is claimed that if you work hard and serve your "masters" well, you may not be rewarded on earth, but you will be rewarded in an afterlife in heaven. One of the primary reasons why millions of Americans are by far more religious than their Canadian or European counterparts is that they are hoping for an afterlife that will be better than their hell on earth. It explains why the poorest people, in America, including the pre-civil war slaves, were and are the most religious.

Despite our long held "work ethic" views, very few American workers will work their way to a better life. America has a hard set and well established class system that we inherited mostly from the English, and which may now be more rigid than theirs. In 2005, the *New York Times* published a series about class and mobility in America which concluded that there was in fact very little upward mobility and "far less upward mobility than most economists or Americans believe."

Most Americans don't even believe they have a class system, despite their subconscious acknowledgement of these classes and their place in them. And most believe that a person can rise in class and income through hard work and talent, although for most it isn't true.

As Malcolm Gladwell stated so very well in his book *Outliers*, "We are too much in awe of those who succeed and far too dismissive of those who fail."

CHAPTER 2. THE AMERICAN CLASS SYSTEM

> "The concept of dignity, worth, or honor, as applied to either persons or
> conduct, is of first-rate consequence in the development of classes and of class
> distinction."—Thorstein Veblen: *The Theory of the Leisure Class*

Many Americans believe we don't have a class system and some believe it is
hidden. I happen to believe it is pretty apparent, if somewhat unconsciously, to
many Americans. The sociologist Paul Blumberg in his book, *Inequality in an Age of
Decline*, said class was "America's forbidden thought." Despite this we use class
everyday to assess and sum up people we meet. To prove the point: if I say mobile homes, apartments, laborers, lunch pails, bowling alleys, work uniforms, lay
away, rent to own, pawn shops, chewing tobacco, used cars, greasy spoon cafes,
and truck stops, most Americans know I am talking about the working class. If I
say soccer moms, the PTA, suburbs, brand name apparel, golf, chain restaurants
and public universities, most know I am talking about the middle class. And if I
say polo, one-of-a-kind designer clothing, tailored suits, Lear Jets, Bentleys and
Rolls, everyone knows I am talking about the leisure class.

Most sociologists agree there are three major classes in America: the working
class, the middle class, and the leisure or upper class. Most also agree that the
first two classes can be sub-divided into two more sub classes each: The underclass and blue collar workers (which also now includes service sector and retail
workers) are subsets of the working class, and the middle class can be divided
into a lower and upper middle class.

The popular myth holds that America is a "middle-class country," which is
not now true nor has it ever been true. For most of the nineteenth and twentieth

centuries the Europeans called America "a nation of farmers." It wasn't meant as a compliment. They meant we were a nation of, and led by, peasants, or a nation of working-class people, and for better or worse it is the reality.

The American class system is defined by cultural traits and by income. And although not all individuals will fit hard and fast into these designated categories, they generally apply to most people. There are fewer exceptions to these generalizations than most may imagine. As this book is being written, American incomes are falling as the country slides into recession, but the household incomes defining the classes and their subsets can be roughly divided according to the 2000 census roughly as follows: The underclass live in households earning less than $24,000. Blue collar worker households earn between $24,000 and $50,000. Lower middle-class households earn between $50,000 and $80,000. Upper-middle-class households make between $80,000 and $1 million. The leisure-class households earn more than $1million per year.

You may note the large range of income in the upper middle class. Although the range is quite large, this class contains only about 13% of the US population. And despite the income range they share the same economic cultural traits and behave very much the same on the upper and lower ends of this income spectrum, although the higher the income the individuals will began copying more leisure-class traits.

As a rule, most Americans inflate their class status as much as possible. Many working-class people claim to be middle-class and most upper middle-class claim to be upper class. These attempts to inflate their status are occasionally conscious but frequently are unconscious.

Using the 2000 Census income guidelines the classes break out as follows: The underclass has 73 million people or about 29.3% of all Americans. Blue collar workers have 69 million people or 27.4% of the population. This means that almost 57% of Americans are working-class people and live in households that earn less than $50,000 annually. We are, as I stated, a working-class rather than a middle-class nation. The working class is the largest and also the fastest growing class, which has accelerated during the current financial crisis as lower middle-class incomes fall.

Although the middle class are the minority it is their culture that is the dominant American class culture giving them advantages over the working class, and this status is preserved as the dominant culture largely because they work as the merchants, bosses and mangers that serve the needs and provide the profits of the very small but powerful and wealthy leisure class. The lower middle class has 73 million people which are 29.3% of Americans. The upper middle class has 32 million people, which is only 13% of the population.

The leisure class has 2.6 million people, which is 1%. Whereas the leisure class is very small in total population, their annual income is still much more than all the 73 million in underclass households combined. They are also in stasis meaning the population has been at one percent for a long time and is projected into the future at about one percent.

Also contrary to American mythology, these income groups or classes have very set limitations which allow for little mobility. This is due significantly to the fact they each class has very different cultures along with the income limits. The people in each of these classes behave remarkably alike and have many shared habits and preferences. These are called class traits.

Now some will argue that some rich people (leisure class) will act like some poor people (working class), or vice versa which may be true of a few individuals but is very rare. Someone who was not raised wealthy but has found a fortune will still exhibit the traits of their former class. And while we are exposed to things such as the television show *The Beverly Hillbillies*, there are actually relatively few exceptions to these classes and their confining incomes. This is why *the Beverly Hillbillies* television show was an interesting show to many Americans. One of the conclusions that can be made from the *New York Times* article *Class in America* is that class traits or behaviors are what define a both person's preferences, associations and income, which is an idea that many sociologists and anthropologists have held for years.

As previously noted, many if not most Americans inflate their class status. One of the reasons we believe we are a middle-class nation is that most of the blue collar working-class will claim to be middle class, while the upper middle-class will usually claim to be leisure or upper class. These individuals will even copy some of the behaviors of the class above them, particularly in purchasing something that may be unaffordable just to show off to others thereby reinforcing the idea that you are higher in class than you may actually be. This class inflation is summarized nicely in the American catch phrase, "keeping up with the Jones.'"

Before we go too far afield, it is important to deconstruct another American myth: that upper class is better than middle class, which is better than working class. Although the leisure class makes more money, which most find desirable, as a class their values or class traits are different than those of the working class but not better. For example, the dominant priority trait of the working class is people. The dominant priority trait of the middle class is their possessions, and the priority trait of the leisure class is rare, old or expensive items. In moral terms, which of these groups has the best dominant priority? In this case most of us would say the working class.

In looking at the classes it is important to know they are different than each other, not better than each other. Each class has some good and some bad class traits that define who these individuals are and how they behave. It is these behaviors that limit their associations and incomes. As an example I have often asked audiences for a show of hands of the people who think that the celebrity Paris Hilton is a better human being than they are. I have never had anyone claim that Paris Hilton is better despite the fact that she is a Hilton Hotel heiress and a member of the leisure class, and most of my audiences are Working or middle class.

I am a diversity lecturer and trainer and I have given many talks and presentations on the American class system, including many to groups of people of color. They are frequently amused that their "diversity trainer" is an old white man. I usually start out these presentations with the statement: "As bad as racism is, America is more classist than racist." This usually gets number of questioning looks, so I make my point by giving the audience the following test to prove my point. First, I tell them that they can be totally honest and that they only have to think of the answer and be honest with themselves. So here is the test:

You just got the job of your dreams and because of this you were able to buy the house of your dreams. In celebration of these two events, you decide to host a dinner party and invite your new boss and the neighbors — whom you haven't met. The neighbors turn out to be Dr. Huxtable and his wife Claire from the television Cosby Show, and I ask my audience would you have a problem with this?

I tell them that, surprisingly, even many white racists wouldn't have much of a problem with this. Why? Because Cliff Huxtable is a doctor and Claire is an attorney and they would probably come with a good bottle of merlot wine. You would have a pleasant time and your boss would have a pleasant time.

But what if you extended the invitation to your neighbors and instead of the Huxtables, Fred Sanford the junk dealer showed up with his old unemployed friend Grady from the television show Sanford and Son. Would you still feel comfortable? Most participants begin laughing or at least smiling at this point; they are not as comfortable with Fred as they are with Dr. Huxtable.

Why is this true? Is it race? Is Fred a thief? Will he hurt you? No, it is none of these. It is because Fred will embarrass you in front of the boss. You are afraid that the boss will think you are low class, "a dirt ball," that you are "trailer trash" or any one of a hundred put-downs. This is American classism. Class is one of the primary factors in how America socializes, works, and most importantly allocates wealth and other benefits.

Chapter 3. The Okies, a Case Study

> "Coming of age in San Francisco, I was always ashamed of my parents and resisted their down home ways. In my view they were Okies, and I was not an Okie. I was born in the city by the Golden Gate, where you saved your paper-route money to buy cashmere sweaters."—*James D. Houston, American writer*

Perhaps one of the most obvious examples of American classism and class discrimination was during the Great Depression and the Dust Bowl, whose story was told very well in John Steinbeck's novel, *The Grapes of Wrath* and captured in 1936 in a Pulitzer Prize winning photograph, Dorothea Lang's *Migrant Mother*.

After several years of drought on the central plains during the Great Depression of the 1930s, tens of thousands of farm families were forced to borrow against their farms to survive. With the continued multi-year drought and loss of crops, many lost their farms to the banks and were forced out of their homes by the county sheriff. They found themselves sitting on the rural roads outside their former homes with all of their possessions and usually with a Ford truck, which was the farm vehicle of its day. This occurred to thousands of farm families from Minnesota to Texas.

Since they were farmers, and the best climate and farmland in the United States was in the Central Valley of California, they made a nearly universal decision to migrate, and they stacked their possessions on those ford trucks and headed to California on Old Route 66, which went from Chicago to Los Angeles. Once in California they would leave Route 66 at Barstow on the Mojave Desert and head west to Bakersfield the city at the southern end of the great Central Valley of California. "The Land of Milk and Honey," they called it.

Since it was the Great Depression, California decided that it didn't want a bunch of poor working class people. In Barstow, men lined the street with clubs and weapons and told the farmers and their families they couldn't stop.

The first group of farmers to arrive in California were mostly from Oklahoma, so the new immigrants were all called "Okies" by the California residents, regardless of where they were from. And soon thereafter the Governor of California declared a state of emergency. They rounded up all the "Okies" and held them in concentration camps. No one protested this illegal incarceration of these farmers and their families who had broken no laws. They were not allowed to leave the camps except when local business people would hire them for the day. They were usually paid in pennies for a ten hour work day. Sometimes they were given a pound of flour for their work. Men, women and children in the camps went hungry and some died of starvation. *"Migrant Mother"* the Pulitzer Prize winning photograph taken by Dorothea Lange at the camps in 1936, shows a distraught woman with two starving little girls and an infant in her arms. The woman had been living for months on desert sparrows they captured and ate and a little flour they brought with them.

The camps were closed at the start of the Second World War and the Okies were set free. Most continued to live in California and they are still discriminated against. A used beat-up pickup truck in California is still referred to by many Californians as "an Okie Cadillac." Any poor white working-class person is still referred to as an Okie. In 2002 my daughter visited friends in California. They asked her where she would like to go, and she replied that she thought she would like to visit Barstow and Bakersfield where I, her father, had lived as a child. They replied, "Why would you want to go there? Only Okies live there."

The previously mentioned television show, *The Beverly Hillbillies*, was a show about this bias. The California writers and producers had the Okies in mind when the show was created. The opening story is the same as that of the Okies; a rural family loads all of its belongings on an old Ford truck and comes to California. Except the creators decided to make them rich from discovering oil on their property back home, so that they could demonstrate that even with money Okies were lesser people. The show was created to make fun of a working-class family. In their show the characters called the swimming pool the "cement pond" and kept ducks in it. They thought the billiard table was a fancy dining table and ate Sunday dinner on it. Jethro, a thirty something man, was so dumb he couldn't pass the sixth grade, and Granny was a superstitious old witch who made potions and moonshine, and Jed, the head of the family, spent all of his time hunting squirrels on his front lawn to the dismay of his Beverly Hills neighbors.

However, an interesting thing happened in that first season. The show, like most television, was watched by primarily working-class people across America and they identified with the "hillbilly" Clampet family. As the writers and producers began to understand their market, the show quickly changed from showing how low and pathetic the hillbilly family was to how "real and unpretentious they were." And the hero quickly became the wise old down-to-earth Jed Clampet the hillbilly, and the anti-hero became Mr. Drysdale, the Beverly Hills banker who only loved money and coveted Jed's. It also served to reinforce the American cultural universal that if you are good and deserve it, wealth will come. The Clampets were good hard-working folks, so they became rich.

CHAPTER 4. CLASS TRAITS

"God must love the poor, otherwise he wouldn't have made so many of them." — Mark Twain

Each class has a culture and these cultures do not overlap to the extent where there is a significant interaction by the classes. In a PBS program on classism that aired a few years ago a leisure-class man was asked why he didn't socialize with middle-class people. His reply, "If we invited them to a party, they would probably drink too much and urinate in the driveway." He wasn't being funny. He believed that this was a likely event. He also admitted that he didn't know any middle-class people. In the race of life, the Haves always start out ahead of the Have-nots. Recognizing his status as a member of the leisure class, a political opponent of President George Bush Sr. once quipped that the former President had started life on third base and assumed he had hit a triple.

As previously mentioned the dominant priority of the working-class is people. The working-class is focused on people and their needs. Their social structure is inclusive and neighborhoods and communities of working-class people tend to be places where everyone knows everyone else's business and everyone tends to interfere in everyone's lives. It is also a place where strangers as well as friends in need are likely to be assisted to the point where they will sometimes take needy friends and relatives into their households. Barbara Ehrenreich witnessed this trait in her nonfiction book *Nickel and Dimed.*

These traits are not true in middle-class communities and neighborhoods. The middle-class trait is to be self-sufficient and they will not usually involve themselves in the lives of their relatives or neighbors. They may in fact not know their neighbors other than to say a polite hello in passing. This is a primary difference between many inner-city working-class neighborhoods and the middle-class suburbs. There are some working-class suburbs which also function like the working-class inner-city neighborhoods, and there are a growing number of gentrified urban neighborhoods that function like middle-class and upper middle-class suburbs. We will discuss urban gentrification later.

Much of the culture and the class traits of the working class are driven by survival. With the underclass households making less than $24,000 per year, survival is of paramount concern. The time frame for the working class is immediate and deals with immediate needs and crisis, unlike the middle and leisure classes which can afford to focus more on the future. Money in working-class homes is meant to be spent on things you need or something you desperately want. Savings is not usually an option for households that have a very difficult time finding enough money to pay for the necessities of housing, food, medical care and transportation.

Money is also like a tool. You need to have enough of it to become comfortable and adroit at using it. The middle class and leisure class tend to believe that saving, budgeting and thrift are common sense behaviors that everyone knows or should know. However, these are learned behaviors, usually taught in middle- and leisure-class households where there is enough money to practice with. Fiscal literacy is like reading, it is taught, and it is not something one acquires at birth. Unfortunately most schools, which should help fill this need, do not have fiscal literacy programs.

The working-class often sees life as fate based, believing that fate, not choice, plays a determining role in their destiny. It is understood that if you are poor, it is because god meant you to be poor. I grew up in a poor working-class household and still have close relatives who make statements like, "I will never be rich and if I ever did, someone would just steal it from me anyway." Or: "I will never be able to have my own house." "I will never be able to go to college." And if you don't believe you can do these things, you won't. They are self-fulfilling prophesies.

Sociologists sometimes refer to this as the "Matthew Effect," based upon the Bible verse Matthew 25:29 which says: "For unto everyone that hath shall be given, and he shall have abundance. But from him that hath not shall be taken away even that which he hath."

In Christian-dominated America, with so many using the literal interpretation of the Bible, particularly among the working class, this verse and the prevailing attitudes that come from it condemn the poor to certain poverty. Fate is a very important dynamic in understanding the limits of the working class. Because it is so ingrained in our culture even working-class people that are not

Christian or religious still subconsciously believe that they are not deserving of a better life. Most social workers and nonprofit employees working with the working class say that instilling this belief that the working class can, and that they deserve better, is the first hurdle to overcome in improving the lives of the poor and working class.

The fate-based philosophy of the working class is strong and gave rise to another class trait, the working-class fear and hatred of authority. If you believe that others control your destiny and they can change your life on a whim, then you are likely to both fear and hate this authority.

Many people feel this way about police, for instance, and for a wide variety of reasons. Recent immigrants speaking limited English know that being pulled over for a simple traffic violation may lead to humiliation and the certainty they cannot defend themselves before the judge. A number of US cities are well-known for police brutality (particularly against people of certain races); and anyone who might be mistaken for an Arab or a Muslim also has good cause to distrust the authorities.

I worked with a large suburban police department not long ago that was having trouble with the new Russian-speaking immigrants. "They all have an attitude and act as if they dislike us," several officers told me. I asked them how they would behave if they had lived under the KGB or in any country where the police were understood to be keeping an eye on you, not "protecting" you, and they began to approach the Russians in a more positive, less confrontational and friendly manner. After that, some progress was made.

When working-class Americans are stopped by the police, they know the officer can pretty do as he likes and they are usually powerless to act. They will not likely retain, nor could they afford, legal counsel to protest and their experience tells them that the officer's word will be taken more seriously in court than theirs. And even something as small as a speeding ticket may mean severe consequences and the payment of a fine which could prevent the working-class person from paying rent, buying food or making a car payment. Because of this powerless and the consequences of such a confrontation, they will fear and hate this authority.

This is a very different mindset than that of the middle class, who generally respect authority, and the leisure class, who tolerate authority as protectors of their person and of their property. A speeding ticket to a middle-class or a leisure-class person is an inconvenience, it is not a life-changing event. And if an officer did abuse his authority, these upper classes can afford to take legal remedies and are much more likely to have their word accepted over that of a police officer. The hierarchy of credibility in a court of law goes something like this: a doctor, a police officer, and last, an unemployed worker. Judges tend to be upper middle-class people themselves, and naturally they favor and relate to their own.

I remember sitting in court waiting to give testimony on another issue, when a working-class woman came to fight a speeding ticket. I had spoken to her earlier. Since she couldn't afford a babysitter, she had brought her four children with her. Before she made her statement, the judge interrupted her with, "I see we had to bring the entire clan today." This remark did several things: First, it said that the judge felt she and her family were hillbillies; second, that they were not welcome in court; and third, they were not likely to be heard or have justice—and they didn't. Courts, like most US institutions and businesses, have a middle-class culture and working-class people are made to feel unwelcome and out of place.

Schools are one of the middle-class institutions that most negatively affect the working class and this brings to mind another class trait, language. The language of the working-class is casual, and the language of the middle class and leisure class is formal.

Early on in school, children learn they cannot use the language of the street, casual language, in school. It isn't tolerated. Young workers learn that this language isn't tolerated in most jobs, except in exclusively working-class environments such as blue collar construction work or the military.

And the casual or street language most unacceptable to the middle class and the leisure class is swearing, or the so called "four letter words" which are frequently used by the working class. These words are also used by the middleclass and the leisure class but much less in public settings. For example it was revealed in his White House Tapes that Richard Nixon used these expletives on an everyday basis. The use of these words have become American cultural taboos, however these taboos have lessened over time.

Language rules, like all manners are largely arbitrary and are dependent on class. They are social indicators of our class and to weed out those who are not of the "right" background. There are many different kinds of expletives some referring to parts of the anatomy, and while these terms are acceptable in working class settings such as the military or some blue-collar jobs, they are forbidden in middleclass settings like the public schools. English is a language of complex heredity, combining words derived from Celtic, Germanic, Latin, Norman French, and other roots, with a great many foreign borrowings as well. Historically, the Celtic and some Anglo-Saxon people were "commoners" or working class with the upper classes being members of, or representatives of, the Roman Empire and later the French speaking Normans. Therefore the longer, Latin-based and Germanic words are considered relatively polite terminology while the shorter words typical of the Celtic languages have been declared crude and unacceptable.

America's class system is derived from England's, and the social interpretation of how one speaks carries these biases.

Not that long ago I was asked to do a class presentation to a group of public nurses who have to deal with bodily functions as part of their jobs. The truth is that many of their patients were unfamiliar with any but the short working class Celtic versions, while the nurses in their middleclass environment were supposed to use words like "urinate." Here, a small class difference can mean we are truly worlds apart.

Food and clothing provide more class cultural differences. In working-class households, food is primarily about quantity. In homes where there is a struggle to pay bills and buy necessities, getting enough food is paramount. If you lived in a house where you were asked such questions as: "Did you get enough to eat?" or "Would you like seconds? or "Thirds?" it means that you either grew up in a working-class home, or your parent, grandparent, maid, or the nanny asking you this question was working class. Working-class folks wouldn't mind going to a church or school pot luck supper, but many middle-class and leisure-class people would consider this "slumming," and would complain about quality versus quantity.

In middle-class households food is primarily about quality. "Did you like it?" "Is it fresh?" "Is it organic?" "Is it free of bovine hormones, pesticides and herbicides?" And so forth.

A Woody Allen joke from his standup comedian days demonstrates this difference. Woody Allen grew up in a poor working-class area of New York City, the Garment District. He talked about his poor aunt and uncle who would save their money all year to be able to go out to a nice restaurant every year for their anniversary. Because going to a restaurant was so rare, Woody's extended family would gather around every year when they got home to hear the tale of their night out at a restaurant. One year Woody recalled that his aunt proclaimed, "It was terrible! We spent so much money and the food was inedible!" To which Woody's uncle replied, "Not only was it inedible, but the portions were way too small."

To them, the quantity was much more important than the quality—even if it was inedible.

In the leisure class, food is about presentation. There is a story that during the Reagan Administration that the President and Nancy were invited to a very exclusive Boston upper-class event. They commissioned a well known sculptor to fashion a life sized bust of Ron and Nancy Reagan out of ice as the center piece of the head table. This made the statement that they could afford not only to hire a well-known sculptor, but to hire him to create a work of art just to watch it melt.

The attendees later joked that Nancy never did melt. This was their leisure-class way of stating that Nancy didn't really belong to their class. The President didn't either, but it is considered poor form to insult the President.

Clothing habits are also different for each class and are subconscious identifiers to which class we belong. Working-class clothing is personal and casual and used to express the individual and their individual tastes, which frequently includes ethnic styles and dress. Working-class dress may include odd or plentiful jewelry and piercings, tee shirts with humorous or other statements, and individual styles of dress like "the man in black." Working-class attire is frequently considered either too casual or too "loud" for middle-class settings, including jeans or sweat suits, or suggestive clothing such as short skirts and plunging necklines and tight pants or shorts, bright colors and other features that may be considered odd, distasteful or unfashionable to current middle-class tastes.

The middle-class is about "dressing for success" and their dress demonstrates their social status or the status they wish to achieve. It is not about the individual, but about "fitting in" or "being appropriate." Current styles and labels are very important. To the middle class, clothing and dress are possessions and possessions are a most important priority. For example, most offices are middle-class institutions and even in those without a dress code, there is an expectation that people will dress a certain way. Even on "casual Friday" when employees are allowed to wear jeans, the brand of jeans may be more important than the dress slacks, the dress or the pants suit worn during the other days of the week.

Leisure-class dress is about style, artistic taste, designer labels, high prices, and individuality. Clothing is tailored and is one of a kind.

Another cultural trait of the working class is the household gender structure. In working-class households, the structure is matriarchal. In the middle class it is more often patriarchal, and in leisure class households it can be either, depending upon which spouse has the higher social status. So what does this mean?

Working with schools and teachers, I have often told them it is best when working with working-class households to begin conversations about a child with Mom rather than Dad, because Mom usually makes all household decisions and most decisions about the children in working-class homes.

The exclusion of fathers in this decision making may be part of why there are many more single women with children in the working-class than the other classes, particularly in the underclass, although there are strong financial reasons to explain this as well. While it is true that most households need two incomes to make a middle-class income or in many cases even a blue collar income, underclass households may have a larger percentage that are female-headed because working-class households are matriarchal, and the principal role of the male is to be the "bread winner." If the "bread winner" isn't making a substantial contribution to the household, he may feel useless or redundant and leave. It may also be the reason that some young women with children choose not to marry the fathers of their children.

In middle-class American households, the male is usually dominant. Remember the television show *"Leave It to Beaver?"* When Beaver inevitably got into trouble, his mother June would turn trustingly to Ward, Beaver's father, and say, "Ward, I am worried about the Beave." And wise old Ward, with his sweater and pipe, would solve Beaver's problems.

In the leisure class it is about social status. A current example: Governor Arnold Schwarzenegger is a member of what family? The answer is, of course, the Kennedy family. Although he is a Schwarzenegger, and his wife Maria is a Shriver, her mother was a Kennedy; and since the Kennedy family has higher social standing than either of the Shriver or Schwarzenegger families, so despite the fact he was elected Governor of California, he is proud to be a member of the Kennedy family.

Place and housing are areas of major differences in class cultures. Later we will look more at housing and the geography of class, but housing needs to be mentioned here as we continue to define the culture of the working class. Housing for the working class is shelter, whereas the middle and leisure classes view housing more as an investment.

The housing and mortgage crisis would have been different if the middle and the leisure class and their lenders had also viewed housing principally as shelter rather than as investment opportunities. The irony is that the working class was blamed for the housing crisis and the bad loans. Many people, such as Congresswoman Michele Bachmann of Minnesota, said that the housing bubble was caused by the government forcing banks to give loans to the poor and "on the basis of race and little else."

These critics ignore the fact that much of the housing bubble was due to failures of "low-doc" and "income stated loans" (called "liar loans" in the mortgage trade). These higher income, good credit applicants usually greatly inflated their incomes on their applications without the banks verifying them. In fact, many lenders actually told these borrowers how much income they would have to put on their applications, whether that income was real or not, so they could obtain the loan. The banks did this because they were making higher fees on these loans and could usually sell the loans off to others without consequences to themselves, while their regulators looked the other way. In fact, there is some evidence to suggest that the regulators actually encouraged these loans. We will explore this and its consequences a little later.

Housing is also much more casual for the working class and more formal for the middle and leisure class. That is to say that working-class housing tends to be a gathering place and a place to socialize, and drop-in guests are welcome, while most guests in middle- and leisure-class homes guests tend to be by invitation only. Even the furnishings and room set up of the middle and leisure class is dominated principally by style and appearance versus the practicality of "everyday" use in working-class homes. In summary, in middle-class and leisure-class homes it is more "look and don't touch."

Working-class homes are likely to have intergenerational and extended families and friends living in them, which is not common in most middle-class homes.

My Irish-American grandmother used to say that in a "Shanty Irish" home (working class), you had at least one uninvited guest for every meal, whereas in a "Lace Curtain Irish" home (middle class) you were "damn lucky to get invited for tea." I remember many, many uninvited guests present for meals at my grandparent's table, including me, my parents and my five sisters; although to their credit my grandparents would never have thought of us as guests.

Since we were also poor, the eight of us lived with my grandparents for several spells, in their little three-bedroom house, as did many other relatives at different times, including my great grandmother, my single uncle, my divorced aunt and her two children, my Great Uncle, and my Dad's cousin and his family, and an elderly blind woman whom we called "auntie" (she was some kind of a shirttail relative). Fortunately for my grandparents we didn't all live there at the same time, but it probably seemed like it to them.

The eight of us, me, my parents and five sisters also lived several times with my other grandparents in their small three bedroom home, along with my uncle who was just a few years older than I. My uncle and I slept in the unfinished basement.

In my early twenties, while I was going to college fulltime and working full time, there were relatives that needed to live in my house. In addition to my wife and three children, my sister-in-law and her two children moved in with us after her divorce because she had nowhere else to go. My young brother-in-law also lived with us for a time when he was going through some trouble. And my youngest brother-in-law and sister-in-law spent so much time there it was as if they lived with us. And few years later after I had graduated from college and was starting my career, I was living in a small three bedroom house with my wife and now four children, and my youngest sister-in-law moved in with her child after her divorce.

Working class homes are not occupied in the same manner as middle-class or leisure-class homes and their living arrangements are sometimes illegal according to local law. Frequently these households are in violation of rental leases, zoning, overcrowding, health and building code regulations, which typically deal with the number of persons per room, or number of persons per bathroom, or the square footage of space per person and "unrelated individuals in the household." These regulations frequently seem ridiculous to working-class people, who believe that leaving their relatives or friends living on the street is a much more significant crime than having them live in their overcrowded homes.

When I was working as the director of a large affordable housing nonprofit corporation in a large city, we had many low income clients with owner occupied homes which contained too many people to meet the city's zoning, building and health codes. However, my organization was the city's largest provider of housing rehabilitation and reconstruction, so we had extra clout with the city and in most circumstances we were able to get the city officials to overlook minor things during building inspections and work with us and the household on the major problems. In fact, this was one of the things that attracted clients to our nonprofit: we were seen as their protectors against the city authority. It is also interesting to note that by design we were a working-class organization, and not a middle-class one like the city. Our language, dress and attitude reflected working-class culture.

In fact a condition of success for nonprofits working in owner occupied affordable housing is that their clients feel comfortable in their institutions and must trust that the nonprofit will not report them to authorities for building code, health or sometimes even immigration violations. These clients realize that if their house is found overcrowded they must force family members to leave to comply, or in the case of building code violations, in order to stay in their own house, they could be forced to make repairs they can't afford. The nonprofit's reputation in protecting clients in these matters is paramount to their success in these programs. And generally unless there is something too egregious, most housing nonprofits will never report these violations.

These rules do not apply as stringently for rental units. If someone is making money or attempting to make money from housing, they are under both a legal and a moral obligation to provide decent, safe and sanitary housing — although I will grant that there may be a few little old ladies renting out one half of their dilapidated owner-occupied duplexes, to supplement their small pension or out of a similar concern to avoid having someone sleep on the street.

An affordable-housing nonprofit has to start with the philosophy that people may be better off in their own dilapidated and overcrowded home than on the street. In many years in this business I can only think of a couple of occasions when I broke this trust and reported violations, and I did because there were severe and immediate threats to children. In both cases I was able to tip off a friendly social worker "who just happened to come over unannounced" to find the problem so the nonprofit wouldn't be blamed, and then in both cases I then worked with the family and their social worker to successfully resolve the problems to allow the families to remain in their housing without penalty.

In poor and minority communities, there is always a concern with the U.S. Census about under-counting. That is to say that poor and minority populations are never fully counted. When the census is conducted these large working-class households will not report additional friends or family members in the household because they either consider them temporary, or are afraid that by revealing their true household numbers or conditions they will be reported for building code violations (despite assurances to the contrary by the Census, who also have a policy of not reporting and keeping confidential the results of individuals in the census).

The working class isn't likely to report "lacking some or all plumbing facilities" or "overcrowding" to the Census if they know they will be reported to authorities and forced out of their housing. And despite the Census policy to not report these violations, many households still refuse to report these conditions.

Education is also a major area of class cultural differences, and while all three classes value education, they do so in different ways and with different expectations. The working class believes that education is largely attainable only by the very smart or very rich. Since the working class largely believes that fate determines what they will be and the success they will have, education may be seen then as making little difference in their lives.

Many social studies have shown little differences in intelligence between classes, and there are many working-class people with high intelligence. When the working class see middle-class people of the same or less intelligence doing better than them, especially their bosses who have usually obtained these positions because of training and education that wasn't available to the working class, they may find this as grossly unfair. This leads to working-class anti-intellectualism, frequently an attitude that is passed onto their children. The derision of "book learning" and "eggheads" in working-class households is a disabling class trait. And it is another of many barriers a working-class child must overcome to get an education.

This anti-intellectualism has real consequences. In his book, *The End of Work*, Jeremy Rifkin quoted the U.S. Department of Education that one of every three Americans is functionally, marginally, or completely illiterate, with 20 million reading at a fifth grade level or less, and another 35 million reading at less than a ninth grade level.

Lonely is the man who leaves his family because of a change of location or a change of class. Neither of my grandfathers graduated from elementary school. My father didn't graduate from high school. I was the first to graduate from high school and I was the first to go to and graduate from college. My father, as proud as he was of my accomplishment, was still very derisive about my education because he was so anti-intellectual and class conscious. It was for him a matter of me either denying or out growing my class. Although I was very conscious about not using my education around my father, he never failed to bring it up in conversation, as in "Is that the type of crap they teach you in college?" Or if I made an error or a mistake, "Apparently they don't teach common sense in college," which of course most college graduates know they don't.

Now, it may appear that because I graduated from college and came from this poor background that I am contradicting myself about working-class mobility and limitations, so please allow me to expand upon my situation.

I was born in Minnesota, but I spent a good part of my childhood in California. My father changed jobs very frequently, like most underclass households, and when he changed jobs we would move to wherever his new job was located. I went to six different elementary schools in the seven years from kindergarten through the sixth grade. We often changed schools not at the end of school years, but rather whenever Dad changed jobs. In the third grade, when multiplication and division are taught, I missed several months when we changed schools, and then I attended a ghetto school with an extraordinary number of migrant farm workers. They didn't teach us multiplication and division, but instead we spent the year learning to make change as if we were cashiers at a fruit and vegetable stand — apparently the highest position you could reasonably expect to achieve as a farm worker's child.

In the fourth grade, I moved to a school where the students had already learned multiplication and division. My teacher, upon discovering my lack of math skills, told me I was lazy and stupid. And rather than instructing me in these subjects, he assigned me extra math homework, apparently thinking that volume would somehow overcome his lack of teaching. Fortunately, I was intelligent enough to learn multiplication and division on my own, but I have disliked math and my fourth grade teacher ever since. He made my life miserable that year, so I returned the favor.

The following year I was placed in a class of "delinquents and trouble makers." In this class we could achieve a grade of C for coming to class and "shutting-up." At the time, this was fine by me.

Unlike my classmates, many of whom were as smart as I was, I was an "egg-head." I liked to read. I would read anything, cereal boxes, children's books, adult's books and even text books, although no one seemed to notice or care, except for my mother who encouraged my reading. I loved the library, and fortunately most librarians liked me. I read most of the children's classics and all of Mark Twain before I finished elementary school. When I was in the seventh grade my grandparents, who had dreamed of being educated, bought a set of *Great Books of the Western World* and the first of these I read was Cervantes' *Don Quixote*. I continued through the *Great Books* and also read William Shirer's epic *The Rise and Fall of the Third Reich* while in eighth grade. I was reading Voltaire and books on religion in the ninth grade. My grades in school were average and I was bored most of the time. I was a working-class "egghead" who didn't fit in at school. My working-class classmates thought I was odd. And it seemed incongruous to most of my middle-class teachers that a child on the free lunch program could read, and dismissed me as "white trash" and largely ignored me. In school I felt like a trained monkey, like a pet. I knew that I was supposed to fulfill the schools meager expectations and nothing else, and because of this, I hated school. I was always told I was bright, but that I didn't "apply" myself. Part of this was true. I had written a paper on communism in seventh grade because I had just read Marx in the Great Books. I received an A on the paper. I turned in that paper for credit in the eighth, ninth, and tenth grades, so that my chosen reading wouldn't be interrupted by "their damn" school work.

In addition to moving and poverty I had other distractions. I went to work at the age of twelve as a dishwasher and busboy in a railroad depot to help my family out. By the time I was in high school I was working a full time job. School was a distant second to my "real" job which brought in the much needed money to buy food. My biggest ambition at that time was to get a decent job on the railroad.

In tenth grade my father was out of work. He decided to leave California and return to Minnesota where I was born and where most of my extended family lived. Because of the move, I had to drop out of school the middle of tenth grade. Fortunately my social studies teacher, who had taken an interest in me, persuaded the school and pushed me to test out the remainder of the year. He knew I would do well in these tests and I did. This allowed me to continue high school the following year in Minnesota in the eleventh grade. I might have dropped out if not for his efforts.

My situation in Minnesota worsened. My father's alcoholism and gambling addiction was becoming progressively worse and our financial situation was deteriorating. We lived in a small town and my father was looked upon as the town drunk and our family as "white trash."

Like many small town groceries of the time, families could buy food on credit. When our unpaid bill reached a significant amount, the grocer had a word with my father. The grocer offered to allow me to work off the family's debt, and since my father had no other choice, he agreed. The other seven stock boys at the grocery were there for the same reason.

While the grocer was a decent man, he was in business for his own gain. The going rate for working in a grocery at the time was the minimum wage, $1.25 an hour. The grocer paid me and the other stock boys sixty cents an hour. Half of my earnings went to pay the existing debt, and I was given the other half each week, which he knew would be spent in his store on food for my family. He knew this to be true because it was for all his stock boys. The stock boys were in practicality nothing more than indentured servants.

I am not complaining, as it significantly helped my family, and after the debt was cleared I was eventually able to persuade him to pay me the going rate by threatening to work for his hated competitor. To his credit, rather than being angry about it, he told me I had ambition and gave me the raise, but only on the condition that I didn't tell the other stock boys. After high school he offered me the opportunity to apprentice as a butcher, which I turned down because my family was relocating again. Most working-class workers don't receive this generosity or opportunity from their employers. The other stock boys didn't get this offer.

The respect that the grocer had in the community was enormous. In addition to owning the grocery store, he was part owner of several businesses in town including the bank, and he sat on the bank board. I believe he also sat on the hospital board. The interesting thing about the grocer and my father is that they were both alcoholics; but the grocer was a middle-class man with money. However, when it came to hard work, few men (including the grocer) could out-work my father.

This is a good place to dispel another myth. A few years ago, I was giving a presentation on poverty to a group of conservative businessmen. In the question and answer session that followed, a very successful business owner asked, "Isn't it true that most of the poor are poor because they are drunks and drug addicts?" My answer was no.

The rate of chemical dependency among the different classes is remarkably the same. It is somewhere between eight and ten percent of the population in each class. I asked this man and my audience if he or anyone else in the room did not know of at least one middle-class person with a chemical dependency problem. None raised their hands. I had made my point.

Does chemical dependency affect the classes differently? Yes, it does. And the grocer and my father are the examples.

A middle-class and leisure-class person can afford their rent, their food and their other necessities and they can also afford their addictions, whereas a working-class person struggles and frequently cannot afford their rent, food, medical care or their addictions. And be assured that a chemically dependent person, regardless of class, will always take care of their addictions first. It is part of the disease. However, if you can afford these addictions, society will treat you much better. The grocer, it was said by the townsfolk, "drank too much occasionally because he worked so hard." But I can assure you that he never worked as hard as my father.

Back to education: In high school, I began to really take notice of the different treatment that the classes received. One day three teachers, pretending to talk among themselves, said loudly enough to make sure I would hear, "There is no use investing education in that one, he'll turn out just like his father." In response to my anger, they laughed and walked away.

Later, one of these teachers tried to goad and provoke me into fighting him so he could expel me from school, and when this failed, he told me he would eventually find a way to do it. This kept up for about a year. He was so cruel that when the school principal overheard him one day, he told the teacher that he was forbidden to speak to me outside of school and was only allowed to speak to me in the classroom if it was about school work. The teacher was also told that I had better receive a passing grade or that his teaching contract would not be renewed. I received an average C, although my tests had warranted a better grade. That teacher moved to a better job at a large suburban school the next year.

In high school, I had two friends and we spent a lot of time together. Two of us were poor working class and the third was the middle-class son of a successful merchant. His great grandfather was the town's founder. His father was small town royalty, making him the same. It was to my friend's credit that he made friends outside his class. We were all bright and capable, but to be truthful, the middle-class friend was less capable than me and my other working-class friend. He was also much less interested in hard work. He was made to work in his father's business a few days a year during vacations and summers and pouted like a baby. We made fun of him for it. My other friend worked summers. But neither of my friends worked during the school year, while I worked full time. I was also allowed and encouraged to leave school early for my job, since the school had determined that menial work was my destiny anyway.

Sometimes, for fun, I would do both of my friends' physics home work which they found difficult. I wasn't in the physics class, being dubbed too stupid. Instead, I was in the Business Math class, which was similar to my third grade math, and amounted to training to be a cashier in a grocery store.

My working-class friend, who had good grades, was smarter and harder working than our middle-class friend, and unlike me he catered to his teachers and always did everything that was expected of him in school. He was, in the words of our teachers, "a perfect gentleman." He got good grades, but not as good as our middle-class friend who, upon receiving a B or even a C, would complain to his father, who would then go to the teacher and the grades would be upgraded. Teachers were well aware of the merchant's status and his influence with the school board.

The results: The two kids who worked harder and were brighter received nothing and our middle-class friend got three scholarships for college despite the fact that his father could more than afford to send him. He went to college. It wasn't based on merit; it was based on class. If he were asked today, he would acknowledge that his two working-class friends were brighter and more deserving. My working-class friend and I didn't go to college after high school. Neither of us could afford it, nor did we think we could get into college. After some tough times and being rejected by his father, my friend moved in with my family and when we moved shortly after graduation, he moved and lived with us.

After high school we both went to work in a canning factory that paid $1.35 an hour. We worked sometimes twenty-hour days with no overtime pay. It was a form of slavery, since there was no other work to be had. This was during the Vietnam War and draft-aged boys had difficulty finding work since employers knew they could spend time training them only to watch them be drafted, and then the employer would have a legal obligation to hire them back if they returned from Vietnam two years later.

Malcolm Gladwell in his book *Outliers* states that intelligence and hard work are never enough to insure success; it also takes luck and opportunity. My friend and I both got lucky and received our opportunity. It was 1967 and I was drafted at the age of eighteen into the Army. My friend was so dissatisfied with his lot in life, and knowing that he too would be drafted shortly, joined the Marines.

At first glance, this doesn't seem that good of an opportunity. While the Vietnam War raged, middle-class and leisure class boys sought the shelter of college or the military reserves. Most of the reserves were not sent to combat during the Vietnam War; their ranks were filled with people like George W. Bush, whose influential families were using the reserves so their sons could avoid Vietnam. It was rumored that you had to "know somebody" to get into the reserves and it was strongly rumored in working-class circles that you sometimes had to pay to join the reserves. Vietnam was fought almost exclusively by young, poor, working-class boys. The average age of the combat troops in Vietnam was nineteen.

There is a scene in the television show *China Beach* about the Vietnam War where the old sergeant is contemplating his troops and says: "I served in World War II with doctors, teachers and lawyers. I served with them in Korea, but here in Vietnam its poor black kids, poor white kids, and big dumb farm boys." It was true.

After training, I had orders to go to Vietnam, but when the North Koreans pirated the US ship the *Pueblo* in international waters, my orders for Vietnam were cancelled and I was sent on emergency orders to the Republic of Korea, where I was much safer than my friends in Vietnam. My friend who went into the Marines served two and a half tours in Vietnam before he could get discharged. He was decorated for his service and he suffered bad health and mental problems for the rest of his short life. But it was also because of this service that we both finally got our opportunity; we had earned the G.I. Bill, and we both could finally go to college.

As a twenty-year-old veteran with the G.I. Bill, I thought it would be easy to get into college. I was wrong. I didn't have the right college prep classes. I lacked the math requirement (apparently learning to make change doesn't count). I was denied access to the University of Minnesota. A friend told me I would get the same G.I. Bill benefits at a junior college, so that is where I enrolled. I completed two years with a high grade point average before the University would accept me.

Being twenty, working class and a veteran, I was also of the "marrying age." My father, for example, was nineteen when I was born. It was expected in the 1960s that people in the working class would be married young. I met Kathy and we were married as I began college. She had just graduated from high school and was also from a working-class family. She was the first in her family to go to college too. My first three children were born in short order while I was in school. In our defense, birth control was not as reliable then as now. Kathy attempted to stay in school after the birth of our first child, but when we became pregnant with the second child, she had to give it up. Kathy would return to college and finish her degree when our youngest and fourth child began school full time. During college I worked full time nights and weekends, and went to school full time during the day, while Kathy was home working full time with first two, then three babies, and she also cared for two other children for extra money. The G.I. Bill was enough to pay my school costs, but it didn't support my family.

A word about my motivation is in order. As much as I loved books and liked to read, my main motivation wasn't about education, and as I now look back upon it, it had more to do with my awakening understanding of class barriers. I saw college as a barrier separating working-class people like me from the easier, more pleasant lives of the middle class and I was insistent that I would cross this barrier and get what I thought my family deserved.

This insistence is not a common working-class trait, and it is sometimes called "the chip," as in "there is a chip on his shoulder." It is not a measure of a willingness to work harder; there are others without this "chip" that have to work much harder; and it isn't about character, because I believe that it takes much more character to raise a family as a farm worker. It is simply a different attitude and a rejection of predestination.

The chip is the result of poverty. Poverty will do one of two things to a person. In most, it destroys self-worth and feeds upon the Divine Right of Kings/fate cultural trait making the poor believe they are getting what they deserve. In a few individuals it will fuel anger to the point that they will see people who work less, or are of less intelligence, and maybe of less integrity, who are getting more and living easier. Those with the "chip" believe they are not getting what they are entitled to have. This "chip" will result in a very driven person. This is what happened to me. In some people this chip can turn to a rage and anger where the victim will simply take what they believe should be theirs, and many of these people end up in prison. I had childhood friends in this category, almost all of them very intelligent. Fortunately, mine turned into what my grocer ex-employer called "ambition."

It was only possible to cross this barrier, I admit, because of the G.I. Bill resources. This was true for many working-class veterans, and it has been rightly argued that the G.I. Bill is what built the American middle class after the Second World War, one of the few times in history where a significant number of working-class people moved into the lower middle class. Unfortunately, today's veterans, still mostly working class, no longer have these same benefits. And many of the children of these lower middle-class workers are now falling back into the working class.

Since I was working full time and frequently had a second job as well, and because I also had children and family obligations, I was not able to completely take advantage of this educational opportunity like most of my classmates, who worked part time or not at all. At one point, I was working a fulltime night job during the week, a part time job during the weekends, and convinced the University to give me a part time student job at school called "work study." I was taking twenty-one quarter credits at the time. When I finished my last exams that quarter, I took off two days off work and was so exhausted that I just slept.

Since I viewed education as a barrier, I was less concerned about learning than completing what I was required to do, no more and no less, to complete graduation and cross the barrier. In fact, with my work schedule and family I couldn't have done any more. But a funny thing happened, despite the odds and my attitude: I got a very good education, and I did graduate with two majors. I am still grateful to the University of Minnesota for this education. I have worked hard and had a pretty good life, and it was due in large part to this education.

Education is now critical for the working class. The most valuable workers today and increasingly more in the future are those who use their minds. An advanced education is necessary for everyone to earn a good living. Today's economy rewards ideas and knowledge over physical production. When I explained this to my father, who was a railroad worker all his life, he said, "You mean some guy sitting on his ass all day in some office that has maybe one or two good ideas a year is worth more than several guys working their butts off every day making something I can use?" And the answer to that, for better or worse is yes.

America began to make the transition from what we think of as typical working-class blue collar jobs to what we see as middle-class white collar jobs in the information age, and the demand for white collar workers in the future will be insatiable. Intellectual properties are worth more than physical properties. Microsoft is a good example. Bill Gates became the richest man in the world without owning huge land holdings, resources, factories, utilities, stores, transportation systems, or other physical things. Very few workers will continue make a good living from their hands and backs. Education was always a way to better yourself, but in this new era it is not a choice, but a necessity for economic survival.

Education has been shown to be the only significant way a poor or working-class person has a chance of improving his income and life. According to the 2000 Census, the annual income a person will average over their forty years of work with differing levels of education is as follows. A person with less than a high school education will average less than $20,000 per year. A high school graduate will average $24,000 per year over the same forty years. With two years of college or a trade school degree, a person will average $30,000. With a Bachelors Degree it jumps to an average of $42,000 per year, and it rockets to an average of $50,000 a year with a graduate degree. A doctorate will give you an average of $68,000, and a law or medical degree will give you an average of $88,000 per year. These are averages with people obviously earning less at the beginning of their work life and usually more toward the end.

Education is one factor in determining income and class is the other. And education is one of the very few things that will provide upward mobility and allow an individual to overcome some of the class barriers.

As much as I then underappreciated my education at the University, I was absolutely right in realizing that this was the barrier I needed to cross to get to a better life.

Chapter 5. One Nation under God

Class, Culture, Predestination and Christianity: How Christian Conservatives Divide the Working Class and Dominate America with an Anti-Working-Class Agenda

> "The national government will maintain and defend the foundations on which the power of our nation rests. It will offer strong protection to Christianity as the very basis of our collective morality. Today Christians stand at the head of our country. We want to fill our culture again with the Christian spirit. We want to burn out all the immoral developments in literature, in the theater, and the press. In short, we want to burn out the poison of immorality which has entered into our whole life and culture as a result of liberal excess during the past few years." —Adolph Hitler, 1942

> "No, I don't know that Atheists should be considered citizens, nor should they be considered patriots. This is one nation under God!" —President George H.W. Bush

President Obama made headlines during the 2008 presidential campaign when he talked about working-class economic frustrations and said, "They get bitter, they cling to their guns or religion." While he was widely criticized for these remarks, the fact is they are true. The American working class loves their guns and they cling to their religion and are dominated by a sense of predestination and the cultural limitations of American Christianity. To begin to understand the limiting effects of class culture and to gain an understanding of American class politics, we need to look at the powerful and very divisive role that Christianity has had on the working class and in promoting anti-working-class politics.

31

Christianity has divided the working class into splinter groups and has thus ensured that the largest group of Americans, the working class, hasn't come together as the largest political force. It has done this by separating the working class by religious divisions: into Christians versus Jews, Muslims, Hindus and Buddhists, and by dividing Protestants and Catholics, and the religious versus atheists and agnostics. Christianity has even played a significant role in the racial divisions of the working class. Contrary to the economic well-being of the working class, Christian conservatives have enshrined big business laissez-faire capitalism as part of the American Christian ethic. It is this history that we will explore.

The benefits of Christianity in America are given to us daily. They are repeated over and over again in history books, schools, newspapers, by government officials, and forced upon us out of the mouths of our presidents and other national leaders. Where many speak for Christianity in our government, few speak for non-Christians. This is one-sided and there isn't any balance or other viewpoints. Christianity has dominated our culture and with it our classes. No one dares speak of some of the unfortunate consequences of Christianity on our culture, politics and particularly upon working-class people. Indeed many, if not most, Americans reading this will be angry that someone has the audacity to even imply that such negatives exist.

The reality is that America has become as much a theocracy as it is a democracy. We are clearly a nation where the Christian god is the supreme authority and Christianity is the dominant culture. America is a "Christian" country and god damn those that aren't. America is fifty-five percent Christian Protestant and twenty-five percent Catholic. And since the Protestant majority sometimes considers the Catholics as Christians, it means that America is eighty percent Christian. The rest of us are as follows: eleven percent atheists and agnostics, four percent Jews, two percent Muslims, one percent Buddhists, and six percent are "others."

Basically, the twenty percent of Americans that aren't Christian don't count. They are sometimes allowed by the Christian majority to "practice" their own religion, even if some of them don't practice or believe in any religion. These non-believers also must pay a price for their different beliefs or lack of them. Congress, which the Constitution clearly states shall make no law establishing religion, passed a law in 1954 requiring the phrase "One Nation under God" in the Pledge of Allegiance. This places non-Christians in a position of choosing between being unpatriotic or unfaithful to their beliefs. Christians and the Christian dominated Congress claim that "god" isn't necessarily the Christian god, which is a lie. Jews, Muslims and Buddhists didn't ask for their god to be put in the Pledge of Allegiance, and since atheists and the agnostics have no god, what does the phrase "One Nation under God" tell them? It means they are not truly free to have their beliefs in the United States. There are many examples of this intolerance: "In God We Trust" was printed on our money by another unconstitutional act of Congress. Our Congress, many state legislatures, and the military have chaplains paid for at the expense of many of us that aren't religious. Churches and church property, and in many cases income-producing church commercial properties (as well as properties designated as Jewish temples), escape local property taxes to pay for their use of the roads, police and fire protection which must be then subsidized by those who do not share their faiths. The Supreme Court, the body that is charged with enforcing the First Amendment, opens each session with a Christian prayer. Despite the First Amendment, we do not have real religious freedom in America.

About eleven percent of Americans are atheists. Atheism is an absence of re-ligion. It is not a competing doctrine searching for souls or converts. An atheist doesn't believe everyone or anyone should share their beliefs. It is not a mission-ary religion. It isn't a religion, but rather a lack of one. Unfortunately, Christian-ity is a missionary religion and there lies one of her unfortunate consequences. Christians are perpetually trying to convert all others or to at least have all oth-ers live by their rules and under their culture and belief system, including the class system. This cultural dominance includes the working-class which is con-trolled through Christian tenets exhorting them to "willingly serve their masters." Christianity has set the class and culture structure for all Americans, regardless if an individual's beliefs coincide with this culture, it is particularly true for the working class.

Islam and Buddhism and a handful of others share some attributes with Christianity and may require obedience by the under classes to their "betters" and enjoin the followers to seek the conversions of non-believers. However very few Americans have been approached by these religions to convert and Ameri-cans have not been forced to live under their rules or by their class and social structures. America is a Christian-dominated nation and to understand her cul-ture and classes, you must understand the American Christian religious culture. The Reverend Franklin Graham, who in 2000 took over the evangelical empire from his aging father the Reverend Billy Graham, the once self-appointed coun-selor to presidents, had this to say about the American church and state:

> Our forefathers never wanted us to eliminate Christianity. They were Christians who came. They weren't Buddhists, Hindus, Jews, or Muslims. They were looking for the freedom to worship God, and they ensured reli-gious freedom for those who followed them.

America is much more fanatical about religion than any other western or industrialized country. According to a recent survey by the Pew Research Center, Americans are more like the third world in their religious fervor, closer to radical Muslims than to Europeans and other first world countries. Even in Canada, our culturally closest neighbor, only thirty-three percent of the population believes religion to be "very important" compared to fifty-nine percent in the US. In a recent Gallup survey of US religious attitudes, eighty-two percent said that god was "very important." In comparison, sixty-four percent of Czechs, fifty-five percent of Swedes, fifty-two percent of Norwegians, and forty-nine percent of Danes said god didn't matter at all.

The *Gallup Poll* also reported that seventy-two percent of Americans regularly attend church, whereas about half of Western Europeans never attend church.

The *New York Times* recently reported that over fifty-eight percent of Americans believe that you must believe in god to be a moral person, compared to only thirteen percent in France. In short, Americans are much more fanatical about religion than most other peoples.

A poll in *American Demographics* magazine found that twenty-three percent of Americans wouldn't vote for a qualified presidential candidate that was Asian-American, fifteen percent wouldn't vote for a candidate that was African-American, fourteen percent wouldn't vote for a woman, and eleven percent wouldn't vote for a Jew. But a 2003 poll released from the Pew Research Center found that well over half wouldn't vote for an atheist!

The real threat to America is that Christianity is becoming the official national religion, as is evidenced by President Bush, who recently said, "For too long, too long, some in government believed there was no room for faith in the public square."

A Christian conservative Web site, dutyisours.com, stated: "Dimpled and hanging chads may also be because of God's intervention on those who were voting incorrectly. Why is George W. Bush our president? It was God's choice!"

Chapter 6. The European Roots of Christian Class Culture, Predestination and the Divine Rights of Kings

> "It would have been better to take more time and do it right than to rush it through helter skelter in just six days for reputation." —*Mark Twain*

Before Christianity came to America, the Europeans had ample opportunity to work out their religious preferences and prejudices in Europe before some of the more devout believers brought their more extreme versions to America. It was these radically religious European colonists that formed American culture and set the American class system. The newly arrived colonists disregarded the Native Americans (like other non-Christians in America today) and their beliefs during the nation's founding. Most early immigrants to the colonies were from radical Protestant sects in northern Europe who felt the need to leave (if not flee) their homelands because their religious beliefs put them at a severe disadvantage, if not risk. Their religious extremes and biases are the cultural consequences that we live with today.

The ancestors of early American immigrants were primarily Germanic and Celtic peoples. Their conversion to Christianity occurred relatively late. These were mostly rural peoples. They were hunters, fisherman and farmers. They lived in huts of rough timber and stones plastered with mud with thatched roofs. They were polytheistic and their gods were associated with their natural environment. They worshiped trees and water, and they were particularly enamored with the sun and the four seasons.

Christianity in northern Europe came at the point of the sword and spear from the invading Roman Legions. It was forced. The Romans called these Germanic

---

and Celtic tribes "Pagus." It is a Latin word that meant "rural." The "four-letter" equivalent might be "hick." It meant an unsophisticated, lower class of people. The word "pagus" became the root of both the word "peasant" and "pagan," the word for non-Christians.

The Germanic and Celtic peoples were slow to convert to the new religion. It is not really surprising, considering that this new pushy missionary religion created in the west Asian desert and forced upon them by the conquering Romans legions, had very little to do with the culture and lifestyles of northern Europe.

However, one thing the new religion had that proved to be attractive to some was monotheism, the belief in one god. Monotheism reflected the existing Germanic and Celtic tribal structures, which were usually dominated by a lone strong leader, usually a male. Monotheism mirrored their belief in a central authority better than nature-worshipping polytheism. This belief in a paternalistic and an unquestioned central authority eventually smoothed the way for European monarchism, which also led to European nationalism. The monarchy in turn would become the strongest supporters of Christianity, and royalty were frequently leaders of the church because Christianity created the justification for their high position and preserved their power and authority over the peasants. The monarchy, because of Christianity, could claim the "Divine Right to be Kings."

"I am King because god wants me to be King and you are a peasant because god wants you to be a peasant — and who you are you to question god?" This was the start of the class system that still governs American culture. Christianity was used to keep the peasants in their place. "Place and duty" are persistent Christian themes. Christianity also promised the peasants a reward in heaven if they obeyed the will of their masters and the church in this life, even if it meant that this life wasn't very good.

Christianity proved an effective means for controlling the people, distracting them from real problems and the deficiencies in their own lives. It was much easier to enforce laws and gain obedience of the masses by fear of an angry god, rather than just by fear of angry men.

Christianity was used by the Roman Legions to divide and conquer. The pagans were much larger in numbers and Roman military tactics by themselves would not conquer and keep the masses in check, so the Romans allowed for some pagans to become citizens and join the Romans if they were subservient and adopted Roman customs and beliefs, particularly Christianity. This is the same tactic used today by Christian Conservatives to divide and conquer working-class America and insures that the much larger working-class will not overcome their leisure-class masters and their middleclass managers.

The first folks to convert to the new religion were town dwelling people that were under control of the Romans. The villagers came to like the central authority that provided security to their town and also promoted new developments around the church. And they also enjoyed the added Roman bonus of new technologies like paved roads, irrigation, new building methods and sanitation. These were the rewards for betraying their people.

The Romans were intelligent in their conquest and allowed for the pagans and peasants to customize their Christianity. The pagans and peasants also changed Christianity. In just one example, they slowly surrendered their sun god, "Invictus" as some called him, but they kept his holy day, and "Sunday" became part of Christianity. They also insisted upon keeping their sun god's birthday, an annual celebration just a few days after the winter solstice. So European Christians arbitrarily declared that December 25 was Jesus' birthday, thereby ensuring their pagan holiday would remain a part of their culture.

Later in Chapter 9 we will see that similar changes made by the American working-class rural population during the Revivalist Movement would also appear to give the working class the feeling of ownership and choice in their religion while still making them subservient to the ruling classes and the leisure class power structure. Religion is also used in America to divide and conquer the working class.

Religion was used by the Europeans to divide large class and ethnic groups and to entice the masses into fighting for various causes, long before nationalism. A king wanting to steal a neighboring kingdom's land could force his peasants to fight, but it was more effective if he could give his masses a religious cause to further bolster his case. Thus the king could assure that if they died in battle they would receive their reward in heaven.

European Christianity has been at war with itself since the beginning. The first major division occurred when Rome and Constantinople split Christianity into two factions, forming the Catholic Church and the Eastern Orthodox Church. The Catholic Church would remain the more powerful, while the Eastern Orthodox would constantly have to fight off Islam and occasional Asian Hordes sweeping westward. The religious difference between Christians and Muslims is which "son of god" they believe and which addendum to the Jewish Old Testament they believe, the New Testament or the Koran. The difference between the sects within Islam and Christianity are even smaller but still frequently as deadly. The two religions have frequently fought internally, as well. In Chapter 28 we will look more at how Americans are divided between their Christian and Muslim faiths.

The second major split occurred in Christianity just as America became available to European settlement. The Protestant movement began in the 1500s. Martin Luther, a smart young German businessman, was headed to law school until he was struck by lightning. Not wanting to be struck again, he decided that the safest course was to become a priest. It was Luther who began the Protestant assault on Rome, and he may have likely felt that he had god's support since he was never hit by lightning again. In Luther's case, the events of history and emerging economics lashed this unlikely religious icon to a movement that would split Christianity.

Europeans in general were beginning to feel the rise of nationalism and capitalism that was contrary to a world controlled by the Christian Church in Rome. One of the basic beliefs of Christianity that it had inherited from Judaism (and shared with Islam) was that it was a sin to lend money for profit. The new nation states and the rising upper- and merchant-class families were extremely hindered by this belief. The Protestants dropped the prohibition on money lending for interest. After the split, the Catholic Church would also drop this holy law.

Over a hundred years ago Max Weber, a German sociologist, published his essay "The Protestant Ethic and the Spirit of Capitalism." Weber pointed out that capitalism was "born from the spirit" of Protestantism.

In America, capitalism and American Christianity have in fact become one single religion. And the marriage of these two philosophies established and defined both economics and class in America and made the preservation of both capitalism and class a central part of the American belief system. In Chapters 14 and 15 we look at non-Christians, particularly Jews, which caused more working-class divisions in America.

Because of Germany's religious division and constant fighting, the Germans, both Protestant and Catholic, would become the largest group of Europeans to immigrate to the United States. Almost a quarter of European-Americans are of German heritage, followed by about one in six who are of Irish and another one in six who are of British heritage. The Germans, like the English Puritans and others, came not to allow others religious freedom, but rather they wanted the freedom to practice their religion. They were zealots.

It was with these strong religious biases that European Christians settled America. Christianity and its subsequent class system would come to regulate most of life's significant achievements. Birth is approved by baptism, puberty is acknowledged by confirmation, and love and sex are only approved by the wedding ceremony and death by the funeral. It is interesting that the only significant event not controlled by Christianity is the public high school or public college graduation and the only reason that Christianity doesn't regulate those events is that they don't wholly approve of non-religious education.

Chapter 7. Christianity and Predestination Comes To America

> "From the fifteenth century to the twentieth, the Christian nations of Europe have been spreading civilization little by little over every part of the world."—Columbia University Historians Carlton J.H. Hayes and Parker Thomas Moon

George Bancroft, one of the first American historians, set the tone for future writers by stating that, "The American Republic represents the culmination of god's wonder-working in the life of mankind."

This quote is just one very mild example of Christian bias that is written into the historical record of America. This has caused the nation to ignore cultural influences that are not Christian. This bias persists throughout our history and today. In 1928, two prominent America historians from Columbia University, Carlton J.H. Hayes and Parker Thomas Moon, summarized the thoughts of the American intellectual community in their book *Modern History* with the following:

> From the time of the ancient Greeks and Romans down to the present day, the leading roles in the drama of human history have been taken by the white men of Europe... From the fifteenth century to the twentieth, the Christian nations of Europe have been spreading civilization little by little over every part of the world.... During this period the European white man began to teach and if need be compel his yellow, black and brown brothers to adopt the ways of the Europeans. A great poet, Rudyard Kipling has called this "The White Man's Burden."... The unprogressive yellow races of the Far East were aroused from slumber to receive their first lessons in European civilization....the benighted black men of Africa were brought under European rule.

These two scholars further wrote that modern American imperialism was the "humanitarian desire to civilize backward races."

Today most of us would be shocked if two prominent intellectuals wrote these words, but the idea is still very much alive. "Predestination" is a Puritan doctrine coined by John Calvin. It is the concept that White Protestants, or at least Christians, as the only true believers, are predestined for heaven. It is the belief that if you are good, you will prosper, and if not, you will be poor — and it is god who makes these decisions. It is a belief still strongly held by the working class in America today. It is interesting to see what "Christian civilizing," as Hayes and Moon called it, has done to America.

Chapter 8. The Early History

> "Quakers prayed for their neighbors on the first day (Sunday) and then preyed on them the other six days of the week." —*Governor Blackwell 1684*

In 1620, the Mayflower brought the Pilgrims and their puritanical beliefs to America. While the Puritans were responsible for the development of New England, their legacy left strong and lasting imprints on the entire nation and its culture and class structure. The Congregational, Presbyterian, Methodist, Baptist and Unitarian Churches, along with the Quakers, are offshoots of seventeenth century English-Scottish Puritanism. The Protestant Ethic, more appropriately called in America the "Puritan Ethic," dominates American culture.

Since it is the major cultural foundation for American society, Puritanism has received much attention from American historians. The greatly respected historian Samuel Eliot Morison wrote:

> Puritanism was hewed out of the Black Forests of feudal Europe and the American wilderness. Puritan doctrine taught each person to consider himself a significant, if sinful unit, to whom god had given a particular *place and duty*, (italics are mine) and that he must help his fellow men. Puritanism, therefore, is an American heritage to be grateful for and not sneered at because it required everyone to attend Divine worship and maintain a strict code of ethics.

Knowing one's "place and duty" are paramount in American culture. Knowing your place is to know in which class you belong, and duty refers to the Christian belief in serving your masters and betters well. Duty and place was enforced by severe methods in the Colonial period including the stocks, the dunking stool, the scarlet letter, branding, and the burning and hanging of anyone different or who protested the social structure.

Several other writers on the subject of Puritanism have not been as generous as Samuel Eliot Morison.

MacCaulay in his *History of England* wrote: "The Puritan hated bear-baiting, not because it gave pain to the bear, but because it gave pleasure to the spectator."

H.L. Mencken wrote: "The great artists of the world are never Puritans, and seldom even respectable."

G.K. Chesterton in a 1936 *New York Times* article wrote: "A Puritan is a person who pours righteous indignation into the wrong things."

The Massachusetts Bay Colony was the first American Puritan settlement. It was a religious merchant colony whose main business was the raising of cattle, corn and foodstuffs to be sold mostly to new incoming Puritan settlers. Since the colony doubled in size every year from 1620 to 1637, business was good. Unfortunately the English Civil War in 1637 greatly reduced the number of colonists coming to America because the Puritans and their radical religious beliefs had finally achieved some acceptance in England.

Immigration slowed to a trickle and the subsequent economic depression in America forced the Puritans to look for new forms of commerce. They were capitalists and they began to diversify into shipbuilding and fishing, but the mainstay of the new economy soon became the lucrative West Indies trade. Rum, tobacco, and slaves were the commodities of the West Indies trade. This trade is very odd for a self-declared devout Christian people with such a supposed strict moral and ethical code. The forgiving historian Samuel Eliot Morison justified this by stating simply,

> Puritanism appealed to merchants because they taught that man could serve god as well in business or a profession, as by taking Holy Orders.

Since god allowed the Puritans to prosper in this trade, they reasoned that the trade was approved by god. If god was not in favor of smokers, drunks and slaves, he was at least he was in favor of his followers being allowed to make money from this trade, or so they reasoned. It is not apparent whether they thought that god also approved of the forced prostitution that also accompanied the slave trade. However it is known that at the time some believed this forced prostitution wasn't sinful since none of the women were believed to be Christians.

America was and is governed by the "Puritan work ethic," which is a strong component of the Puritan ethic. It means that you are expected by god to work hard, as in, "If any shouldn't work, neither should he eat." The "work ethic" supports predestination and that "the Lord would not suffer a sinner to prosper," and therefore all economic success was a sign of proof that the prosperous were chosen by god for salvation and therefore chosen by god to be masters. This fatalistic trait is deeply imbedded in American class social structure and is the foundation of the class structure.

The contradiction of Christians supporting morally questionable business activities is a prevalent theme in American history. The ultimate Christian capitalist, Henry Ford, the father of American mass production, declared in 1930:

> "There can be no conflict between good economics and good morals, as we know anything that is economically right is morally right."

This is the cultural equivalent of, "If it makes money, it is apparently blessed by god."

Henry Ford was also a rabid anti-Semite and he financed hate groups and Christian supremacist movements. He was also a Nazi sympathizer and an admirer of Hitler. One rarely sees a Ford parked in a Jewish driveway, which is only fitting. You also don't find many Volkswagens, a car that was named by Adolph Hitler, parked in many Jewish driveways. Fortunately for the two automakers, most Americans don't seem to mind as much.

For people who came to America for religious freedom, the Puritans were horribly intolerant of others. It was a trait that would remain entrenched in Christian America and cause many rifts, conflicts and biases within the American working class.

The Puritans didn't believe in religious freedom for anyone but themselves. The Reverend Roger Williams, who later founded the Rhode Island Colony, Samuel Gorton, and Anne Hutchison, were banished from the Bay Colony for promoting "religious freedom for all Christians." The leaders of the Bay Colony were also angry with the Reverend Williams, because they said he had also had committed heresy for advocating that the Indians should be free to follow their own non-Christian beliefs.

Banishment in those days was a penalty that was worse than death. It meant being thrown into the hostile wilderness with no food or possessions except the clothes on your back and given no chance to ever return and therefore very little chance of survival. But Roger Williams did survive the ordeal. He eventually founded his own Rhode Island Colony where he would allow some limited religious freedom. However, like the Bay Colony Puritans, Reverend Williams only allowed male colonists the right to vote and only if they were members in good standing of his church.

Religion also dominated education. The Bible and Christian teachings were part of the American school system from the beginning, and the Christian influence on intellectual America was entrenched with the founding of Harvard College in 1636. John Harvard, a Puritan minister died and left his collection of four hundred books and half his fortune to start a college to educate Puritan ministers. Harvard was and still is the standard to which all American universities are measured. The first printing press in the American colonies was set up in the Harvard College yard. The first two printings were the "Bay Psalm Book" and followed by the entire Bible printed in the Indian language of Algonquin. It was reported that this was the first Bible printed in the new world and the first translated into "a pagan language" since the fourth century when it was printed in Visigoth.

In 1685, Louis XIV of France repealed the Edict of Nantes, which had provided for French tolerance of Protestants. And soon the newly outlawed French Protestants, the Huguenots, began their immigration to America to seek religious freedom. They settled in the American South mostly in the two Carolina Colonies.

Grateful for their new liberty, these people would soon begin trading in slaves like the Bay Colony Puritans. The Puritans bought slaves in Africa to sell in the West Indies; however the Huguenots were the first to bring slaves in large numbers into America. Some of the first slaves were brought in to grow rice on the Carolina coastal marshes. Eventually the slaves would also be used to produce tobacco and cotton. Like the Puritans, the Huguenots had little trouble with moral dilemmas when it came to economics. They too were Christian capitalists. They had made the determination that the African people were of lower-class status and believed that since they were not Christians, they had no souls and were not fully human and could therefore be exploited.

In the Christian world of the seventeenth century, intellectuals and the clergy believed that people could make deals with Satan to their benefit, or commit evil on their enemies with Satan's help; this was called witchcraft. Even prior to the Salem Witchcraft Trials in 1692, there were forty-four people found guilty of practicing witchcraft and three hangings of witches in Massachusetts. There were even three cases in Anglican Virginia, but none were hanged.

The leader of the Puritan movement in America, the Reverend Cotton Mather, was enamored on the subject of witchcraft. He wrote a book called *Memorable Providences* in which he described in detail a trial and execution of an old woman for witchcraft. It was well read and circulated in its day.

In the book, Mather wrote that he was concerned that the old woman's accusers, a group of malcontent children, could have started a witch-hunting epidemic. Unfortunately for the people of Salem, most editions of his book included very detailed information on how the "possessed," those supposedly under the witch's power, were supposed to act. After reading the book, a group of not very nice girls from Salem accused a defenseless half-Indian and half-Black slave of being a witch. Their performance of being possessed was taken right out of the Reverend Mather's book. They convinced the town and church authorities that the woman was a witch and had possessed them. The church officials beat the old woman until she finally confessed, and they threatened her with death unless she gave the names of other witches. She gave them the names of two others, to save her life. One would guess she named people she didn't like anyway.

Governor Phipps of the Bay Colony was notified, and he appointed a special court to try the two accused witches the old woman had named while being tortured. These two were also beaten and threatened with death if they didn't name other witches. They accused others, and the ungodly process of people being accused and naming others continued throughout the summer of 1692. The final count resulted in fourteen women and five men being hanged as witches. They also hanged two dogs for "devil worshiping." Apparently, the dogs died without accusing other dogs, even though witnesses at the time claimed to hear them clearly speak and cast spells. Four other accused witches died because of mistreatment in prison and one little girl was jailed with her mother who was accused of witchcraft. The poor child went insane in the prison shortly after they hanged her mother.

Sixty-five of the accused managed to escaped hanging by pleading guilty and naming others. One brave man, Giles Cory, stubbornly refused to admit guilt or accuse others, so they crushed him to death by slowly piling large rocks on him over a two day period. My ancestor, Martha Carrier, a defenseless widow with two children, was accused as a witch. Her neighbors on either side accused her so that they could claim her farm. She gave a fiery speech about the hypocrisy of the church and their belief in witches. She was hanged quickly to shut her up. Her two young sons were also beaten and imprisoned.

The accused witches began to realize that it was mostly lower-class people who were accused, for entertainment or so that others could steal their property. They started getting wise. They began to plead guilty and began accusing a number of wealthy merchants, several prominent members of the clergy, and perhaps the most brilliant ploy, Governor Phipp's wife, as being fellow witches. The Governor and the Reverend Cotton Mather who had presided over the trials quickly consulted with other clergy, including the three that were accused, and dissolved the Witch Court and freed the Governor's wife and a hundred and fifty other lower-class people who were awaiting trial.

Perverse sexual interest also played a part in the witchcraft trials. Not on the part of the "witches," but the colonial leaders, particularly the clergy and the men of the church, who would exhaustively "search" the sexual parts of the lower-class females accused of being witches for "signs of the Devil" to prove their guilt.

Apparently, men's sexual parts and upper-class women didn't exhibit these signs. This amounted to horrible sexual abuse by the clergy of the defenseless women. Sexual repression led to perverted sex so frequently in the Puritan Bay Colony that William Bradford their leader and first historian of the colony lamented: "Human nature dammed in one direction, would find outlets in another."

In 1711, the General Assembly and the Governor agreed to compensate Martha Carrier's two sons and twenty other victims. The two boys were given seven pounds six schillings for the loss of their farm and death of their mother. In 1957, the writer Arthur Miller and others who were upset with the Communist "witch hunt" trials led by Senator Joseph McCarthy of Wisconsin televised a re-enactment of the Salem witchcraft trials to show their similarity with the McCarthy proceedings. Included at the end of the performance was the fact that the Massachusetts General Assembly and the Governor had found the victims innocent and compensated their heirs; the re-enactment implied that this would be the likely future outcome of the McCarthy proceedings. It so angered the Republicans, and the Christian conservatives and the churches at the time, that they pressured the Massachusetts General Court into taking the unusual action of declaring the Governor's and the General Assembly's actions of 1711 illegal and to uphold the original convictions of the Salem witchcraft trials. Apparently, in Massachusetts, at least as late as 1957, they still believed in witchcraft.

Religious tolerance was very slow to come to Puritanical America. In 1692, the largely Catholic colony of Maryland passed a law allowing for religious tolerance, mostly intended for Catholics, but it was repealed after a very short time when it was discovered that it could apply to non-Christians as well.

In the late seventeenth century another Puritan group, the Quakers, began immigrating to the American colonies. Although they were a branch of the Puritans and were Christians, every colony except Roger William's Rhode Island passed a law outlawing the Quakers. The punishment for being a Quaker in most colonies was flogging or imprisonment. In Massachusetts they were hanged. The Bay Colony felt that if they were willing to hang their own for witchcraft, that they should be willing to hang Puritans for being different. One of the differences was that the Quakers were pacifists, a trait disliked by most Christians —who believe that Christian nations have the right to conquer non-Christian lands, a sentiment immortalized by the hymn "Onward Christian Soldiers." The Puritans believed that taking land from the Native Americans by force was acceptable to god because they were heathens. But the Quakers disapproved of violence.

George Fox founded the Quakers in England. Charles II had tolerated the Quakers because they were the only Puritans to not take up arms against the Crown during the English Civil War. The Duke of York owed a debt to Admiral

Penn that he could not repay, so in partial settlement of the debt he gave Admiral Penn's son, William, a proprietary province in America called Pennsylvania. It meant Penn's Woods.

William Penn had converted and became a Quaker. Soon Quakers from England, Germany, Wales and the Netherlands began immigration to Pennsylvania. Already occupying the land were several hundred Swedish and Finnish Lutheran settlers that were the left over remnants of the New Sweden Colony in America. Needing their cooperation to start a successful colony Penn quickly allowed them their religious freedom.

The colony was tolerant of these other Christians until a crime wave in 1698. The Quakers were adamant that Quakers didn't commit crimes and blamed the non-Quakers. Pennsylvania then proceeded to ban all other religions and passed a Code of Ethics based upon strict Quaker beliefs. The Code was so severe and rigid that the very conservative governing English Privy Council rejected most of it.

The Quakers, like the other Puritans, soon adopted a strong merchant culture. They too were Christian capitalists and believed in "place and duty," reinforcing America's growing class culture. Ironically, the Quakers became such ruthless businessmen that Governor Blackwell, the second Governor of Pennsylvania, in 1684 lamented, "Quakers prayed for their neighbors on the first day (Sunday) and then preyed on them the other six days of the week."

The generous and charitable founder of the Quaker colony in America came to a sad end. William Penn's fellow Quakers eventually cheated Penn out of all his money and his property. He was then thrown into debtor's prison. There he became ill from the frigid conditions and poor diet and he almost died. Upon his release from prison, he spent the six years until his death as a penniless beggar and an invalid who was unable to work or properly care for himself. The Puritans, as Christian capitalists, do not believe in welfare. They refused to help him and reasoned that since Penn had become poor and of ill-health, that it must have been god's intention.

Chapter 9. The Revivalist Movement

The more extreme religious movements have always been populated mostly by the working-class. These working-class religious extremists were the fuel of America's Revivalist Movement.

One of America's first charismatic preachers, Jonathan Edwards, began his first fire and brimstone sermon at North Hampton, Massachusetts in 1734, and from it the Revivalist Movement was born. In 1736, Edwards published a book entitled, *A Faithful Narrative of the Surprising Work of God in the Conversion of Many Hundred Souls in North Hampton.* It was printed in Boston, London and Edinburgh and translated into both German and Dutch. This new kind of Puritan preacher so inspired John Wesley that he broke away from the Church of England and founded the Methodist Church based upon Edward's teachings. He preached primarily to the lower-class masses.

The Revivalist Movement was slow to take root in the older and more established cities and villages with their middleclass and upper classes, but the working class, who were mostly rural folks, particularly those on the frontiers, embraced the Revivalists.

Many traditional ministers who worked in these "backwoods" areas refused to make the transition to the Revivalist Movement and soon found their working-class congregations quitting and founding their own "New Born" or "New Light" churches with working-class lay ministers. Most of these new churches would affiliate with the Baptist or Methodist Churches. The Revivalist Movement would give rise to three new American universities, Dartmouth, Princeton and Brown. Their founding continued to cement the link between Christianity and the American educational institutions that was started at Harvard.

The working class comprised mostly rural folks (well over eighty percent of Americans at this time lived in rural areas). Mostly self-sufficient farmers, they were naturally attracted to the Revivalist Movement. They lived too far from the town churches to attend on a regular basis, and were likely to be looked down upon in the more formal churches because of their dress and status. The new religion was accepting of lower-class people and offered social interaction and entertainment that was otherwise unavailable to working-class people living in sparsely populated areas. The Revivalists brought religion to them through the "tent" or "camp meetings." These meetings were frequently the only time they heard music or came together with their friends and neighbors.

The Revivalist "circuit rider" and the camp meetings were designed to give the working-class rural Americans what they wanted. The Reverend George White-field was the first "Road Revivalist." It was said that his voice was so loud and strong that it could carry to twenty thousand people. He was working class. He was very animated in his sermons. He would dance, sing, spit, rant and rave, challenge the devil to fight, and make violent threats, and he also claimed he had the ability to heal the sick. He introduced sermon participation, whereby he would ask a question and the audience would answer in loud unison. He strongly encouraged his followers to participate by crying, screaming, rolling around in incoherent fits, and generally "carrying on in the name of the Lord." He became the model for the modern Revivalist preacher. The social acceptance of everyone who attended, the social contact, and entertainment of the most intense kind drew a large following. This was a religion that was designed for the working class as opposed to the more staid and formal middle-class and leisure-class churches of the time.

Another working-class pioneer circuit rider, Francis Ashbury, was said to ride his poor horse over five thousand miles per year to bring the word of god to rural folks in the rural the South. Some of these "camp meetings" were enormous. One meeting in Bourbon County, Kentucky, in 1801, was said to have over thirty thousand attendees. The working-class country people came for days from a range of over a hundred miles. Seventeen preachers preached continuously for seven days. It was reported that at one time three thousand followers lay on the ground in "unconscious swoons" while another five hundred people "jerked and barked like dogs in unison." One particularly emotional prayer was said to fell three hundred people.

Another of the main attractions of these "camp meetings or tent revivals" was sex. Historian James Truslow Adams wrote the following about nineteenth century camp meetings and tent revivals:

> Religious frenzy often passed into sexual orgy, and as dusk came on, the preacher played on the emotional nature of his hearers, he would be surrounded by a mass of humanity in which all intellectual control had been released, some falling insensible, some writhing in fits, some crawling and barking like dogs, some having the "jerks" and others throwing themselves in couples on the ground or among the trees in frenzies of passion.

In some sense it could be argued that tent meetings were replaced by rock concerts in the twentieth century.

Before the Revolution of 1776, the United States had an official state Church that was supported by tax dollars. It was dominated by the leisure and middle class. It was the Church of England, which is also known as the Anglican Church. It even had an enforced monopoly on weddings in the Southern colonies. After 1776, the Americans decided against the use of tax dollars to support churches. However, this was not because Americans valued the separation of church and state (a popular but false belief), it was in reality a result of hatred for British domination, including the Church. They wanted to end the subsidy of the Anglican Church.

The very first law that enforced freedom of religion, other than the brief and failed attempts in Rhode Island and Maryland, was the Virginia Statute of Religious Liberty, written by Thomas Jefferson in 1786, which made it unlawful to "compel any man to support by contribution of monies any religion he disbelieves." It further provided that all men were free to believe as they saw fit. Jefferson also acknowledged that his law would have never been passed if it were not for Virginia's extreme anti-British attitudes and the dislike of the Church of England at that time.

Jefferson was also the author and champion for Article One of the Bill of Rights, which established freedom of religion and free speech before even the freedom of the press, the freedom to assemble, or the freedom to petition the government to address grievances. It was the first freedom of the first article because Jefferson felt it was the most important. Jefferson wrote: "Congress shall make no law respecting an establishment of religion." Unfortunately, this right under the Constitution has been repeatedly violated by Congress and the federal and state governments. The most obvious violation was in Congress passing a law in 1954 adding the words "One Nation under God" to the Pledge of Allegiance. In the same year, Congress also had the words "In God We Trust" placed on US money.

In 2002, when a US Appeals Court said that the 1954 law was unconstitutional, President Bush denounced the court ruling as "ridiculous." Democratic Senate Majority Leader Tom Daschle called the decision "Just nuts!" The Senate then stopped in the middle of debate on another issue to unanimously pass a resolution denouncing the court decision. President Bush had his spokesperson point out that even "the Supreme Court itself begins each of its sessions with the phrase "God save the United States and this honorable court."

In the United States the Executive Branch, Legislative Branch and the Supreme Court are all Christian-dominated institutions. The fact that the Supreme Court regularly asks god to save the country and their court gives little comfort to those Americans outside the Christian faith.

Supreme Court Justice Oliver Wendell Holmes summarized Congress and their proclivity for ignoring First Amendments rights in a 1919 opinion:

> If you have no doubt of your premises or your power, and you want a certain result with all your heart, you naturally express your wishes in law, and sweep away all opposition.

He further commented in the same opinion, "I think we should be eternally vigilant against attempts to check the expression of opinions that we loathe."

CHAPTER 10. THE CATHOLIC EXPERIENCE IN PROTESTANT AMERICA, AND GROWING CONFLICTS WITHIN THE WORKING CLASSES

"The Pope Reigns In Philadelphia!"—A Philadelphia newspaper headline upon the decision of the Philadelphia School Board to not force Catholic children in public schools to participate in Protestant religious exercises.

In early America, Catholicism was mostly confined to Maryland. Then in 1820 and through the 1840s, Catholics began coming to America in large numbers. The majority were Irish and German. Protestant Americans resented these newcomers and their religion. Religion aside, many working-class Protestants saw these new immigrants as increased competition for their jobs and as a threat to their status because some of these new immigrants were middle class. The Germans tended to move inland and into their own newly-created communities, but the Irish settled mostly in the existing cities. The growing Irish populations in these cities were indeed willing to work for less money and competed with the existing working class for their jobs. This caused a wave of anti-Catholic and anti-Irish sentiment across America.

Eventually the Irish would become the second largest group of Europeans coming to America and today there are more Americans of Irish heritage than there are Irish people in Ireland. In the mid-nineteenth century, when Irish-Catholic immigration swelled because of the Potato Famine, it put pressure on the existing workers who were already in competition with the new Black working-class population (comprised of free Blacks and the soon-to-be-freed Black slaves). This heated competition for jobs and status lasted in many of these cities until at least well into the 1960s. And today's Latino immigrants are the most recent form of this dissention.

To make matters worse, America had an economic depression in the years 1837 to 1840, making these new Irish Catholic immigrants even more unwelcome. It was a common sight to see signs in doors and windows of businesses that said, "No Catholics or Irish allowed." A wave of anti-Catholic violence also took place during this time. A Catholic Convent near Boston was burned to the ground by a working-class Protestant mob as the working-class police stood by and watched. In New Hampshire, three Catholic churches were torched by Protestant mobs. In Maine, a crowd stripped a Catholic priest naked, painted him with boiling tar, covered him in feathers, tied him to a rail and carried him far out of town.

In 1843, the anti-Catholic sentiment melded with an anti-immigration movement. The new "American Republican Party" was created at this time to pass new and more stringent immigration laws and to require a minimum residency of twenty-one years before granting citizenship.

In 1843, the Catholic Bishop of Philadelphia had obtained permission from the Philadelphia School Board to allow Catholic public school students to forgo required Protestant religious exercises and to be exempted from having to purchase and use Protestant Bibles. Newspaper headlines in Philadelphia and other cities read: "The Pope Reigns in Philadelphia!" It was followed by more working-class Protestant riots and acts of violence.

The following spring in Philadelphia, the American Republican Party staged a protest in front of a polling place in an Irish-Catholic neighborhood and tried prevent the Catholics from voting in the election. The angry Irish-Catholics chased the American Republicans out of their neighborhood.

The American Republicans gathered up a large group of thugs and toughs and held a large anti-Catholic rally in Kensington, the main Irish-Catholic neighborhood. A riot started and the rioters came at each other with knives, clubs and a few guns. One Protestant was killed by a gunshot.

The American Republicans used this incident to rally an even larger Protestant army to invade the Irish Catholic neighborhood. They burned thirty Irish-Catholic homes and businesses to the ground and badly damaged and looted over a hundred others. They also burned both St. Michael's and St. Augustine Catholic Churches. The conclusion left over two hundred people homeless and the Irish-Catholic business and religious community destroyed.

The American Republicans' actions in destroying Kensington were hailed by Protestant America with a giant rally and a parade. They decided to attack another Irish-Catholic neighborhood. They made speeches and promised they wouldn't stop until all the Irish-Catholics in America were dead. Federal authorities feared a wholesale slaughter and ordered the militia and the Blue Jackets from the U.S.S. *Princeton* to defend the Catholics. In the riot that followed, thirty people were killed and another hundred and fifty were seriously wounded.

The American Republicans were generally condemned for fighting with the militia and the federal troops. They lost public support. In Baltimore, because of declining numbers, they were forced to form an alliance with the smaller and also declining Whig Party to out vote the city's Catholic dominated Democratic Party. The American Republican Party was also racist and campaigned against the growing abolitionist movement in Baltimore to attract more white working-class voters.

To win elections in Baltimore the American Republicans kept "Coops" during elections. A Coop was an unused building where they gathered derelicts, drunks and drug addicts and held them against their will for several days before an election. The kidnapped detainees were denied food, drugs and liquor. The men became desperate with starvation and their addictions. When the election came, the American Republicans forced them to go from polling place to polling place to vote, and promised them food, liquor and drugs if the American Republicans won the election. They were forced to vote under different names and as many times as possible.

Edgar Allen Poe arrived by steamship to Baltimore five days before an election. He was very ill and intoxicated at the time and was easily kidnapped by the American Republicans and thrown into a coop. The conditions of the coop where Poe was kept were so bad, and his health and addiction problems so advanced, that he was released from the coop and hospitalized; he died very shortly afterward.

Another Protestant, anti-immigration and anti-Catholic group was formed in 1850. Like the Ku Klux Klan, it was a secret militia. The members were instructed and swore an oath that if they were ever questioned about the existence of the organization or its activities, they would claim to know nothing. They became known ironically as the "Know Nothings." They attracted both the working-class and some influential businessmen who played significant role in influencing government against immigration and policies against non-whites and Catholics. They recruited working-class urban Protestants by playing on their economic fears.

CHAPTER 11. OTHER AMERICAN WORKING-CLASS CHRISTIAN MOVEMENTS

"Religious insanity is very common in the United States." —Alexis De Tocqueville

As in Roman times, Christianity in America has been used to divide and conquer. The working class has been subdivided into splinter religious sects that have allowed the leisure class and their middle-class managers to dominate the American political and economic agenda. It has recently spawned the phrase "values voters" to mean working-class people who regularly vote against their own economic and political interests for religious and "moral" reasons. Religion made the working-class subservient to the upper classes and divided them along sectarian lines. In many sects, it also further divided the masses along gender lines, with women being markedly subservient and in some sects they became the property of men. These sects began to influence American culture, politics and economics.

The more influential of these sects were inventions of power-hungry individuals that preyed upon the misery and fears of the working class to gain recruits. Their institutions were working-class friendly, unlike the more middle-class mainstream Christian churches. The main purpose of these sects was to separate their followers from the rest of American society and make them dependent upon their church hierarchy and to follow blindly the directives of their leaders. These sects helped give rise to the Christian conservatives who have dominated American politics and now divide the nation into "Red" and "Blue" states.

The World Ecumenical Movement started in 1846. It was the first attempt to unite the world's Christians. It was driven by the mainstream Churches who watched as Christianity continued to fragment the faithful and as the more extreme sects attracted a growing number of working-class believers. The Evangelical Alliance that was formed failed amid the bickering between the splintered and self-righteous groups. Each of the groups refused to allow that anyone but their own followers would gain access to heaven. The Ecumenical Movement struggled for a hundred years, and eventually formed the World Council of Churches in 1948.

However, only the Protestant and Eastern Orthodox Churches joined the Council; the Catholic Church steadfastly refused to join. The Catholic Church agreed to work "cooperatively" with the Council. The Council is not united and frequently feuds over such things as the role of women in church and society, and feuds about the rights of gays and "other liberal influences" by the more politically conservative sects.

In America, new Christian groups particularly catering to the working-class seem to form around every new charismatic preacher, and for some unknown reason a working-class area in upstate New York along the Erie Canal, a place that became known as the "Burned Over District," was the largest producer of new splinter working-class Christian Groups. Many of these groups had and still have a significant impact on American culture, class structure, economics and politics.

One of the splinter groups that originated in Palmyra, New York, is the Church of The Latter Day Saints, better known as the Mormons. The Mormons today play a key role in the Christian conservative movement that dominates American politics and economics. The Mormons influence and some would argue control the largest bloc of Red states outside the South: the rural Rocky Mountain States of the West.

The Mormons are a good example of the role of sects in American culture and politics. The Mormons recruited vulnerable members of the working class, first in upstate New York, with some converts coming from the Midwest as they moved westward. When they ran out of new recruits, they went to the slums of London to entice the very poorest of the English working class to convert with paid passage to America and a promise good life once there.

The Mormon Church has isolated its members from the rest of society and made them totally dependent upon church elders. They have, practically speaking, enslaved their women making them second-class people subject to the whims of men, including forced polygamous marriages of underage girls (legally, they say they have stopped that practice). They use banishment to punish any young men who show the slightest hint of rebellion, which then makes more women available to the remaining men.

Its founder, Joseph Smith, a "ne'er do well" who had an insatiable desire for women, bounced around New England, moving ten times before coming to Palmyra, New York.

Smith claimed an angel of the Lord came to him one night when no one else was present and showed him where god had hidden some "magic golden plates" buried uncannily on his parent's farm. He said they were written in a strange "Indian" language. Fortunately for Smith, he also claimed to have a pair of "magic spectacles" handy, and these magic spectacles allowed only Smith to read the golden plates. He called it the book of Mormon. Smith had it printed in 1830.

Smith organized the Mormon Church as a cooperative theocracy with himself as the "head prophet." He moved his band from Palmyra to Kirkland, Ohio. After a short stay in Ohio, he moved first to Missouri and then to Illinois.

In Illinois he received another revelation from god. This time it was in favor of polygamy. He convinced his male followers that they too were allowed to do this, and the Mormon men wholeheartedly agreed this was a directive from god. Like most Christians at the time, the Mormons didn't consult the women, who may have had a very different inspiration. Christian and Mormon doctrine held that women were subservient to the men. They were property of their fathers or husbands. Smith then proceeded to marry twenty-seven women within five years, some of them just children as young as ten years of age.

Mormon marriages were arranged by men. Women were traded like cattle. Fathers traded their daughters with other fathers, or would trade them for property, or would have daughters marry someone to enhance their own class standing in the Church. A Mormon can raise his class standing by marrying his daughters to men of higher community standing. Widows were also given away to other members of the tribe, usually without their consent. These practices continue today as is evidenced with the 2002 conviction of Tom Green, who was thirty-seven when he took his thirteen-year-old stepdaughter as a wife. Green was at the time of his conviction living with five wives and twenty-nine children in a cluster of trailers in Utah. He was also convicted of failing to pay child support and welfare fraud.

Ironically, Green was only caught because he appeared on a half dozen nationally televised talk shows to talk about the "Mormon lifestyle." In Utah, the local authorities, most of them Mormon, have always turned a blind eye to both polygamy and pedophilia, although the Mormon Church "officially" banned these practices in the 1890s as part of a deal with the federal government to grant Utah statehood.

Joseph Smith, the founder, was killed in a dispute with the Illinois locals. It was Brigham Young, his second in command, that led a bloody war of retaliation for the next two years. He also married five of Smith's twenty-seven wives.

The Mormons began losing members during this war of retaliation, and Brigham Young feared the eventual collapse of the Mormons. In 1840, with all of the resources of the Mormons, Young went to England and recruited four thousand of England's poorest working-class people. He promised them passage to America and a farm of their own in the wilderness if they would convert to Mormonism and follow him. These destitute people without a future in England readily joined the Mormons.

In 1847, he moved his small band and the recently arrived English converts into Mexican territory, around the Great Salt Lake. He called it "Deseret," but it would become known as Utah. After the war with Mexico in 1848, it became part of the United States and Brigham Young was named the Territorial Governor.

Young became a Mormon dictator. He clashed with the federal judges and marshals that the Federal government appointed, and he eventually had them all driven out of Utah.

In 1857, President Buchanan and the US Congress had had enough of Brigham Young. They appointed a new Territorial Governor, new judges, federal marshals, and sent the Army under the command of Colonel Albert Sydney Johnson to occupy Utah and to establish and support the newly appointed government. In 1862, because of the Mormons, the Congress passed legislation outlawing polygamy. However, Mormonism still prevailed in Utah and so did polygamy. The Mormons became a very powerful element in the rise of the Christian conservatives in America.

In the Burned Over District of New York, another large and interesting religious event occurred in 1843. William Miller of Hampton, New York had a revelation that the "Second Coming of Christ" would happen on October 22. He managed to convince thousands of mostly working-class people in New York. He urged them to rid themselves of all their ungodly material possessions and to find the highest ground on that night to assure their ascent into heaven. Thousands gave away their goods and money and sat on barn and house roofs, up in trees, and on hilltops. When midnight passed and nothing happened, and they realized that they had given all their money and possessions away for nothing, they got off their high perches and began to riot.

In Lebanon, New York, a working-class woman who called herself Mother Ann Lee, and her friend Jemima Wilkinson from Jerusalem, New York co-founded the Celibate Shaker communities. Unlike the Mormons, they were anti-sex. They believed that sex was the original sin and sexual urges should be repressed to improve one's relationship with god. This seems to have been a less appealing platform than polygamy, and the movement died out after only one generation.

In 1848, the same district produced one of the few working-class socialist and anti-capitalistic Christian societies. Called the Oneida Communities, they were founded by John H. Noyes and specialized in quality craftsmanship. They produced silverware, steel traps and craft goods. In 1881, they were doing so well that they gave up socialism, embraced capitalism and reorganized as a joint stock company. American Christianity has not since strayed from capitalism.

Another Burned Over District resident was Mary Baker Eddy. In 1866, she attributed her miraculous recovery from an undiagnosed and an unknown illness to her reading the New Testament of the Bible. In 1875, she published a book called "Science and Health." It really wasn't about either. It was about what she called "Divine Laws" based upon the biblical acts and sayings of Jesus.

Strangely, the followers of Eddy are called Christian Scientists. In 1879, the first Church of Christian Science was formed in Boston. Their name is an oxymoron, as the Church is anti-science and against modern medicine. US courts have been intervening on the behalf of children against their Christian Scientist parents since that time to insure that they receive real medical care in-life-and death situations and not just the support of their parent's prayers.

Two others, the Fox sisters, took advantage of the gullible residents of the Burned Over District to introduce "Spiritualism" in 1848 through their claimed ability to speak to the dead in "Séance sessions." During the next ten years in America over sixty-seven newspapers and magazines would be devoted exclusively to the subject. After a hundred and fifty-some years the interest in the occult and Spiritualism is still believed and practiced by many in America.

The nineteenth-century Christian religious movements weren't totally confined to the Burned Over District. In 1851, the Young Men's Christian Association, the YMCA, was founded. The organization was created to inspire Christian beliefs among working-class boys and young men. They provided temporary housing, recreation, summer camps, Bible study groups, and Christian education. In 1894, their sister agency, the Young Women's Christian Association was formed.

The Salvation Army was imported to the United States from England. William Booth, a London Evangelist, founded it in 1865. Its purpose was to provide Christian services to the many working-class poor who lived in London. His son Ballington Booth brought the Salvation Army to America in 1887. He served as the first "Commander" in America. His sister Emma Moss Booth-Tucker replaced him after his resignation in 1896. She served as its Commander until her death in 1906 and another sister, Evangeline Cory Booth, served as the Commander until 1934. The Salvation Army uses social welfare benefits to attract the working-class poor to its Christian education and missionary programs. And although they do charitable work with the poor, the primary mission is Christian recruitment and conversion of the poor.

After his resignation from the Salvation Army in 1896, Ballington Booth and his wife founded the Volunteers of America, which became another national religious non-profit corporation serving the working-class poor. It is today the largest owner of subsidized affordable housing in America. They also deliver a variety of social service programs. It is also organized as a church so that many of their employees can chose to become ordained ministers, and thereby receiving unfair tax breaks on their income taxes and housing. The organization promotes these tax advantages as part of their employee compensation to new hires. Like the Salvation Army, it is also a missionary organization.

Today the Mormons and these other splinter groups provide much of the impetus of the Christian conservative movement that has dominated the Republican Party and US politics. They have attempted to control American culture through these politics by campaigning against such issues as women' rights, the rights of gays, teaching science and evolution in schools, and in favor of promoting Christianity in public places and the government.

But perhaps their greatest influence is felt in getting their working-class followers to ignore their own best economic interests for those of the leisure class, including voting against taxes on the wealthy, supporting the deregulation of business, disdain for consumer protections offered on their behalf, and opposition to health and welfare programs for their own benefit.

Is this manipulation merely a by-product of Christian culture or a deliberate manipulation of the working class by the rich and powerful? I would argue the latter. Karl Rove, the most powerful architect of the recent political successes of the Christian conservative movement, is himself an atheist. Rove, like many in the power elite, uses religion to control the working class by manipulating them and side-tracking them with Christian cultural issues to make economic and political gains for the leisure class and to advance their own agendas. It is a lesson learned from the Romans, to divide the masses and subdue them.

Chapter 12. The Ghetto Complex

> "Rome supported what is now called by Catholics themselves the 'ghetto complex,' trying to keep Catholics living together and forbidding them to take part with Protestants in secular American activities."—*Historian Samuel Eliot Morison*

There were twelve million Catholics, mostly working class, in Protestant-dominated America by 1890. This dramatic increase was due to continued immigration of Irish and German Catholics, as well as from Poland, Italy, the Baltic States, and some French Canadians. The Catholic Church in America was splintered into groups around nationalities and these groups wanted to hear their Mass and give their Confessions in their native tongues.

A movement started to organize around nationalities instead of the usual Catholic geographic area. It was led by a Catholic layman Peter P. Cahensley. The supporters of the movement were mostly German priests, who considered themselves better Catholic scholars and more middle-class than their Irish counterparts, but it was the Irish working class who had dominated American Catholicism. However the Irish, to the anger of the Germans, were better politicians and were claiming most of the Bishoprics in America.

The two main adversaries of the German approach based upon ethnic groups and nationalities were Archbishop John Ireland of St. Paul, Minnesota and Bishop James Cardinal Gibbons of Baltimore. They were powerful men who were able to defeat the ethnic movement despite its popularity with the majority of American Catholics and with support from Rome.

The Vatican considered the American democracy a bastard cousin of the French Jacobism which was anti-clerical and felt that America was also an anti-clerical society, where even American Catholics had little regard for the leadership of priests. The Vatican wanted to keep America divided into ethnic groups loyal to their homelands.

The Vatican had also become very alarmed that in Protestant-dominated America, over a million and a half Catholics had converted to Protestantism during the years 1820-1900. The Vatican developed a strategy to combat these conversions. It was called the "Ghetto Complex." It was instituted just before the twentieth century. It was also a policy that insured most American Catholics would remain poor and locked in the working class.

American Catholics were instructed by their priests to have as little contact with Protestants as possible. They were to patronize only Catholic businesses when possible, live in Catholic neighborhoods, to pay for and attend only Catholic schools instead of the free public schools, and under no circumstances were they allowed to date or marry non-Catholics unless their partners agreed to convert to Catholicism.

In 1899, Pope Leo XIII in a Papal Letter condemned "Americanism" and "liberal American priests" for their advocacy of Catholics participating in a secular American society. He also condemned priests for accepting honorary degrees from Harvard and other Protestant colleges, and for participating in the Congress on Religion at the World's Fair.

By 1908, the US became the largest contributor to Catholic Charities. Pope Pius X, realizing the growing importance of American Catholics, finally bowed to American pressure and removed them from the jurisdiction of the Propogand Fedei, where American Catholics were governed as second-class Catholics, and reluctantly gave American Catholics the same status as the Churches in France and Spain. However it would be another fifty years before Pope John XXIII would recognize the American concept of separation of Church and State and allow the Catholics to participate in a secular Christian America and loosen up the Ghetto Complex policy.

CHAPTER 13. CHRISTIANITY VS. SCIENCE AND MODERNISM

> "In these times it has almost become a requirement for the sophisticated and intelligent to take a swipe at the nearest Christian."—Reverend Franklin Graham

> "If the Bible told me that two and two were five, I would believe it!"—Reverend Billy Graham

Charles Darwin published *The Origin of Species* in 1859. It provided the theory of evolution through natural selection and stated that man was the product of development from lower forms of life. The Christian community was outraged.

The American intellectual community, led by Asa Gray from Harvard, pushed Darwin to include that evolution was part of "a grand design by an omnipotent god" to appease American Christians. Although Darwin was a Christian, as a scientist he could not accept this "compromise" and refused to co-mingle religious philosophy with scientific fact. Darwin's bravery inspired other scientific writings such as "Mans' Place in Nature" by Thomas Huxley, "The Geological Evidences of the Antiquity of Man" by Charles Lydell, and the "Principles of Biology."

The Origin of Species was published in 1859 and became a best seller from 1860 to 1900. The American Christian establishment rejected Darwinism and other scientific discoveries as blasphemous. A number of states passed laws banning the book and prohibiting the teaching of evolution in the public schools.

In 1925, John T. Scopes, a science teacher in Dayton, Tennessee, was accused of teaching evolution. He actually had done so at the urging of the American Civil Liberties Union, who wanted to take the issue to court. The State of Tennessee chose William Jennings Bryan, a staunch Christian and a famous working-class populist and former presidential candidate as the prosecuting attorney. Clarence Darrow became the defense attorney. From the beginning, the trial was more circus than legal proceeding. It gained worldwide recognition and was mockingly dubbed by Christians as the "Scopes Monkey Trial."

The trial was before a jury of working-class Christians, and Bryan played on their class fears and emotions and asked frequently how many of them would like to claim that they were the heirs of monkeys instead of being made in god's image. He won the trial on pure emotionalism. But Darrow was a very shrewd attorney. He lost the case but was successful in having Scopes' conviction thrown out on several legal technicalities.

At the trial's climax the Judge ironically allowed Bryan to take the stand as a "Biblical expert" and Bryan affirmed among other things that a whale had actually swallowed Jonah and that he had lived inside the beast, that Joshua actually made the sun stand still, and that the world was created in seven days in the year 4004 B.C. (Scientists and non-Christians prefer the term B.C.E. which means Before the Christian Era. Bryan's testimony became the subject of widespread ridicule, most notably by the witty newspaper columnist H.L. Mencken. Fortunately for Bryan, he never heard these criticisms. He died. Mencken and others offered two theories: First, god, apparently impressed with Bryan's defense of Christianity, had called him home several days after the trial, or second, god killed him because he was such a pompous ass.

State laws prohibiting the teaching of evolution remained in effect until 1964. However, in the 21st century a new Christian conservative movement is attempting to pass laws that would require the teaching of "Creationism," the religious Christian six-day belief of creation, to be taught by science teachers along with evolution. Incredibly, this is being sold as a freedom-of-choice issue for students who would then be forced to choose between science and religion. Expanding on this argument some educators have suggested with tongue in cheek that we should also include Native American, Hindu, Buddhist and other ideas of creation in our science classes too, thereby allowing an even greater choice for students. Science is not the rubric under which to teach religion. Most science teachers are unqualified, unprepared, and do not wish to give Christian religious instruction as part of or instead of their science courses.

Tom DeLay, Republican House Majority Leader until his ignominious departure in 2005, summed up Christian educational bias with the infamous comments he made shortly after the Columbine school shootings. He suggested that the tragedy occurred "because our school systems teach our children that they are nothing but glorified apes who have evolutionized out of some primordial mud."

Paul Krugman, writing for the *New York Times,* summarized DeLay's comments by stating that according to DeLay, "Guns don't kill people; Charles Darwin kills people." DeLay's comments also give credence to President Obama's unpopular remarks about the US working class' emotional dependence on their guns and religion.

In 2003, the US Justice Department under President Bush began an investigation of Michael Dini, a biology professor at Texas Tech University, for supposedly violating the constitutional rights of his students. His crime was that he required any student entering a career in biology and who wished a reference from him to believe in the biological principle of evolution.

Chapter 14. Jewish Impact on America, Anti-Semitism and More Class Conflict

> "God Almighty does not hear the prayer of a Jew."—The Reverend Bailey Smith speaking at a news briefing of the Religious Round Table
>
> "The Anti-Christ is already among us and living as a male Jew."—*Pat Robertson*
>
> "Therefore, I am convinced that I am acting as an agent of our creator by fighting off the Jews, I am doing the Lord's work." —*Adolph Hitler in Mein Kampf*

Jews were not welcome in America. The religion was banned in America in the early days. It wasn't until 1777 that New York became the first state to allow Jews. A hundred years later, in 1877, New Hampshire became the last state to enfranchise Jews. In the states that were admitted to the union after 1877, it was no longer an issue. However, their enfranchisement didn't mean that Jews were fully accepted.

During the late nineteenth century, there were very few Jews in America. As the Jewish immigrants rose in numbers, American anti-Semitism also began to grow rapidly. Most American Christians, like their European counterparts, felt that the Jews "deserved" to be victims of vengeance for betraying Jesus. Jews were called "Christ-Killers." A significant Jewish immigration to America began in the late nineteenth century. While most immigrants were working class, the Jewish immigrants were of mixed classes, including middle-class tradesmen, and professionals. The Americans working class was even less tolerant of these middle-class Jews. As the differences between the working-class American and the middle-class Jews became apparent, the working class began to describe Jews as "cheap, cunning, and avaricious." American working-class slang would use the word "Jew" as a verb to mean cheated out of something, as in: "He Jewed me out of it." Or to get a bargain, as in: "I was able to Jew him down from the price." This anti-Semitism has created another division in the working class.

In 1895, President Grover Cleveland attempted to save the troubled economy and the gold standard, which was the basis of the value of the American dollar. He secretly negotiated to buy gold in Europe. He authorized the Secretary of the Treasury to sign an agreement with J.P. Morgan and Company, August Belmont and Company, and N.M. Rothschild and Sons. Radicals and working-class Christian populists like William Jennings Bryan fixated upon Rothschild (who was Jewish) and claimed that there was "an international Jewish conspiracy to dominate America." Incredibly, a hundred years later, some rightwing Christian conservatives still promote this concept of a "Jewish World Conspiracy."

"The Jewish Conspiracy" was blamed for everything wrong in working-class people's lives and led to even more widespread anti-Semitism in America. In 1902, on New York City's lower East Side, a Jewish funeral procession for Rabbi Jacob Joseph triggered one of the most anti-Semitic incidents in American history.

The Rabbi was one of the first prominent leaders of the American Jewish community. He was very well known and liked. His funeral attracted over a thousand Jewish mourners. As the mourners followed the funeral procession to the graveyard, they passed a large factory, which employed mostly working-class Irish-Catholic laborers. The Irish-Catholic workers began pelting the mourners with nuts and bolts, then blocked the street and refused to let the Jews pass. The police were sent to restore order—but the police officers were also mostly working-class Irish-Catholics and sided with the factory workers. They began to beat the Jews and were joined by the workers. In this police riot, well over two hundred Jews were seriously injured.

Anti-Semitic hate groups flourished during the first half of the twentieth century. Open and widespread anti-Semitism became common during the period. The automaker Henry Ford became a leader in the anti-Semitic movement. He had his Dearborn newspaper publish "Protocols of the Elders of Zionism," which renewed the claim that there was "an international Jewish conspiracy" that Ford said was trying to destroy "American Christian Civilization." Ford also wrote and published a book, *The International Jew* that blamed most of the world's problems and like Hitler, he blamed World War I on Jewish plots.

Henry Ford was also a supporter of an anti-Semitic and fascist Catholic priest, Reverend Charles E. Coughlin. In 1926, Ford helped Coughlin start his radio show, "The Shrine of the Little Flower." It was a sweet name for a hate-driven show. Coughlin was the first mass communication Christian Evangelist.

He became known across America as "the Radio Priest." His show attracted a large working-class audience across America.

He was a shameless self-promoter and his first mission was to raise money for himself and his show. In a typical letter written to a donor he wrote:

"My Dearest Friend;
   With this letter, it is my privilege to send you a souvenir crucifix. As I announced over the air it has touched a relic of the true cross.

   Devotedly yours in Christ, Fr. Charles E, Coughlin

   P.S. If a friend wants a crucifix let me know. C.E.C."

In just three months after joining the CBS Radio Network, he was receiving over eighty thousand letters a week containing over twenty thousand dollars a week in cash. He would employ more than a hundred and fifty clerks just to open letters and count his money. By 1934, he would have over forty five million radio followers and make a half million dollars a year during the Great Depression. Most of the money came from poor working-class people.

Coughlin would build a towering church in Royal Oak, Michigan. It was ironically called the "Charity Crucifixion Tower." The tower contained a large statue of Jesus illuminated with spotlights and the word "charity" written under the statue in large letters. Coughlin's operation had little to do with charity. Jesus overlooked a bizarre commercial scene that included: "The Little Shrine Super Gas Station," "The little Shrine Inn Motel," "The Little Flower Hot Dog Stand."

Inside Charity Crucifixion Tower there were many other commercial vendors who sold souvenir post cards, crucifixes "personally blessed" by Coughlin, and a large quantity of anti-Semitic literature.

Coughlin's second mission was even darker than hocking goods and begging money from poor people during the Great Depression. He was a violent anti-Semite and a White Supremacist and a Christian fascist even before Hitler. Some newspaper reporters of the day were so disgusted with Coughlin and his Charity Crucifixion Tower that they began calling it "The Gross Silo" and began calling Coughlin "Silo Charlie."

During his radio show Coughlin sat on stage chain smoking with his Great Dane dog lying beside him. He preached rabid anti-Semitism and other right-wing causes while soliciting money for his "Christian causes."

In the 1930s, conservative upper-class businessmen including the newspaper publisher William Randolph Hearst and *Time* and *Life Magazine* publisher Henry Luce began the "whispering campaign" that started the rumor that Franklin Roosevelt was a really a Jew named "Rosenveldt." To their delight, Father Coughlin began repeating these lies on his radio show and claiming that "Rosenveldt" was part of the Jewish conspiracy to enslave Christian Whites. Coughlin was also a racist and ranted about how "Rosenveldt" wanted to employ only "Jews and niggers" at the expense of White Christian people. He soon became the official spokesman for the American Fascists.

There were many complaints and CBS was concerned about Coughlin, but they bowed to the fact that he had forty five million followers. CBS refused to take action on these complaints until Coughlin, in 1935, advocated to his audience that "Rosenveldt should be eliminated by the use of bullets." It was only then that CBS finally pulled the plug on Coughlin.

Coughlin immediately founded an independent radio network that started with sixty affiliated stations. It was claimed at the time that Coughlin's flock was the largest in Christian history. *Fortune Magazine*, a Henry Luce publication, called Coughlin "The biggest thing that ever happened to radio." Coughlin's personal fortune became so great from his contributions from his poor working-class listeners that he became the largest speculator in silver. He called it the "Christian metal." He warned his listeners to "Think Christian, Act Christian, Buy Christian and beware of World Jewry! Call this inflammatory if you will, it is inflammatory! But we will fight and we will win!"

Coughlin began his own religious and political group called The National Union for Social Justice. At its peak, it had over seven and a half million working-class White followers. He had a magazine published called "Social Justice" that was a hate filled publication of anti-Semitic and racist articles. His Union for Social Justice had a large paramilitary organization within it. They were organized into platoons of twenty-five and wore "brown shirts" like Hitler's Nazis. The platoons roamed the streets vandalizing Jewish businesses. Their favorite tactic was to find someone they suspected of being a Jew and offer to sell them the magazine Social Justice. If they refused to buy, they would be severely beaten by the Brown Shirts.

Father Coughlin was also anti-labor union. He said unions were anti-Capitalistic and therefore anti-Christian. He called labor leader John L. Lewis "a communist stooge," and called the American Federation of Labor "socialists." Coughlin advocated on his Radio show and in his magazine that America should follow Hitler's lead in outlawing unions. He failed to mention that Stalin had also banned labor unions.

Coughlin, like many conservative Americans at the time, was an admirer of Hitler. After New York Mayor LaGuardia publicly criticized Hitler as a dictator, Coughlin stated that La Guardia was "threatening world peace and breeding international bad feelings." On his radio show he mockingly awarded La Guardia the "Ill Will Award."

Anti-Semitism was not just isolated in the Coughlin's Detroit or in the South. Even in very tolerant and liberal cities like Minneapolis there were large anti-Semitic movements. The Reverend Luke Rader and his son Paul, like Father Coughlin, were two of the first "radio evangelists." They worked out of the Lake Street Tabernacle in Minneapolis. They had over seventy-eight thousand followers in their heyday. Their radio show went on the air twice a day. They became so popular that the Reverend Paul Rader was drafted by his followers as a candidate for Mayor of Minneapolis and came in a very strong third in the election as an independent candidate against the Democratic and Republican candidates despite never campaigning for the office.

The Rader's claimed that the Anglo-Saxons were the "true" Israelites, and Jews were created by Satan. They referred to the Roosevelt's New Deal as the "Jew Deal." In 1946 after the Holocaust, Paul Rader justified Hitler's actions and the Holocaust by saying, "Jews weren't fit to live." The Raders were also anti-communists and in 1963 when Russian Church leaders visited Minneapolis, Paul Rader organized a large protest against them. On that Sunday he delivered a radio sermon called "The Red Anti-Christ in the Pulpit."

The Rader's Tabernacle on Lake Street was so feared that Jews in Minneapolis were afraid to anywhere near the building. In 2002, the Rader's old and abandoned Lake Street Tabernacle was scheduled for demolition. The Minneapolis Heritage Preservation Commission and the City Planning Department insisted that in order to allow its demolition that the developers should agree to build a display area in the new replacement building "commemorating the two Raders as pioneer televangelists." Several Jewish organizations complained that it would be a monument to anti-Semitism, but the City Planning Department held its ground until a number of Minneapolis leaders finally weighed in on the side of the Jewish community.

Another unlikely hero to the American working-class was Fritz Lieber Kuhn. Kuhn came to the United States in 1927. He was forty years old and a veteran of the Kaiser's Army. In World War I he was decorated with Germany's highest honor, the Iron Cross. He was a graduate of the University of Munich with a Masters degree in Science. Henry Ford hired him at the Ford Motor Company. Like Father Coughlin, Kuehn found a niche in the anti-Semitic Conservative Christian society that flourished in Detroit. He also had the full support of Henry Ford.

In 1936 he founded the German-American Bund. Fritz Kuhn became the leader and he was dubbed the "American Fuehrer." Kuhn received financial support from Hitler and the German Foreign Ministry in his efforts. Kuhn and a group of his American supporters were invited to go to Germany at the expense of the German government and received political training in Berlin. Kuhn was also given a personal audience with Hitler and given a photograph of himself with Hitler as a memento of the trip.

On February 20, 1939 the German-American Bund held a rally at Madison Square Garden. Twenty-two thousand attended. Kuhn opened the rally with a Christian prayer and called for "a socially just and White Gentile ruled United States." He then went on to praise Father Coughlin and Henry Ford. He castigated Roosevelt, Treasury Secretary Morgenthau and Labor Secretary Francis Perkins as forces of evil in the World Jewish Conspiracy." He also preached hard and long about purity of thought and Christian morality, a favorite subject.

Kuhn was convicted later that year for stealing funds from the Bund and the German Foreign Ministry. During the trial it was discovered that Kuhn, the preacher of Christian morality and purity, and a married man with two children, had spent large sums of money on women "of questionable reputation." It was also discovered that seven hundred dollars of the stolen funds were spent on long distance phone calls to a German prostitute that he had become infatuated with during his Nazi political training in Germany.

One of the more humorous disclosures during his trial for theft was that although Kuhn had taken a public position that Jazz was a "Negroid mongrelization of music and a contamination of the White race," he had on many occasions spent large sums of the stolen money on liquor in after-hours Jazz nightclubs, and that he particularly liked the Jazz tune "Flat Foot Floogie With A Floy-floy." It was disclosed in testimony that he had requested the song multiple times at a Jazz club one evening while escorting a former Miss America. Kuhn was imprisoned and the German-American Bund was dissolved.

However anti-Semitism was still prevalent in America after the Bund's demise. As early as 1942, the military and the American government knew about Hitler's plan to exterminate the Jews. The American government did nothing. America not only turned its back on the plight of the Jews in Europe, but it also refused to take in new Jewish immigrants. One of the most famous incidents was a ship called the St. Louis. It arrived at Miami, Florida with a thousand Jewish immigrants that had fled Hitler's wrath. The ship was turned away and forced to return to Europe. Most of those aboard returned to Europe and died in the Nazi concentration camps.

At this same time the State Department had set a quota to allow European immigration and Jews into America. America never used its full quota, and at the war's end, ninety percent of the quota was left unfilled. The Jews were turned away because they were Jews.

The American military knew early on about the concentration camps, but chose to do nothing. At the end of the war there was pressure put on the American government by the American Jewish community and others to destroy the crematoria at Auschwitz and to destroy the rail lines leading to the camp. The American military insisted it was "unfeasible," even though at the time of the request there were bombing missions less than a few miles away on much more highly defended targets. The real reason they refused to bomb these targets was that the military didn't consider them a priority. The death toll at the camps reached ten million, including six million Jews. Had the Americans bombed the crematoria and the rails lines to the camp tens of thousands who died would have survived to be liberated.

It was only in the aftermath of the exposed horror of the Holocaust and the Nuremburg Trials that American anti-Semitism began to abate. It was out of this debt and guilt about the Holocaust that America in 1948 would recognize the Jewish state of Israel, and then ironically would be accused by many as being "pro-Jewish."

Chapter 15. The Ku Klux Klan & Other White Christian Supremacists

Klansman James True invented the "Kike Killer," U.S. Patent Number 2,026,077. It was a club made in two sizes, "a small for ladies and a large for gentlemen."

The Ku Klux Klan, the post-Civil War Southern White hate group was organized as a "White Christian protection group." It remained a strong force in the South until the 1970s, and has made a recent comeback with the "Skinheads" and other White Supremacist Groups. These groups are mostly populated by working-class Whites who believe their status and well being have been stolen by Jews and non-Whites. It is an unfortunate legacy of the American class system.

After flourishing in the South after the Civil War, the Klan was "reborn" at Stone Mountain, Georgia in 1915 when William J. Simmons paid workers to start carving a Confederate Memorial on the northeast wall of the mountain. It was finally completed in 1967 and is now one of the most popular tourist attractions in Georgia. Simmons reorganized the Klan at the turn of the century as a working-class "White Christian Organization" and expanded its mission of hating blacks to also hate other people of color, and to hate Catholics and particularly Jews. The phrase K.K.K., he said, meant that they were against "Coons, Kikes, and Catholics." He pronounced that it was a religious organization to protect White working class Christians. The Klan also ironically became advocates for the prohibition of alcohol. Simmons eventually lost control of the organization to a Dallas dentist, Hiram Wesley Evans who said that the Klan was also about "Americanism." He expanded their hate list to include Latinos and all new immigrants. He declared that America was for only "native-born White Protestants." Others weren't welcome. He was also against the Women's Movement, which he said was led by women of low moral standards who practiced "the new morality." The Klan spread from the South to the Southwest, then into the Midwest and the Northeast.

The Klan for the first time was able to market itself successfully and to spread in the northern states. It was because large numbers of rural southern working-class Blacks moved north to new factory jobs and began to compete with whites for these jobs. The southern Black farmers, many of whom were sharecroppers and didn't own their own land, were much more vulnerable to the decline of farming, and this change in the economy from agriculture to industrialization forced their migration north into the large central cities. Southern whites were also part of this migration and further increased the job competition for the existing working-class population.

The country song, "Detroit City" reflected this southern working-class migration. The lyrics of the song are: "Last night I spent the night in Detroit City, and I dreamed about those cotton fields back home." The song goes on to express the loss he felt from the separation from home, family and friends. It became popular because the song reflected the experience of hundreds of thousands of people who made this migration.

Before this migration, the north had a very small black population, but after the migration most industrialized northern cities had significant black populations. And with this migration the Klan became a significant force nationwide in the 1920s. The Klan elected Governors in the states of Illinois, Wisconsin, Indiana, and Oregon. During this time Klansman James True invented the "Kike Killer," U.S. Patent Number 2,026,077. It was a club made in two sizes "a small for ladies and a large for gentlemen."

The Klan became so prominent in the North that Governor David Stephenson of Indiana replaced Evans as its leader. Stephenson became "The Grand Dragon." He preached sobriety, chastity, and Christianity along with the hate messages. He was also the reason for the Klan's decline. One night while drunk he raped and murdered a young Black Indiana girl. His highly publicized conviction for her rape and murder began the decline of the Klan in America.

However white supremacy would be revived again in the mid twentieth century and flourish in the form of "White-Christian organizations" like the Skinheads, the Neo Nazi Movement and a host of paramilitary organizations. They even have their own music that has become known as "Hate Rock."

In 2002 Joseph Rodriguez, a video producer and director for the University of California at Berkley was shopping at a Target Store near Sacramento, California, while shopping he spotted shorts with human skulls that had "88" emblazoned on them. He had just seen a documentary about Hate Rock and knew that "88" was Neo Nazi and Skinhead Code for "Heil Hitler." "H" is the eighth letter of the alphabet and the hate groups use it as their private code on clothing, flyers, letters and email addresses to identify each other.

The Target Corporation is a Minneapolis based company. At the time they also owned Marshall Field's Department Stores. The store was selling these Nazi shorts for $12.50 and hats for $7.99 with the 88 codes emblazoned on them. Rodriguez complained to the local store managers who dismissed and rejected his concerns, so he complained to the Target Headquarters in Minneapolis. These contacts also failed to produce any results.

"The more I tried to do something, the less response I got and it turned to anger." He said.

He finally contacted the Anti-Defamation League and the Southern Poverty Law Center. They put enough pressure on the department store chain to pull the offensive clothing and offer a refund to people who may have bought the items not knowing their significance. The company denied any knowledge of the significance of the skulls and 88 symbols. However it begs the question why did the retailer put skulls and symbols on clothing if they didn't know what they meant? The department store chain has never responded to Rodriguez who suggested that the company at the very least needed diversity training.

He said, "I think they need to start at the very top and work their way down."

The Target Corporation isn't the only company to have problems with hate and intolerance. Earlier in 2002 the teen clothing chain, Abercrombie & Fitch, had to recall a line of their tee shirts that had pictures of Asians depicted in racist cartoons on their front.

CHAPTER 16. CHRISTIANITY & CAPITALISM, THE CREATION OF AMERICAN
ECONOMIC AND CLASS CULTURE

> "Children are being subjected to psychological manipulation which moves them
> away from their Judeo-Christian mind-set and moves them into a humanistic
> mould into the socialist worldview and ultimately into the Communist
> International."—Pat Robertson

It is extremely telling that "In God We Trust" is on the nation's currency.
Christianity was and is synonymous with Capitalism in America and they have
become one religion. Because the Puritan "work ethic" stated, "the Lord would
not suffer a sinner to prosper," it was assumed that economic success was proof
of a person's salvation. Although some rightwing conservatives of the working-
class lean toward fascism, capitalism along with Christianity is the American
creed.

Interestingly enough, where Christian conservatives disavow Darwin's Theory of Evolution, Christian Conservatives have adopted "Social Darwinism" to justify capitalism. In 1900 a social philosopher, Herbert Spencer, coined the phrase,
"survival of the fittest." It was a corruption of the biological theories of Charles
Darwin and often this quote is mistakenly attributed to Darwin. Spencer believed that social processes, like society and economics, were natural forces and
these natural forces only failed when government tried to "artificially" regulate
them. The Christian conservatives seized upon this theory to justify their version
of capitalism with "less government regulation" and "free markets." They would
vehemently oppose any regulatory or social legislation by their government. Alan
Greenspan the former Chairman of the Federal Reserve Bank and arguably one

of the most influential people in American economics was a staunch adherent of this free market philosophy.

In the 1990s an Evangelical Christian research group, the George Barna Group, found in a poll of American Born Again Christians, that they ranked "Living a comfortable lifestyle" almost as important as "Having a close relationship with God." Christian conservatives are apparently equally capitalistic as they are religious. Christian conservatives are also mostly from the working class.

The Communist Revolution in Russia and the rise of socialism upset American concepts of class and society particularly among these Christian conservatives who have come to dominate the Republican Party. The leaders of the Republican Party, the upper and middle-class business owners who disliked the unions used the fear of communism to make much of the working-class paranoid about the American labor movement. The unions were socialist they argued, and they would artificially limit free markets. They also argued that the union movement unchecked would eventually lead to a communist revolution in the United States.

They also reasoned that since the Russian Communists were atheists, then all atheists are communists. Communism has become synonymous with atheism in America.

America was solidly anti-communist during World War I, the American Army invaded Russia's Arctic ports in 1918 during the Russian Revolution with an expeditionary force of eight thousand men. Ironically Russia was an ally against Germany at the time. It was a strange way to treat an ally. It was called an "intervention" and deemed for the Russian's own good.

One of the main purposes of the intervention was to help the Czarist Russians to push out the communists. The intervention failed because there was little Russian support for the rapidly declining and repressive Czarist government in Russia. And it was from this American "intervention" that the Russians would harbor long-standing suspicions about the United States. It was the actual start of the Cold War. America had made the first strike in what would be a long cold war. The acrimony between the two nations would continue despite the fact that they would again be allies against Nazi Germany in World War II.

During World War I the federal government, at the urging of Christian conservatives and their politicians, suppressed the free speech of communist and socialist groups in America. And the Christian conservatives, along with business leaders like Henry Ford, went after labor unions and labor leaders as well.

During this campaign, Attorney General Thomas W. Gregory, a man sworn to uphold the Constitution and the First Amendment, made the incredible statement, "Free expression is dangerous to American institutions." During his term as Attorney General, Gregory would prosecute over 1,500 people for exercising their right to free speech. He justified these prosecutions under the newly passed Sedition and Espionage Acts. Very few of those prosecuted had anything to do with the either the war or espionage. Most were working-class people involved in union activities and a few were socialists.

Most of those prosecuted were new immigrants. They were mostly Eastern and Southern European Catholics and Jews. A few others were Buddhists from the new East Asian immigration to the West Coast. Immigration was becoming a concern to Christian conservatives who viewed the new comers as "socialists," and as a threat to capitalism and their religious beliefs. In the year 1869 immigration to America was just a little over 350,000 people, but by 1884 over 1,500,000 new immigrants came to America.

The vulnerable working-class Protestants became easy recruits to the growing Christian conservative anti-immigration movement. Many of the working class were economically vulnerable and feared the new competition meant less for their families and were also intolerant toward the growing number of Catholics, Jews and non-Christians. One of the most highly public anti-immigration incidents happened in 1920.

The police were unable to solve a payroll robbery and murder, and in their questioning of witnesses it was discovered that there were two neighborhood residents that had claimed to be anarchists. The two were libertarians who disliked all forms of government and they had come to America because they felt that the American democracy had the least intrusive and most libertarian government. The two were recent Italian-Catholic immigrants, named Nicola Sacco and Bartolomeo Vanzetti.

With no actual ties to the crime and despite no evidence, they were arrested and charged with the robbery and murder. During the trial the judge repeatedly referred to them as "the anarchist bastards." Without evidence and with an obviously biased judge, they were found guilty by the jury. Although there was an international outcry that the two men were found guilty for their libertarian views and not from any evidence, the two men were executed. Many Christian conservatives were pleased by the results of the trial. They felt the guilty verdict justified capitalism and defended America from these new immigrants who wanted change. It began new era in American intolerance.

Toward the end of Woodrow Wilson's last presidential term he was so sick that he became virtually incapable of running the country. The government was left in the hands of his wife and cabinet. A Pennsylvania Quaker named A. Mitchell Palmer was Wilson's third Attorney General. He was a ruthless and ambitious man who desired to be President when Wilson left office. He decided that openly attacking the "godless communists," who he labeled as the "Red Menace," was his ticket to the White House. He was urged on and would be greatly assisted by a young fanatically anti-communist member of his Justice Department named J. Edgar Hoover. Hoover would later be named to the very powerful post of Director of the Federal Bureau of Investigation.

The Red Menace campaign would be repeated and copied and repeated by Senator Joseph McCarthy of Wisconsin in the 1950s who was also encouraged and assisted by the Christian conservative J. Edgar Hoover.

Wilson who was very ill at the time, warned Palmer, "To not let the country see red."

Unfortunately as Wilson became more incapacitated, Palmer had the freedom to do as he pleased. One winter night in 1920 Palmer ordered raids by federal agents in thirty-three cities across the country. He arrested over four thousand people. Most of those arrested were new working-class immigrants who were union leaders and Jews. Palmer alleged that they were all "communist atheists" and charged them with "armed revolution and conspiracy."

They were held in jail for up to a week, some without food. All of these "communist-atheists" were found innocent of any wrong doing by the courts. Despite this fact, a wave of anti-communist paranoia swept the nation. The New York Legislature in a panic expelled five of their legally elected members for "suspected socialist ties."

Despite his nonexistent conviction rate, Palmer continued his arrests throughout the spring of 1920. Since he couldn't get convictions out of the courts, he began to deport new immigrants that he arrested as "undesirable aliens." Deportations of undesirable aliens fell solely under his jurisdiction as Attorney General. He was assisted in these mass deportations by his aide J. Edgar Hoover.

Palmer suffered a setback when two Senators, Charles Evans Hughes and Warren Harding denounced the arrests and the deportations. Labor Secretary William Wilson and his deputy Louis Post also took exception to the deportations. Post bravely took on the Attorney General. Post released over two thousand people from jail on his authority and was labeled a traitor by Palmer. During the chaos Palmer still managed to have another six hundred people deported, and arrested another two thousand that he planned to deport pending hearings.

Palmer was enraged by Post's interference and appeared before Congress to demand that Post be fired for "his tender solicitude for social revolution." Congress angrily demanded that Post appear before a congressional committee to explain his actions. Post appeared and made such an impassioned case for the protection of individual rights and liberties that the Committee backed down and did not recommend his termination. But the committee and Congress turned a blind eye when it came to stopping Palmer.

Palmer doubled his efforts buoyed by what he thought was the Congressional approval of his deportations. He stepped up his anti-communist campaign and warned the nation that he had inside information that on May 1, 1920 the communist workers would seize control of the nation. The nation took this warning seriously. The army and many state National Guard units were put on alert. In New York City they were so fearful of the revolution that the entire police department was put on overtime in an immediate twenty-four hour alert.

Palmer had finally overplayed his cards. When May 1, passed without a single incident Palmer became a national joke. The police and military units that had been called up were angry, and his credibility in government was permanently damaged. Palmer faded from significance. The nation's first "Red Menace" scare was over.

Chapter 17. The First Sexual Revolution

> "Unbalanced by prolonged contemplation of New England Puritanism, a generation of Americans has arisen whose great illusion is that the transalvation of all human values may be effected by promiscuity."—*An Irish Journalist Visiting America in the 1920s*

The first American sexual revolution came just after the turn of the twentieth century and this sexual revolution would begin as a protest against prostitution. The hypocrisy of the Christian sexual ethics of the time held that virginity for girls and women before marriage and chastity after marriage was absolute however these same standards didn't apply to boys or men. It was argued that men should delay marriage until they were occupationally established and could afford to properly support a wife and children. Men were therefore given "liberties" from these standards so that their sexual needs could be satisfied outside of marriage.

Public opinion, which at the turn of the century was given by only men, condoned the use of prostitution for men while at the same time hypocritically and unfairly condemning the women prostitutes for their immoral promiscuity.

Most American cities and many small towns and rural areas had their local whorehouses. New Orleans printed an annual guidebook to its brothels to attract men from all over the South. The New Orleans guidebook was one of America's first printed attempts at tourist promotion and was very successful. Many cities like San Francisco had famous "Red Light Districts" where whores displayed their charms in sidewalk display windows. American Christians believed that the women of the lower classes, certain races, religions, and ethnic groups were more susceptible to immoral behavior and therefore suitable for prostitution. The horrible truth was that many prostitutes at this time were young girls from working-class homes or were orphans who were frequently kidnapped from rural areas and small towns and brought to far away cities and forced into prostitution.

In 1910 Wright Kauffman published a novel called "The House of Bondage." The book gave a factual account about how young innocent girls were kidnapped and sold into prostitution. It also illuminated the dangers of venereal disease, particularly syphilis. It was the book that gave America the phrase "White Slavery." House of Bondage caused a moral uproar across the nation.

The new Women's movement took up the cause of anti-prostitution and this abuse of women, and was able to persuade their clergymen to support their efforts. Despite their efforts many Americans still entertained the notion that that most prostitutes were willing vendors who were new immigrants and people of color and were not white Christians. They were so sure of this the U.S. Immigration Service was forced to conduct an investigation to prove this. And although the U.S. Immigration Service study confirmed that many young foreign girls through a variety of unseemly illegal ploys were brought into the country and forced into prostitution, they also found that the majority were very young white American girls, many about twelve or thirteen from poor working-class homes or orphans that were the victims of these same illegal ploys and kidnappings. Most prostitutes entering the business were under-aged, white rural working-class girls. The study also confirmed that there were a good number of organized prostitution rings throughout the nation that traded in these under-aged girls. They were slaves.

Once the report became published an outraged American public lead by the Women's Movement forced the Congress to act. They passed the Mann Act which made it a felony to import or transport women across state lines for prostitution. The State Legislatures also felt the public pressure to outlaw prostitution, and by 1914 forty-five states had passed laws to do so. However even in the states where prostitution was outlawed many brothels still continued to operate with the help of friendly local law enforcement officials, but most of the large Red Light Districts in American cities were permanently closed.

At this time, a young man's first sexual encounter was considered a rite of passage into manhood. For their first sexual experience, young men were frequently taken by their fathers, or by older brothers, or by friends to the local whorehouse. With the passage of the state laws banning these establishments, young men were now on their own to accomplish their "passage into manhood." World War I was to become the next event in America's first sexual revolution.

The young mostly working-class American troops who went overseas were greeted by experiences that were denied them in America. It seemed French girls, and not just French prostitutes, had a much more relaxed attitude about sex than the Americans. French girls were as eager love partners as their male counterparts and they had fewer taboos about sex before marriage than American girls. This coupled with the heightened desire of young men at war who didn't know if a sexual encounter would be their last, led to widespread promiscuity among the American troops. The American army feared a widespread epidemic of venereal disease and was also very fearful of the consequences of American troops fathering thousands of children with the French women. So they began issuing condoms to the troops, and this ability to have sex without consequences made sex even more appealing to both the young American men and the French girls.

However it wasn't just the working-class American boys who were engaging in this sexual activity. In the First World War an unprecedented army of young single mostly working-class American women also went to France. They went by the thousands to France as nurses, and as Red Cross workers who were known as the "Donut Dollies" because one of their duties was to give hot beverages and pastries to the American troops. There were also many young women that were sent to France by American Christian groups, like the Knights of Columbus and the Y.M.C.A., to support and entertain the American boys. These young women were also seduced by the young desperate men going into combat and also found themselves eager sexual participants, particularly since the army also discretely provided them with condoms which took away much of their fear the unwanted consequences of pregnancy and venereal disease.

The question was aptly put into a song of the times, "How do you keep them down on the farm after they've seen Paris." These young men and women returned from France with a different outlook about sex and a new ability to express their sexuality without risk. They returned at a time when America enjoyed a period of economic prosperity in the "Roaring Twenties." Dancehalls, theaters, Jazz music and "night life" began to thrive in America. Prohibition made the hidden hip flask "hip," and speakeasies and illegal liquor seemed to make these establishments even more enticing and exciting to America's young.

These young Americans felt that if they could challenge America's ethics on liquor, then they could challenge the sexual ethics as well. Naughty became fashionable. The automobile added to this new sexual freedom by providing easy courtship spots away from the family, neighbors, and others. Parking became an American institution and America's love affair with cars, may have began as a love affair in cars.

Americans also began reading Sigmund Freud and Carl Jung and began studying sex outside the narrow Christian viewpoint. Many young Americans began to see the suppression of their sexual impulses as "unnatural." This new sexuality spread rapidly among young.

Americans prompted a visiting Irish journalist to write, "Unbalanced by prolonged contemplation of New England Puritanism, a generation of Americans has arisen whose great illusion is that the transalvation of all human values may be effected by promiscuity."

The literature of the times also promoted these new sexual ethics particularly in the books by F. Scott Fitzgerald, William Faulkner, and by James T. Farrell in his "Studs Lonnigan Trilogy." The famed exotic dancer, Sally Rand, who started her career in the Roaring Twenties, was asked by a reporter why she danced nude, and she replied, "Because I never made any money until I took off my pants."

America's first sexual revolution ended with the harsh realities of the Great Depression. Many Christian preachers said, "I told you so!" and claimed that the Great Depression was god's retribution for the sins of the Roaring Twenties. The era of the Roaring Twenties was disavowed and greatly disliked by Christian conservatives in America. This caused one more rift and split in the working class.

Chapter 18. Prohibition

"They pray for prohibition, but then they vote for gin."—Words to a 1930s folk song.

The Revivalist Movement that attracted the rural working class put a unique American stamp on Christianity. Although it was the Puritans that institutionalized Christianity in America, it was the new Puritan offshoot, the Revivalist Movement that began to dominate American Christian thinking in the nineteenth century. The Prohibition Movement was a child of the Revivalist Movement. America's first Prohibitionist Movement of any significance started in 1824 and in just seven years over a thousand societies for the prohibition of alcohol flourished across the nation. The Prohibitionists would be a constant source of agitation in America until their brief and painful success in the early twentieth century.

The Evangelical Churches had pushed prohibition of alcohol since 1820, but in the early years the campaign was fairly weak since many of their most ardent followers were both consumers and makers of these beverages. Crops like corn and wheat were more easily preserved and transported by small farmers when converted into liquor and usually alcohol paid better than the raw foodstuffs. For these reasons legal liquor and later illegal moonshine became a staple rural crop for the small working-class farmers in America.

In 1851 Maine did pass a prohibition law. But by and large the rest of the nation was unaffected. At the turn of the century the powerful right-wing Christian organization, the Ku Klux Klan began to support prohibition and they were joined by the Woman's Christian Temperance Union and the Anti-Saloon League who all lent their support to the Prohibition Movement. By 1917 there were twenty-seven dry states with others allowing for local governments to enact local laws prohibiting alcohol. The Volsted Act, named after its author, Congressman Volsted of Minnesota, was passed October 28, 1919. It outlawed alcoholic beverages nationwide. It became effective January 1, 1920. The only state that refused to ratify the Prohibition Amendment to the Constitution or to later enforce Prohibition was the State of Rhode Island.

Over the next thirteen years the federal government arrested over a half million people for the manufacture or sale of alcohol. The Volsted Act would establish organized crime in America by giving them a product that Americans would buy legal or not. It would entrench organized crime in America, and their power and influence would last long after Prohibition. Some remnants of organized crime that were created during Prohibition still thrive today.

Americans never seem to remember their history and therefore are doomed to repeat it. The Prohibition of alcoholic beverages didn't work and this prohibition and its consequences would later be repeated in the American drug wars that would start in the 1960s, and whose consequences we suffer today. America's drug gangs are patterned after organized crime that was created during Prohibition.

When it became obvious that Prohibition was failing, President Hoover became concerned, and he created the Wickersham Commission to study Prohibition's effects on America. After much study the Commission concluded that Prohibition was not enforceable, it was widely unpopular, and that it was financing and growing organized crime. After presenting this conclusion to the President, the Commission and the President received pressure from religious groups to change the Commission's conclusion. The Commission refused, but under immense pressure from Christian conservatives they reluctantly agreed to state that although it was unenforceable that it should be continued for "moral and ethical reasons."

Prohibition was continued through the Hoover years until Franklin Roosevelt was elected President. Roosevelt orchestrated the passage of the Twenty-First Amendment that ended Prohibition in December of 1933.

Chapter 19. War on the Working Class: The War on Drugs

"Just say no!"—Nancy Reagan

The working class is the biggest victim in the War on Drugs. And although chemical dependency effects all classes, the working class are the most likely to be caught up in this trade. And some of the most addictive drugs such as crack cocaine and meth amphetamines are specifically targeted to the poor working class. In many very poor neighborhoods and ghettos the illegal drug trade is the dominate economy and because of these economic conditions more working-class people are imprisoned for their participation in the drug trade.

"Just say no" is the Christian conservative's simple answer to the complex problem of drug addiction. Richard Nixon declared war on drugs over thirty-five years ago. America now spends almost $20 billion a year on the drug war, and what do we get for our money? Are we winning the war? Is there light at the end of this tunnel?

The National Academy of Sciences has declared the war on drugs a financial and social disaster. Despite the billions of dollars spent, custom officials admit that they stop less than 20% of the drugs that come in, and this doesn't take into account the domestically produced products. The supplies of drugs are now so plentiful that today's marijuana, cocaine, and heroin are of higher quality and selling for lower prices than ever. Meth amphetamines can be cheaply and easily made in any kitchen or bathroom. Millions of people take or have taken illegal drugs, including Presidents Bush, Clinton and Obama, who have all admitted taking illegal drugs in their youth. In St. Paul, Minnesota in the 1990's a debate of the two mayoral candidates was over which one had smoked marijuana more recently. The winner of this debate became mayor and later the U.S. Senator from Minnesota.

In California, voters made marijuana legal for medical purposes. The State has allowed its use for cancer patients, glaucoma, depression and other medical uses where marijuana can do what no other drug can replicate. After much planning and monitoring by the State and local law enforcement agencies, a farm in the Santa Clara Mountains was approved to grow medical marijuana. It is heavily monitored and its product is strictly accounted for to assure that no marijuana is used for any other purposes.

In September of 2002, federal drug agents, without notifying the state and local authorities, raided the farm. They confiscated all the marijuana plants and charged the owners with drug trafficking. It was not a mistake. The federal agents knew the farm was for medical marijuana and legal under California law. They also knew that the farm was monitored by local law enforcement agencies, which was why they didn't notify them of the raid. The raid was made because Christian conservatives in the Bush administration had felt that marijuana regardless of its medical use or legality was immoral. Christian ethics have become good or bad, black or white and there are no gray areas. Interestingly, this action came from the administration of a President who has had his own addiction problems with drugs.

Drugs have replaced communism as the new international conspiracy in Christian conservative circles. Just like communism, it is an easy target. No one is leading a campaign in favor of drug addiction. And also like McCarthy's "Witch Hunt," where enemies were labeled as being "soft on communism," Christian conservatives now label their enemies as being "soft on drugs and crime."

The campaign has become so emotional that reason and common sense no longer play any role. It is an all out "War on Drugs." Unfortunately, it is a very long and very costly war that we are losing.

America failed to remember our lesson on the excesses of anti-communism during the Red Menace Campaign of the 1920s, and we were forced to repeat it in the 1950s under McCarthy. Unfortunately America has also forgotten or never learned the lesson from Prohibition in the 1920s, and we are again forced to repeat our mistakes in the "War on Drugs."

Prohibition didn't stop people from taking the drug called alcohol. Nor did it stop alcoholism. Alcoholics Anonymous has done many times more to abate alcoholism than did Prohibition. Mothers Against Drunk Driving did more to stop drinking and driving than did Prohibition. However in the War on Drugs, just like Prohibition, we have eschewed drug addiction treatment and drug prevention education in favor of arresting drug addicts. And when any alternatives to prohibition are brought forward, the official making the proposal is accused of being "soft on drugs and crime."

Just like Prohibition financed and expanded organized crime in America, drugs have done the same. The Mafia was financed and flourished by the illegal liquor, and today's drug gangs and criminals are well financed and flourish from the illegal drug trade. It has turned neighborhoods into battlegrounds. No one is for drug addiction, from alcohol or any other drug, but the fact remains, prohibition doesn't work, because like Presidents Bush, Clinton and Obama in the end not enough of us "Just say no."

After getting a Supreme Court ruling that there would be no exemption from federal drug bust laws for patients using marijuana to ease pain or treat glaucoma, the Bush Administration in 2003, began to pressure the Supreme Court to allow them to revoke the prescription licenses for any Doctor who tells patients that they may be helped by using marijuana as a medical treatment. Christian conservatives feel that the Christian version of morality is much more important than medicine or common sense.

CHAPTER 20. THE CHRISTIAN CONSERVATIVES TAKE CONTROL OF AMERICAN POLITICS

"We have enough votes to run the country, and when the people say, 'We've had enough,' we are going to take over."—The Reverend Pat Robertson

Perhaps the largest rift in America's working class that has been caused by Christianity has been the political rift caused by the very socially Christian conservatives. The Republican Party with its bias for big business and the middle and leisure classes has used this religious movement to attract large numbers of working-class Americans whose best economic interests are not served by the Republican Party, but have devoted themselves to the Republicans based entirely upon these Christian conservative values and issues. These are voters who one would think of as unlikely Republican supporters because of their class and economic interests which conflicts with the Republican big business agenda and the promotion of low taxes on the rich at the expense of the working class.

These working-class Christian conservatives have become known as the value voters. Their opposition to issues such as abortion and women's rights, and gay rights, are the staples of this religious movement, but it also includes other issues they oppose like diversity, affirmative action, immigration, and issues that they promote such as and English as the national language, prayer and Christian creation theory in the public schools, and the unquestionable support of the military and military adventurism.

This leisure class and big business strategy of culling the Christian conservatives has worked and divided the working class by region: north and south. And by place: city versus suburb and rural areas. We now call these red and blue states or red and blue counties. It is a very deliberate strategy of the Republicans, the leisure class and big business that was developed over time.

In the 1950s the connection between the working-class value voters and the Republicans began to form. During the height of McCarthyism the New York State Legislature passed the "Religious Corporations Law of New York." It transferred the control of the Russian Orthodox Church from Russia to a convention of American Orthodox Churches. The object of the legislation was to protect American churches from the infiltration of communist-atheists. It had wide support especially among the working-class Christians. The Supreme Court struck down the law in 1954 as a violation of the First Amendment and government interference in religion.

About this time, the Gallup Institute of Public Opinion surveyed America about religion with the following results: ninety-five percent believed in prayer, ninety-four believed in god, sixty-nine percent wanted the phrase "under god" added to the Pledge of Allegiance and "In God We Trust" printed on the currency. Congress acted upon their desires and passed laws granting both. Democrats bowed to these demands for fear of being called communists or atheists.

Christianity was at an all time high in the 1950s. Even the movie magazine, Modern Screen, would entice its working-class readers by a popular series on "How the Stars Found Faith!" This was also the decade that "Dial-A-Prayer" and drive-in Sunday services came into vogue. Now working-class families could get prayers on the phone or attend "Dusk to Dawn" drive-in movies on Saturday night and receive a Sunday service right there in their car before going home.

In 1952, the Gallup poll showed that the number of adults that said they belonged to a church was at seventy-three percent. In the late 1960s and 1970s church membership steadily declined to a low of sixty-seven percent in 1982. However by 1985 it had rebounded to seventy-two percent.

Through the 1980s Christianity and Republican politics became synonymous. Although there was the independent 1988 campaign by the Reverend Pat Robertson for the presidency, most working-class Christian conservatives had now firmly aligned themselves with the Republicans. They played a major role in Reagan's election in 1980 and 1984, and George Bush in 1988.

Working-class Christian conservatives were the major force in the election of George W. Bush in 2000 and 2004. Bush erased most of the lines between church and state even to the dismay of some in the Christian community. The Reverend Welton Gaddy, the President of the Interfaith Alliance Foundation, a Christian lobbying group, complained about Bush in 2003 at a news conference, "The presence of inappropriate religious language reflects the President's fuzzy vision of the connection of religion and government." Agreeing with Gaddy at the same news conference Elaine Pagels, a professor of religion at Princeton University, said about Bush, "He's placing those who disagree with him in the realm of evil and placing himself at the axis of good, and suggesting that someone who doesn't agree with him is morally deficient."

Unfortunately, unlike Gaddy and Pagels, the Christian conservatives cheered the President's "Faith-Based Initiative" and the promotion of Christianity as the national religion.

"You don't need an evangelical lobby if you have an evangelical in the Oval Office," said Richard Cizik, the Vice President of the National Association of Evangelicals.

CHAPTER 21. MORE POLITICS AND THE DECLINE OF THE LIBERALS AND
MODERATES

> "There will never be world peace until God's house and God's chosen people
> are given their rightful place of leadership at the top of the world. How can
> there be peace when drunkards, drug dealers, communists, atheists, New
> Age worshipers of Satan, secular humanists, oppressive dictators, greedy
> moneychangers, revolutionary assassins, adulterers and homosexuals are on
> top?"—*Reverend Pat Robertson*

The Southern Strategy that sacrificed civil liberties for Southern votes continued to pay dividends for the Republicans. It drove the liberals and moderates out
of the Republican Party. Non-Conservatives and Non-Christians Republicans
now find themselves on the fringe or outside of the Conservative Christian dominated Republican Party. In 1980, Congressman John Anderson defected from the
Republicans to start and independent movement. Later Ross Perot and Governor Jesse Ventura of Minnesota would try to establish an independent party, although both were much more conservative than their followers appreciated.

Originally it was the Southern conservatives who were the outsiders in the
Democratic Party. In 1968 the success of George Wallace with Christian conservatives in both the North and South would cost Hubert Humphrey the election
and gave the Presidency to Richard Nixon. The South then moved into the Republican column in 1972 and would vote Republican in most presidential elections thereafter. The exception would be the 1976 election of the "Born Again"
Southern Baptist politician, Jimmy Carter. Carter's openness about his "Born
Again" religion was as attractive to Christian conservatives.

They felt that the election of Carter was at last mainstream acceptance for evangelicals in main stream America. However, when Carter bucked the Christian conservatives to support the rights of women and gays, and supported amnesty for anti-war youth, the Christian conservatives and the South would forsake Jimmy Carter. They abandoned "one of their own," for Ronald Reagan in 1980. They did it because Christian conservatives would rather vote for a divorced movie actor who was willing to say he was against abortion, homosexuality, communism, and who called the Soviet Union "the Evil Empire." Reagan evoked a folksy "John Wayne" back to the 1950s mentality that harkened the Christian conservatives back to what they saw as their "Golden Era." As simply as can be put, they liked him because he told Christian conservative s exactly what they wanted to hear.

They called him "The Great Communicator." They called him this not because he was knowledgeable, witty, intelligent, or well spoken. In fact he was none of these. He was called "the Great Communicator" because he spoke in plain informal working-class English and said exactly what Christian conservative America wanted to hear. He said it whether it was true or not, and whether he could actually do anything about it or not. Reagan said exactly what they wanted to hear. Reagan and his advisors understood that reality meant little when the majority of voters wanted very simple remedies based upon their faith and simple dogmas and spoken to them in their language. Everything was black and white, good or bad, with no gray areas right down to Reagan's improbable hair color. Christian conservatives felt it was the gray areas and ambiguity that threatened their religious beliefs.

The 1960s, contrary to popular belief, actually gave rise to Christian conservatives, not liberals. The excesses that Americans saw in the 1960s which in their opinions included permissive sex, the acceptance of drug use, the "unpatriotic" anti-war youth, civil rights disturbances, calls for women's rights, abortion and gay rights all gave rise to the growing power of the Christian conservatives. The 1960s revolution was a conservative, not a liberal one. The country took a decided right turn. Even the leisure and middle-class youth that were the source of most of these excesses would soon give up their rebelliousness less than a decade later and turn to conservative politics.

In the 1960s, the working-class, including their young, were already conservative. The many young working-class soldiers who served in Viet Nam, and returned to a country that spit upon them for their service, became even more conservative. And although their economic interests would have been better served by the Democrats, the majority of the working class became conservatives and Republican because they believed their traditional Christian values were threatened.

They also feared their economic livelihoods were threatened. Working-class men were much more vulnerable and more afraid of losing jobs to women, Latinos, Asians or Blacks than middle-class men and they found sympathy from conservatives. America also became increasingly more Christian as church membership rose steadily through the 1980s. By the 1990s, the Christian conservatives controlled America and her politics.

From its first days, American Christianity has had problems with violence and radicalism. In the 1970s, radical Christian cults became a threat to main stream America. People were seduced into religious cults, brainwashed, relieved of their possessions and money and deprived of their rights. A new occupation, called "deprogrammers," was created to assist families in "reprogramming" a captured loved one from the religious cults. There were many cults and sects, and some became newsworthy. In the 1970s the two most well known were the Unification Church of the Reverend Sun Myung Moon, and the People's Temple of the Reverend Jim Jones.

The Unification Church members became known as the "Moonies." Their mode of operation was to seek out the working class particularly the lonely, the disenfranchised, and the unsatisfied and promised them that whatever they were seeking could be found in their church. They shaved their heads and wore robes, and collected money in public places. They had mass weddings and drove traditional Christians and the family members of these converts crazy.

The Moonies were mostly non-violent. The Reverend Jim Jones on the other hand was a very sick man. He was also a charismatic tyrant and attracted a large mostly working-class following. His abuses of his flock were so severe he came under watch by California authorities. To escape this interference he moved his entire flock to Guyana. The abuses continued and in 1978 a California Congressman went to investigate the abuse complaints in Guyana. Upon his arrival, Jones and his followers killed the Congressman. Jones then took his own life after he killed many of his followers including women and young children with poisoned Kool-Aid.

In 1959 David Koresh formed the Branch Davidian sect, which was a splinter group that broke away from the Mormon Church. He was another charismatic leader who set up a working-class commune near Waco, Texas. Over the years Koresh, like Jones, became more dictatorial. He claimed to be a messiah and declared that all the women followers were his god-given wives and property. This included young girls below the age of consent. In 1993 the rumors of child sexual abuse and the stockpiling of weapons by the Branch Davidians created a crisis.

Koresh and his followers refused to allow authorities to enter his compound to investigate these allegations and a siege was born. The aftermath left four federal agents, Koresh, and seventy-four of his followers dead. This siege outraged many Christian conservatives and their right wing militias who blamed the government. This outrage included the men who were to later bomb the Federal Building in Oklahoma City, who cited the Waco incident as one of their justifications.

Is Christianity becoming increasingly more conservative and more radical? The answer appears to be yes. A religious census conducted by Glenmary Research Center of Nashville, a Catholic research group, found that during the past decade the evangelical and Mormon Churches grew very rapidly while the mainstream Catholic and Protestant Churches shrank. Protestants are leaving mainstream churches in record numbers in favor of the Evangelicals and the Fundamentalists. The New York Times reported that since 1960, the fundamentalist Pentecostals have increased fourfold, while the membership of the mainstream Episcopalians have dropped almost in half.

The radicals are becoming the mainstream. The Reverend Franklin Graham, the son of Billy Graham, when speaking about the "under God" clause in the Pledge of Allegiance and the removal of prayer in the schools said that the strength of his opposition is proof to him that "evil exists in the world." He also threatened that, "Those who ridicule or demean the Name (god) and His followers must not understand what they are doing and whom they are dealing with!"

Chapter 22. Christian Conservatives vs. the Civil Rights Movement

"They put the Negros in the schools, and now they have driven God out."—Congressman George W. Andrews of Alabama

It may at first seem incredible that civil liberties and civil rights are have been thwarted and opposed by Christians, but it has. And with this opposition it has divided the American working-class along racial lines.

In April of 1963, the Reverend Martin Luther King Jr. urged Black Christians to join with their White brothers and worship with them in the white churches of Birmingham, Alabama. Before that Sunday, the Birmingham police threatened to arrest any Blacks that trespassed into a White church. On that Sunday, seventeen White Birmingham churches turned away the Black worshippers, only four allowed them to enter and to sit and worship in the back of their church.

Over a decade later the President of the Mormon Church would state, "There is a reason why one man is born Black and with other disadvantages, while another is born White with great advantages. The negro, evidently, is receiving the reward he merits." Unfortunately this statement sums up the historic Christian conservative philosophy on civil rights.

One of the most shameful acts of a political party in American history was that of the Republican Party's "Southern Strategy." The Republican Party, the Party of Lincoln that had preserved the Union and freed the slaves, decided to sacrifice the civil rights of African-Americans in favor of bigotry and segregation to win the votes of Southern whites who had always voted Democratic.

The Republicans had been growing ever more conservative, and by the 1950s Christian conservatives took control of the Party. The Christian conservatives and the Republicans had been frustrated by the Roosevelt and the New Deal, and by the election of Truman in 1948. They were also frustrated that sizable numbers of Southerners, especially Christian conservative Southerners, had remained loyal to the Democratic Party. Although they had some success in presidential elections in the South, the congress and state governments were still heavily slanted to the Democrats in the "solid South." These old loyalties to the Southern Democratic Party were very hard to break.

In the 1940s Theodore Bilbo, the United States Senator from Mississippi wrote a book called *Segregation or Mongrelization: Take Your Choice*. As much as it may seem ridiculous today, it was a serious question in America until the 1970s. President Eisenhower would summarize Republican opinions at length in a 1957 news conference where he sympathized with whites who he said, "see a picture of the mongrelization of the race." He left little doubt that he was also concerned and against this "mongrelization."

To the credit of the Democratic Party, northern liberals, moderates, and even many of their conservatives, supported civil rights. Also to their credit there were also a few liberal and moderate Republicans from the North that also supported civil rights, but they were small minority within their party. The Democrats also had a few Southern members that began to quietly support the civil rights movement. Senator Lyndon Johnson of Texas was one of these. Johnson, a Southerner, was an unlikely civil rights advocate, and yet without Johnson the civil rights movement may have failed or at least have been delayed for decades.

After the death of President Kennedy, President, Johnson vowed to keep Kennedy's promise to Dr. King and other civil rights leaders to pass a civil rights bill. Johnson strong-armed the passage of the Civil Rights Act in 1964 and the Voting Rights Act in 1965.

Johnson was no fool. He appreciated the consequences of his actions. After signing the Civil Rights Act in August of 1964, he told his Press Secretary Bill Moyers, "I think we just delivered the South to the Republican Party for a long time to come." His words were more than prophetic and immediate. That fall, Johnson, a Southerner, lost five states in the "Deep South" in the 1964 election to Barry Goldwater. The only other state to vote in favor of Goldwater was his home state of Arizona, which he carried by a very slim margin.

The dissatisfaction over civil rights by the Christian conservatives was becoming strong in the North as well as the South. In the presidential primaries of 1964, George Wallace, a staunch segregationist, carried working-class conservative voters in Wisconsin, Indiana, and Maryland. And with these victories Wallace's support continued to grow. In the 1968 presidential election Wallace ran as an independent got 13.5% of the vote compared to Nixon at 43.4% and

Humphrey at 42.7%. Wallace carried much of the South and did well in Northern white working-class Christian conservative neighborhoods that had previously voted Democratic. Because of Wallace, Nixon very narrowly beat Hubert Humphrey in the 1968 election. This divide was a harbinger of things to come.

In 1972, Wallace won the Michigan and Maryland presidential primaries in the North, but was then shot and critically wounded in Maryland ending his presidential campaign.

On the advice of Patrick Buchanan and other Christian conservatives Nixon then stole Wallace's campaign themes. Nixon immediately came out against school busing for racial integration and against affirmative action. He then told the working-class Christian conservatives that the Democrats were the party of "acid, amnesty and abortion." He emphasized "his traditional values" to make sure that Christian conservatives fully understood his new intentions and referred to them as the "Silent Majority." He received well over eighty percent of the former Wallace voters.

It seems ironic that the civil rights movement that was started in Christian churches and was led by Reverend King and other Black Christian ministers was rejected by Christian conservatives, but most fundamentalist organizations and the white working-class Christians were anti-civil rights and many were adamant segregationists believing that non-whites somehow degraded their Christianity.

In response to white Christian politics the Black ministers became active in politics to promote the civil rights movement. The immediate reaction from the conservative white Christian churches, despite their own political involvements, was that the Black ministers should not be involved in politics and demanded that the Black ministers be men of god and not men of politics.

The politically active Reverend Jerry Falwell would hypocritically claim that ministers should not be involved in politics. He said: "Believing in the Bible as I do, I would find it impossible to stop preaching the pure saving Gospel of Jesus Christ and begin doing anything else, including participating in civil rights reforms." He also said, "Preachers are not called upon to be politicians but to be soul winners." In his autobiography Falwell stated that Southern preachers had rightly condemned, "lawyers, politicians, abolitionists, and suffragettes alike..... We are here to serve Jesus.....don't get bogged down with unbelievers and their unrighteousness." Falwell included King and Black ministers in the civil rights movement as "unbelievers and unrighteous."

Falwell's attacks on civil rights and the Black ministers were of course themselves a political action. And Falwell also found it possible to "stop preaching the Gospel" long enough to rename Richard Nixon's Silent Majority to the "Moral

Majority" and lead them against the rights of women and gays and to promote other Christian conservative political causes.

Falwell and others labeled King and the civil rights leaders as radicals and communists. J. Edgar Hoover was convinced that King and the civil rights move-ment was part of a communist inspired conspiracy. Hoover and the FBI inves-tigated King and the civil rights movement exhaustively, but never found any connections to the communists or any other conspiracy. When Hoover's FBI investigation showed no connection between the civil rights movement and the communists he forced the Agents involved in the investigation to disavow their own findings and state that the investigation found no connection because it was flawed. This lack of proof didn't stop Hoover or the other Christian conservatives from insisting that King and his followers were communists.

CHAPTER 23. CHRISTIAN CONSERVATIVES VS. THE JUDICIARY

> "The legislative and executive branches of our government have acted in a manner demonstrably at odds with our Founding Father's blueprint for the governance of a free people and our Constitution.....when the fervor of political passions moves the Executive and Legislative branches to act in ways inimical to basic constitutional principles, it is the duty of the judiciary to intervene ...We must conscientiously guard the independence of our judiciary and safeguard the Constitution."—*Judge Stanley F. Birch Jr., in his 2005 ruling against the wishes President Bush and the Congress in the Terri Schiavo case.*

The Christian conservatives have tried force their culture on America by taking over the judiciary and campaigning to remove judges whose opinions they dislike. The ruling by Judge Birch made in the Terri Schiavo Case was labeled as "unwarranted judicial activism" by Republican House Majority Leader Tom Delay and other Christian conservatives, who then demanded that Judge Birch be impeached for his "liberal" ruling. Ironically Judge Birch is a conservative Republican who was appointed to the federal court by President Ronald Reagan. The Christian conservative movement against "liberal judicial activists" started with the campaign to impeach Earl Warren the Chief Justice of the Supreme Court because of Supreme Court decisions in favor of civil rights. Other judges were also targeted. Earl became a particular target when the Supreme Court struck down separate but equal, and ended school prayer in the 1950s. Ironically Earl Warren was a also a Conservative Republican and former Governor from California who was appointed to the Supreme Court by President Eisenhower in 1953 at the recommendation of then Vice President Richard Nixon and other Republican conservatives. After the civil rights decisions by the Supreme Court, Christian conservatives labeled Earl a "judicial activist," saying he advocated positions that they disagree with and what they believe are contrary to a nation founded by Christian doctrine.

The Christian conservative campaign against "activist judges" became even more frenzied when the Supreme Court struck down laws against abortion in Roe vs. Wade. The Christian conservatives began advocating that judges be impeached for judicial decisions contrary to their Christian beliefs. The decisions causing this wrath are now numerous and include such important working-class subjects as: women's rights, abortion rights, birth control, sex education, the rights of gays and lesbians, fluoridation of water, immigration, the death penalty, religious monuments in government buildings, prayer in school, teaching evolution in schools, civil rights, the rights of Muslims and foreign detainees in the War on Terrorism, and gun control laws.

In 2005 a national conference, "Confronting the Judicial War on Faith" was held and the keynote speaker was Republican House Minority Leader Tom Delay who decried "a judiciary run amok." He charged Congress with "constitutional cowardice" for failing to impeach "activist" judges like Stanley Birch Jr. and Supreme Court Justice Anthony Kennedy. Kennedy, like Earl Warren and Stanley Birch Jr. is also a conservative Republican who was appointed by President Reagan. U.S. Senator Tom Coburn of Oklahoma said, "I am in favor of mass impeachments if that is what it takes." His aide Michael Schwartz supplied a potential list that included: Supreme Court Justices Anthony Kennedy, David Souter, Stephen Breyer, and Ruth Bader Ginsburg. Schwartz stated that the President or Congress should be able to oust these "activist" judges for bad behavior. He said, "The President gives them a call and says, clean out your desk, the Capitol Police will be in to find your way home."

The former House Judiciary Committee Chairman Republican James Sensenbrenner told the New York Times that there was serious consideration being given to cutting off court funding to gain the submission of the judges. "When their budgets start to dry up, we'll get their attention."

Even Republican moderates like Senator Rick Santorum of Pennsylvania said when asked about congressional action against the judiciary, "I think that's a legitimate area for oversight, sure."

President George W. Bush began unprecedented campaigns against the judiciary and U.S. Attorneys who disagreed with his Christian conservative agenda. His Administration's actions are now being investigated for their illegal and improper political influence on the judiciary and the legal system.

Chapter 24. Father Knows Best, Christianity vs. Women

> "There is, however, a backlash typified by the 'right-to-life' movement. It has occurred partly because men have realized the significance of changes and fear women will lose their subservience."—*Professor Bonnie Bullough*

The working class has been further divided by gender. The ban on abortions and the subservient role of women by Christian conservatives have divided politics along gender lines. It is not surprising that a solid majority of women now vote Democratic because of the Christian conservative takeover of the Republicans.

Pat Robertson argues that feminism encourages women "to kill their children, practice witchcraft, destroy capitalism, and become lesbians." He says feminism is anti-family. "Pro-Family" has become a Christian conservative and Republican standard. "Pro-family" is like "clean air," in that few people, regardless of their environmental philosophy, would claim to be against it. And in the national debate on lifestyles, few people in America are against families. It is a value voter catch phrase that has little real meaning.

What Christians conservatives mean when the use the word that they are "Pro-Family," is that they are against women's rights, abortion, birth control, sex education, homosexuals, health care and welfare in general, and in particular if it supports female headed households. Christian conservatives are a male dominated who believe according their scriptures that women are commanded to obey their husbands and fathers. It should be realized that our northern European ancestors accepted Christianity in the first place, because Christianity the concept of one god, very closely matched their culture where their tribes were led by a strong male leader. Although it is now changing in some denominations male dominance is a Christian cultural norm.

Susan Kellogg and Steven Mintz wrote in their book, *Domestic Revolutions: a Social History of American Family Life*, that the women's rights movement was born from the Christian "purity crusade" against prostitution and venereal disease. The women's rights movement that challenged male dominance could not be contained once it started. It continued to flourish during Prohibition and in the Woman's Right to Vote movement. And the women's movement began to cause Americans to consider sex in a different way. It emphasized individual health and happiness over the traditions and the controls of religion placed upon them by men and the society they controlled. These new attitudes on sex flourished in the Roaring Twenties as the young men and women returned from France in World War I, where they experienced a much different attitude about sex than the Puritan model that they were born into and that their parents had accepted. And with the introduction of the condom, during the war, birth control and protection from disease meant that sex was no longer just about babies. Like men, for the first time, women could now have sex without life-changing consequences. It began to change the dynamics of society and male-female relationships.

It was not by accident that both the women's rights movement and the sexual revolution occurred when America was changing rapidly from an agrarian society to an industrial society and from a rural and small town nation to an urban nation. These changes of the economy and location also promoted the changes in women's roles.

Women did not begin working because of the women's movement, as is often asserted by the Christian conservatives. On the contrary, in agrarian cultures working-class women worked alongside their men, doing farm work as well as taking care of the domestic chores and raising children. What changed in the industrial age was that they could no longer work at home. For women to work in the new economy they needed to do work that would take them out of the home and away from their children for eight or more hours a day, and five or six days a week. Women were still expected to raise children and do domestic chores despite these changes. It was a situation that became unmanageable for many.

The pressure on working women abated somewhat during the Great Depression, when there were fewer jobs and most of those were given to men. Then, during the War, when so many men were called up, women were needed in the factories. In the post-war economic boom of the 1950s, gains from the labor movement and the subsequent increase of wages allowed a brief time where working-class women could become housewives and concentrate entirely upon domestic duties and childrearing. However, the economic realities of the 1970s once again required working-class women to go back into the workforce as a large number of working-class families suddenly could no longer afford to live on one income. The number of female-headed households was also rapidly rising.

During the 1950s, marriage rates hit a high point in American history with seventy percent of all women married by the age of twenty-four. In the 1940s, this number was only forty-two percent. The divorce rate in the 1950s was also at an all-time low. Christian conservatives have adopted this unique decade as their norm and set this as their goal of what America should be like. Television exalted this 1950s lifestyle with shows like "Leave It to Beaver" and "Father Knows Best." Christian conservatives nostalgically view this decade as the "Golden Age of America."

In an opposing view, Betty Friedan summarized the era in her book The Feminine Mystique: "It was a strange sense of dissatisfaction, a yearning that women suffered in the middle of the twentieth century in the United States. Each suburban wife struggled with it alone. As she made the beds, shopped for groceries, matched slip cover material, ate peanut butter sandwiches with the children, chauffeured Cub Scouts and Brownies, as she lay beside her husband at night, she was afraid to ask even herself the silent question, "is this all?"

Women didn't need to ask this question for very long, by the 1970s most would be required to work to help provide their family with enough income to live. Working-class wages, after adjusting for inflation, began to decline in 1973. By the 1990s two thirds of American families would have household incomes less than $40,000 a year and 82% of all families with incomes between $25,000 and $50,000 had two wage earners. The debate over women in the workplace has become moot. In order to support their family most women need to work.

Christian conservatives resist any type of government regulation of the free economy, and they have also resisted any type of government action to reverse wage gender discrimination and overall declining wages including opposing raises in minimum wages despite inflation. These issues affect more women then men. And many Christian conservatives still insist that the decline in family income and the need for women to work is a myth.

The Christian churches have been slow to recognize the new realities of women especially in their own institutions. It wasn't until 1956 that the Methodists and Presbyterians became the first churches to ordain women. It took until 1974 for the first female American Episcopal Priest to be ordained, and of course the Catholics and some Protestants churches still steadfastly refuse to do so. Christianity on the whole remains a male dominated culture.

After considering the consequences for five years, the Pope, on July 29, 1969 rejected the use of contraception and abortion in an encyclical entitled, "Human

Vitae" which in Latin means human life. This encyclical began a political movement that would be one of the most divisive in American history and set the dogmatic agenda for Christian conservatives for the next four or more decades. This stand against contraception and abortion united the long divided working-class conservative Catholics and the working-class Protestant Fundamentalists, this is the issue that solidified the Christian Conservatives and divided them from the rest of the nation. Catholics, who had been traditionally progressive Democratic voters, were encouraged by their priests to shift to vote Republican.

It was however a very slow change. In 1969 because of polls that showed that 70% of American Catholics approved of birth control, the Pope insisted that his encyclical especially applied to American Catholics. A letter of protest signed by 142 American priests was submitted to Cardinal O'Boyle protesting the encyclical. The Catholic Church responded. Cardinal O'Boyle delivered a sermon on obedience at St. Matthews Cathedral. During this sermon over two hundred Catholic women became angry and walked out.

In 1973, the Supreme Court issued the Roe vs. Wade decision that struck down the nation's abortion control laws. Christian conservatives went berserk. Jerry Falwell called it a "national sin." He changed Nixon's "Silent Majority" in to the "Moral Majority," and declared that the time of silence was over.

The Christians conservatives are very adept at commercially packaging their rigid dogmas in positive rather than negative statements. They do this so that they will sell better to working-class America. Anti women's and gay rights became "Pro-family" and anti-abortion became "Pro-life." The women's movement called their side "Pro-choice."

One of the more unfortunate consequences of the Christian conservative's pro-life stance has been their "all or nothing" attitude about abortion and their persistent calls for action that have encouraged political dissention and even violence and murder. An example of a call to violence was by the Reverend Pat Robertson in 1998 on his television show, The 700 Club. He said the following:

> "The word I got is that if the judges appointed by man will not deal with those who take innocent life, then the Lord is going to enter in and bring justice. And when that happens the innocent will suffer along with the guilty."

This was a thinly veiled call to arms by a leader of the Christian conservative movement, and it served to justify harassment, violence and murder against abortion clinics.

To understand the zealousness of the Pro-life movement, you have to first recognize that it is a strong religious movement in its own right that lives within and is justified by Christianity. It is an emotional faith based argument versus an intellectual argument. The Pro-life movement is therefore believed to be by its followers, "God's work." They fully believe that god is compelling them to fight against this "horrible immoral act." This fact helps explain how a person who is opposed to "killing" (abortion) can kill doctors, nurses and patients by bombing abortion clinics without remorse. The perpetrator feels that god, and perhaps religious leaders like Reverend Robertson have approved their actions, and since it is in god's name, only those who god wants to die will die by their actions. It is the equivalent of saying that "if god didn't want it done, than he wouldn't let me do it." It is very similar to the way Islamic suicide terrorists believe.

Throughout the 1980s and 1990s abortion clinics were picketed, bombed and vandalized. Doctors, nurses, and patients were exposed, embarrassed, hurt, threatened, harassed, and killed. Christians committed all of these acts, in the name of their god. These actions somehow belie the title of being either Pro-life or Pro-family.

In 1994 Paul Hill, a Presbyterian Minister and father of three children, murdered Dr. John Britton and James Barrett, a retired Air Force officer, and wounded Barrett's wife. They had been with the doctor outside a Florida clinic were Britton performed abortions. Dr. Britton survived the first attack by Hill's shotgun, so Hill calmly reloaded and shot him again. Hill was convicted and given the death penalty. In 2003, on the eve of his execution, an unrepentant Hill stated, "I expect a great reward in heaven. I am looking forward to the glory. I don't feel remorse. More people should act as I have acted."

The Reverend Michael Bray, of Bowie, Maryland, an author of a book justifying abortion killing, said that Hill is a martyr. Bray said that Hill "will be recognized after the fact as the honorable man that he is." Florida officials carrying out the Hill execution received threatening letters containing rifle bullets from outraged Christian conservatives.

Quoting a pro-choice spokesperson, *Newsweek Magazine* reported in September of 2003 that there had been seven murders and seventeen attempted murders just since 1998 by Pro-Life advocates.

Ironically, these same pro-life people are also opposed to sex education in the schools and they are also against birth control. It is ironic in that if both were implemented properly, they would prevent abortions. The Christian conservatives are in reality anti-sex. They campaign that schools should teach abstinence versus sex education. "Just say no." The problem with just saying no is that it doesn't work. If it did, there would likely be at least a billion fewer of us on the planet to argue about it.

The Christian conservatives want the government to regulate sex. In 2003 when the Supreme Court struck down state laws prohibiting anal and oral sex between consenting adults, Focus On The Family's Vice president of Public Policy Tom Minnery predicted that, "If the people (the Christian conservatives) have no right to regulate sexuality than ultimately the institution of marriage is in peril, and with it, the welfare of the coming generations of children."

A few days prior to the Supreme Court decision on sodomy, Representative Marilyn Musgrave, a Colorado Republican, sponsored a bill to amend the Constitution to ban sodomy and gay marriages. Republican Senate Majority Leader Bill Frist announced his support of the amendment several days after the Supreme Court action. He said that sodomy laws are best addressed by the state legislatures.

When asked to comment on the Supreme Court decision striking down sodomy laws Frist said on television: "I have a fear that criminal activity within the home would in some way be condoned."

Chapter 25. Class and the Gay Movement

The Gay Liberation Movement was started predominately by middle-class gays just as the Women's Movement was started predominately by middle-class women. Working-class people, as we have seen, rarely challenge society. They are uncomfortable with confrontation with authority and are taught "to know their place." Consequently the Gay Liberation Movement and much of what is considered gay culture is associated with the arts and creative community and assumes and emulates the culture of the upper middle class.

An excellent example of this can be seen in the award winning PBS documentary "Flag Wars," by Linda Goode Bryant and Laura Poitras. "Flag Wars" is about the gentrification of a Black working-class neighborhood in Columbus, Ohio by mostly white gays and lesbians. It is more a story about class conflict than racial conflict or sexual preference issues. As the gay community began to gentrify this old historic neighborhood, they persuaded the city to enforce more restrictive building codes to reflect their upscale tastes and to protect their investments, and as a consequence a great deal of stress is placed upon the original Black working-class residents who in many cases were financially unable to update and repair their properties to meet these codes. Many Black working-class residents were forced out of their neighborhood. It created a huge controversy and sent the neighborhood into class warfare.

The documentary got its name because when gays purchased a home in the neighborhood they would fly the Gay Pride flag. In response to this the Black population in the neighborhood began to respond by flying the African Black

National Flag. *Flag Wars* is about class conflict and like many places in America was further complicated by race and sexual preference issues.

Chapter 26. Class Warfare: Christian Conservatives vs. the Working Class Poor

> "For unto everyone that hath shall be given, and he shall have abundance. But from him that hath not shall be taken away even that which he hath." — Matthew 25:29

> "If any shouldn't work, than neither should he eat."—The Puritan Work Ethic

The Puritan "work ethic" also stated, "The Lord would not suffer a sinner to prosper." The working class according to the Puritan Ethic is getting what they deserve. And although Christian conservatives reject evolution, they have ironically accepted Herbert Spencer's corruption of Darwin's work. It is called Social Darwinism, which provides for the "survival of the fittest" a theme that is often misattributed to Darwin. Spencer believed that social processes, like society and economics, were natural forces and only failed when government tried to "artificially" regulate them. And Christian conservatives see welfare and minimum wage as the unwanted "artificial" regulation of the natural -economy, they are interfering with what god has determined that poor people deserve.

They view the economy as a natural or god given phenomenon rather than a social and political creation of men. They have attacked welfare, food stamps, the W.I.C. Program, subsidized housing, and a variety of other social services as unnatural regulation that interferes with god's natural order and claim it causes dependency in the working class. They have brought forward and made popular the currently accepted theory that it is welfare and not lack of income that causes poverty. Their Puritan "work ethic" tells them that people are poor because they don't work and are undeserving.

"Why would you work when all the people on welfare drive Cadillac's, watch big screen televisions and live in subsidized housing?" they ask. This is the argument that was put forth by President Reagan in his campaign against "Welfare Queens." And it ultimately led to the demise of America's safety net under President Clinton with the welfare to work program.

Christian conservatives see welfare as being "anti-family," because a large number of women on welfare are single mothers with children. They deny these women birth control and abortions, and then claim that they are having children just to get increased welfare. And although Christian conservatives feel women should be home raising their children, they have insisted poor women and women without husbands should go to work for minimum wage. This is the basis for Welfare to Work.

These are many of the same Christian conservatives who steadfastly refuse to raise the minimum wage to a living wage because it would be interference with the "natural free market and destroy small business." In America the corporation is becoming more important than the individual. The large corporations are now the masters and individuals are their slaves. Wal-Mart, the nation's largest and many would argue the worst employer, is an example of this.

The arguments against raising the minimum wage belie all factual evidence that shows the real living wage for working-class families has fallen since 1973, and that most households now need two incomes just to survive. Over 82% of American households with incomes between $25,000 and $50,000 and now have two wage earners. And contrary to the Christian conservative ideas about work, most single mothers will not be able to adequately support their families even with a job unless they have some additional assistance. The income of the wealthiest one percent has doubled in the past 25 years, while the income of the poorest 20% has fallen by 12% in the same time period when adjusted for inflation. Only 62% of all Americans receive health insurance through their employer. The number of people with public health care is over 86 million and the uninsured is 46.3 million according to a study by Families USA, which is one in three people under the age of sixty-five, and yet the Christian conservatives also fight health care reforms. The gap between the rich and the poor is growing. These actions aren't as Pro-Family as the Christian conservatives claim themselves to be.

The middle-class is shrinking while the working class, particularly the underclass continues to grow. The working-class income is declining at the expense of the wealthy. More than 67% of all food shelf users work full time. And the Columbia University Center for Poverty reported that 25% of all American children live in poverty. They also report that American child poverty rates are two to six times higher in the United States than in most other western nations, and these reports were before the current economic crisis.

In 2003 the Democrats attempted to raise the minimum wage from $5.15 to $6.65 per hour by attaching it to a highly supported Republican foreign operations bill. The Republicans lead by the Bush Administration then sidetracked their legislation to defeat the increase in minimum wage. They claimed that a raise would hurt business. The minimum wage hadn't been raised since 1996 and it wasn't until after the Democrats took over the Congress in 2006 that it was finally increased giving the working poor their first raise in more than ten years.

One of the kindest things Congress did was to declare a War on Poverty. One of the most selfish and unkind was to stop welfare for the needy at the insistence of the Christian conservatives. The late Senator Paul Wellstone of Minnesota summed it up by saying, "Congress didn't surrender in the War on Poverty, but rather they switched sides and decided to make war on the poor."

In 2003, Conservative Christians organized against proposed low-cost prescription drugs for seniors. The Traditional Values Coalition, a self-proclaimed "Christian Advocacy Group" representing over 43,000 churches teamed with the pharmaceutical companies to lobby against the bill. They unfairly claimed that the senior citizen prescription drug bill would allow RU-486, called the "abortion pill," to flow into the United States. Tony Rudy, who is a lobbyist for the drug companies, led the Christian Coalition efforts. The real reason they opposed this bill was that the drug companies stood to lose $630 billion if cheap imported drugs were available to poor seniors. Rudy was also a former top aide to Republican House Majority Leader Tom Delay. They oppose health care reform only to protect the insurance and drug industry.

In 2003 Alabama Governor Bob Riley, a Christian conservative Republican, began a campaign to raise taxes to improve the lives of the state's poor. Alabama has an income tax that taxes families with annual incomes as low as $4,600 a year. Alabama also has a very substantial sales tax that applies to groceries, including infant formula. The result of these taxes are that people who make less than $13,000 per year pay 10.9 percent of their income in state tax, while those who make over $229,000 pay only 4.1 percent. The Governor wanted to change this and was strongly opposed by Alabama's powerful Christian Coalition and the Republican Party. They called his proposal "reckless" and they called the Governor a "Judas" to their cause.

If you are poor then god must have meant you to be.

CHAPTER 27. CHRISTIANITY VS. ISLAM

> "The God of Islam is not the God of the Christian faith. The two are as different as lightness and darkness." —*The Reverend Franklin Graham*

> "Christianity is a faith in which god sends his son to die for you, (while Islam is) a religion in which god requires you to send your son to die for him." Attorney *General John Ashcroft in 2002*

> "We should invade their countries, kill their leaders and convert them to Christianity."—*Christian conservative author Ann Coulter*

At the time of this writing we are sending another generation of mostly working-class young men and women into wars in Iraq and Afghanistan. In these conflicts the greatest supporters and victims are the working class. It is their votes and bodies that are needed to fight these wars. Christianity, terrorism, and fear of others are inflammatory emotional issues that are used to cause fear and to inspire both the electorate and the soldiers, but when governments decide to make geopolitical investments as big as war, they are generally driven by other calculations, those having to do with long-term economic and political agendas at the highest levels.

The Reverend Franklin Graham is the son of Reverend Billy Graham and is heir to his religious legacy. He became the chief executive officer of the Billy Graham Evangelistic Association in 2000. Even before September 11, 2001 he attacked Islam as "evil." Recently he has reaffirmed this hatred in his book, and in his speeches and public appearances. When criticized by the American Islamic community for his intolerance, he responded by saying, "There is no tolerance under Islam. I've been to Jordan, Saudi Arabia, Lebanon, Iraq, Iran, Pakistan, Afghanistan, Bangladesh, and Malaysia. Muslims in this country haven't traveled as much as I have. I know." Graham also defended his intolerance by incredibly claiming that Christianity is under attack in America and that Islam is getting better treatment in America than Christianity. He said, "When you mention Mohammed in a room, everyone says that's nice, but when you mention Jesus it polarizes the room."

In his writings, he argues that mainstream Islam cannot separate itself from the extremists because the "Qur'an is inherently violent." He also wrote, "Much is said and published about how peaceful-oriented Islam is, a little scrutiny reveals quite the opposite." He defended his remarks in a later interview, "You buy the Qur'an and read it for yourself. It is in there. The violence that it teaches is in there."

Graham's remarks have been echoed by other Christian conservatives. Pat Robertson has called Islam a "violent religion." In his booklet "Why Islam Hates America and the West," the Christian conservative Paul Weyrich wrote, "Islam is quite simply a religion of war." Even the former Nixon aide and convicted Watergate conspirator turned evangelist Chuck Colson said that Islam "breeds hatred." Reverend Jerry Falwell said in a 2002 television interview that Mohammed, the founder of Islam, "was a terrorist and a man of war." Rev. Jerry Vines, the former President of the Southern Baptist Convention called Mohammed "a demon-possessed pedophile."

The most ironic thing about Christianity's attacks on Islam is that they are the same arguments made against Christianity by the radical Muslims. The strange assertions cited above, and especially Graham's claim that in America Mohammed is more welcome than Jesus, are ludicrous and untrue. This is a Christian conservative tactic to enrage rally the working class Christian masses. It is a tactic that they have used to justify their attempts at taking away others' rights. In this case, it is the rights of the Muslims. It is being used by Christian conservatives to spread their Christian mission and to use the blood of the American working class to these ends. As Ann Coulter said to them in her book, "We should invade their countries, kill their leaders and convert them to Christianity."

After the September 11 attack on the World Trade Center and the Pentagon, the Reverend Jerry Falwell said that "god allowed the enemies of America to give us probably what we deserve."

Two days after the attacks, Pat Robertson on his television show, The 700 Club, said about the attack, "We have allowed rampant secularism and the occult, etc., to be broadcast on television. We have permitted somewhere in the neighborhood of 35 to 40 million unborn babies to be slaughtered in our society. We have a court that has essentially stuck its finger in god's eye and said we are

going to legislate you out of the schools. We are going to take your commandments off the courthouse steps in various states. We are not going to let little
children read the commandments of god. We are not going to let the Bible be
read, no prayer in our schools. We have insulted god at the highest level of our
government. And then we say "Why does this happen?" It is happening because
God Almighty is lifting his protection from us."

CHAPTER 28. CONCLUSIONS ABOUT CLASS AND CHRISTIANITY

Although Christian conservatives dominate American government and politics, there is an almost a hysterical quality from American Christians in asserting their religion. In the aftermath of September11, it is important to realize that militant Muslims are not the only radical religious movement that America needs to worry about. And while Christians will bristle at being compared to their Islamic brothers, their militancy comes from the same root cause.

Both Islam and Christianity are in fact becoming more radical and militant. The common bond that they share is that they both correctly perceive that their faith is threatened by modern society and its cultural evolution, and by science, which has made their desert nomadic religious beliefs obsolete. These two very old religions were both based upon the Old Testament of the Bible. The followers of both correctly perceive that they are facing cultural irrelevance if not extinction. It is this threat of extinction that is making them more radical and militant. It is for them a fight for survival.

Genesis and the six-day creation are no longer defensible or relevant in the light of modern science. How can anyone with even a passing knowledge of science believe that all mankind came from just Adam and Eve? It is difficult to the point of absurdity to believe that there was a flood from an angry god that forced all the animals on earth two by two into an ark. And that all animals are descended from the animals on that Ark, and all humans are descended from Noah's children. People who believe do so out of blind faith. A poll by the George Barna Research Group found that 12% of all adult American Christians believe that the name of Noah's wife was "Joan of Arc." The Bible actually does not give her name.

Science is the search for truth, knowledge and understanding. Since many of the men and women of science were and are religious, including very many of them Christians and Muslims, the undoing of their religion was an unintentional byproduct. But in the light of their discoveries it is becoming increasingly difficult to reconcile their religious beliefs to the scientific understanding of our world. This also begs the question does modern society and culture still need these religions?

Faith aside, religion was necessary to man's cultural development. Unlike animals, humans can understand the past and the future. Even a chimpanzee, the most intelligent animal and our closest relative on the evolutionary tree, must see something to know it; there is no past before his birth and no future once he dies. Man on the other hand, through language and shared knowledge can understand things that happen out of his sight and time, including the distant past. Man, unlike animals, also knows there will be a future even after his own death.

It is this intelligence and understanding that was the birth of religion. Religion is the concept that there is something greater than self. This understanding also gave man the ability to put him in other people's positions, and to imagine their thoughts. This is empathy and the basis of ethics. Man often confuses ethics with religion. It is important in understanding human cultural development to realize that it was empathy and ethics that caused the invention of religion, rather than the Christian and Islamic notion that we have empathy and ethics because of religion.

It is this misunderstanding that causes Christian and Islamic followers to feel that without their particular religion that there is no good in the world, and that anything outside their religion is immoral or bad.

It is probable that religion was a cultural necessity in man's development. Early man understood that it was impossible for a man to impose law or ethics upon others. The concept of an angry god was much more effective than an angry man when it came to the enforcement of laws and ethics. Culture also received an evolutionary lift from religion in art and music, and it can be argued that writing and literacy were also greatly assisted by religion. Culture has greatly benefited and evolved because of the world's religions.

However, religion is no longer needed for our culture to advance, and because of the anti-modernism of Christians and Muslims, it can be argued that religion now actually keeps our culture from advancing. It can be argued that it is religion and the Divine Rights of Kings and the Puritan "work ethic" that keeps the working-class poor and in their place. It is one of the major barriers to class mobility.

The religious will argue the masses, particularly the working class need religion to have morals and make them law abiding. The truth is that even if we once did need this that we no longer need religion to behave. Atheists and agnostics are as unlikely to break the law or to be unethical as Christians, Muslims, Buddhists or Jews. For example: The George Barna Research Group found that the divorce rate for Born-Again Christians and atheists was exactly the same. It could be argued that atheists and agnostics are even more ethical and individually accountable because they don't have god, Jesus or Mohammed to forgive them of their sins. The original need for religion has passed and Christianity, Islam and other religions are losing relevance with the rapid expansion of mankind's knowledge and science. Christian culture is a barrier to the advancement of the working class.

In evolutionary terms, when something relatively new, like American scientific culture is created, the old like Islam and Christianity, will become endangered or extinct. This extinction can be either a slow process or a cataclysmic event. It remains to be seen which will happen to Christianity, Islam and other religions. It is clear that if these religions are to survive for any time they must also evolve, change and adapt or they will die or destroy themselves.

America and the world are on the verge of a cultural transformation based upon our rapidly increasing knowledge base. It is greatly advancing the evolution of man and his culture. Man has the ability transform humanity, and wipe out disease and want within the next few several generations, we may even save ourselves from global warming, another event denied by the Christian conservatives. The key is our growing knowledge. Knowledge, not religion, is now the basic building block of our culture, but knowledge and progress can be stopped, suppressed and even lost to religious intolerance. The current religious militancy that we are experiencing from the Christian conservatives and Muslims could grow large enough to cause another religious "Dark Age" and a period of global intolerance. The wars in Iraq and Afghanistan that are killing our working class as well as Muslims are examples of this intolerance on both sides. Hopefully America will find his way through this challenge. And hopefully man will overcome the religious resistance to the scientific renaissance, and continue to evolve to the next level. It remains to be seen which direction America will take. These are indeed perilous times.

Chapter 29. Class and the Military

> "Without discipline the Army would be a bunch of guys wearing the same color clothing." —Major Frank Burns from the television show M*A*S*H

> "Expect a breakdown in morale as heterosexual men and women are forced to share barracks and showers with openly homosexual persons. Expect a dramatic rise in AIDS cases among military personnel and a subsequent jump in the taxpayer-financed military health care price tag!"—*Reverend Jerry Falwell*

The military has always been home to particularly poor working-class men, and recently women who have few or no other economic options. Currently another generation of mostly young working-class people are being sacrificed to war. As this is written the National Priorities Project reports that we have spent over $943 billion in the wars in Afghanistan and Iraq, these are monies that could pay for their health care and provide for better primary education and college tuition for working-class people who instead are killed and maimed on the battlefield at great cost to our society.

And although some of America's soldiers, air corps and navy are from the other two classes the majority and almost all enlisted ranks are working class.

When I served in the Army I had a friend from Mississippi, who was drafted like me and who also greatly disliked the Army. The Army wasn't what we wanted and we talked about how we couldn't wait to finish our two year commitment and go home. At the end of his two years, he shocked me by re-enlisting. When I asked him why, he sadly told me: "Back home I don't have nothing, sometimes we don't even have enough food, we live in a rundown house somebody else owns, and nobody has enough work or enough money, and we have take orders from bosses and everyone else just like the Army anyway. I don't like the Army, but at least here I got food, clothes and a roof over my head and a few bucks for beer and cigarettes, and in twenty years I'll have me an Army pension and I can go back home and live better than anyone else I know."

I lost touch with him when I left the Army. It was at the height of Vietnam and I hope he survived long enough to get his Army pension.

American classism is demonstrated vividly in the military. All of the military branches have strict class structures, with their officers almost exclusively from the leisure and upper middle class, and the enlisted ranks, most notably the lower enlisted ranks, are mostly from the working class. The officers are called "sir" or "ma'am," which are terms that came from the English upper-class royalty, while the enlisted are referred to by their rank, last names or a derogatory or funny nickname. The enlisted are treated as mindless children.

It was first my drill sergeant and later my officers who told me, "In the Army you don't think, we do your thinking for you!" In the Army, you are in fact a real slave. You are told on your first day that you no longer have civil rights and that "you are property of the United States Army." You are a "G.I.," meaning that, like your clothes and equipment, you are "government issue" or government property and no longer a person. "There are no individuals here!" you are told usually by a loud very belligerent voice.

America's military-class system is also reinforced by Christian culture. From the beginning the American military was a Christian dominated institution. The army and navy commanders were free to appoint chaplains as long as they were from a "Christian church." The military was from its beginnings was mostly Protestant dominated but allowed Catholic chaplains to serve in units that were completely Catholic. In 1862, after a year-long debate in Congress, the first Jewish chaplain was appointed to serve the Jewish soldiers of the Union Army. By the Civil War 2,300 Chaplains served with the Union Army. The Confederate Army had about 600 chaplains. The difference was that the Southern Chaplains preferred to serve in the ranks and fight the Yankee abolitionists, versus the Union chaplains who served primarily in a religious capacity. Oddly there were sixty-six Union chaplains who died in the war and three were awarded the Medal of Honor, while the South lost only fourteen Chaplains in battle.

American military posts from the beginning had churches and chapels built with tax dollars. Sunday worship was a requirement of the soldiers and sailors. Even during the 1960s and 1970s, soldiers were often given the choice of participating in Sunday worship or kitchen duty. The kitchen duty (called K.P. for kitchen police) was generally given to new recruits, draftees and used as a punishment in the army. It consisted of getting up at 3:00 AM in the morning and working until 10:00 PM that evening. Church attendance was almost always mandatory during army Basic Training. "There are no atheists in foxholes," the army is fond of saying. Chaplains also give talks on obedience and patriotism. These talks were also mandatory and usually followed by Christian prayers. American soldiers are expected to be reverent.

The Army is the largest branch of the military, and some would argue the most hazardous, and frequently has the worst duty of the four branches, or five if the Coast Guard is included, and it is quite possibly the most classist of the four. That isn't to say that the Marines, Navy and Air Force are free from classism and free from hazardous or bad duty assignments, but less so than the Army, which is why the Army has problems with enlistments from time to time, and needs to resort to involuntary service, known as the draft. While it is true that the other branches have had some draftees in times of war, such as during Vietnam, but their drafts were very small compared to the Army, and the three other branch's enlistment rates actually benefited significantly during Vietnam because of the desire of young men to not be inducted into the Army.

The induction letter notifying you that you had been selected, and were required by law to serve, started with the following sentence: "Congratulations! You have been selected by your friends and neighbors to serve in the U.S. Armed Forces." And I know for a fact none of my friends and the little old lady next door didn't select me for this duty. The local draft board did, and local draft boards had their biases concerning who was selected.

Boys who were "adrift," meaning they came from working-class homes, were the ideal candidates, since their draft boards deemed that they didn't have that much going for them anyway. During Vietnam very few middle-class and leisure-class boys were drafted or served. They usually obtained exemptions for attending college or belonging to the reserves. For example former Vice President Dick Cheney and Defense Secretary Donald Rumsfeld, both war hawks, were the recipients of these deferments and avoided being drafted and serving. Serving in the reserves was also a way for middle-class and leisure-class boys to avoid service. Very few reserves were used in combat during Vietnam, and it has been widely argued that it was largely because they were filled with the sons of influential people. In fact the reserves sometimes never served in any actual military capacity. Former President George W. Bush for example served some of his reserve duty during the Vietnam War working on a Republican Senate campaign in Alabama.

As in the case with George Bush, most members of the reserves in the Vietnam years became reserves through the significant influence of their families and friends. The reserves were filled with mostly influential upper middle-class and leisure-class boys, and there were many rumors that some reservists paid to get into the reserves. These injustices were a source of considerable dissent in the regular Army. The enlisted draftees referred to reservists as the "week-end warriors," and would say they were "rich guys who put on the uniform and pretended to be soldiers."

When my very previously mentioned smart working-class high school friend was serving in Vietnam, he got a Christmas card from our not so smart middle-class friend who was at college. He was so outraged by the irony of it that he sent a postcard in response which said the following: "Jingle Bells, mortar shells and V.C. (Viet Cong) in the grass; so take your Merry Christmas Jack and shove it up your ass!" It may have been rude but it said a lot about the times.

In the Army, the boys who had these exemptions were collectively called "Jody." And it was said that back home "Jody" was getting all the girls and maybe even yours. And "Jody" was usually the reason given for any "Dear John" letter, as in "Jody stole my girl."

The tension between the reservists and the regular Army sometimes boiled over when the reservists were required to take basic training with draftees. Eight weeks of basic training and sometimes vocational training were the only active duty required of most reserves during Vietnam.

The day I was drafted, I arrived at Ft. Campbell, Kentucky after midnight in the late winter. It was about forty degrees, but felt much colder because of the pouring rain and wind. I was with a large group of other draftees, and a smaller group of Army reservists. The drill sergeant separated us into draftees and reservists. The reservists were then allowed to go into the warm barracks and go to bed. We draftees were made to do jumping jacks, pushups in the mud and other exercises in the freezing rain for two more hours before going to bed frozen to the bone at 2:00 am, only to be forced to get up at 4:00 am. It was following this cold and virtually sleepless night that we were then all expected to stay awake next day and take our written intelligence, leadership, Army vocational tests. You can probably guess which group did better on their tests. And the tests were important because in 1967 recruits who did poorly on these tests became infantry and were primarily sent to combat units in Vietnam.

In basic training drill sergeants will assign student NCOs to lead the other recruits during basic training. Our drill sergeant, as was common practice, picked the reservists to fill this role, which in turn the reservists also favored their own, so when the night guard duty roster was prepared it was comprised of all draftees. Night guard duty is particularly brutal because you have to "donate" two of your six hours of sleep to walking guard. The K.P. duty roster was also all draftees. Kitchen Police or K.P. was duty where you got the privilege of getting up an hour early and working like a dog to prepare meals, serve meals, wash pots and pans, swill garbage, mop and clean from 3:00 am until well past 10:00 pm at night. It wasn't fun.

Like most G.I.s you learn to pace yourself or slough off when the authority isn't looking. Toward the end of basic training, our student NCO became angry that we pretty much ignored anything he had to say unless the drill sergeant was present. I was particularly insolent to his authority and one night he said, "You are an insubordinate bastard! If I was your sergeant in Vietnam I would shoot you in combat!" My response was, "Well that's never going to happen since I am going to Vietnam and you and all your chicken-shit weekend warriors are going home to Mommy."

These were fighting words and all the reservists in the barracks rose to their feet and for a moment I thought I was going to be beaten senseless, but in response to this, all the draftees rose to their feet and one particularly large and tough draftee said, "You reserves can shut up for the rest of basic training or we will kick the shit out of all of you, and the student NCOs will be the first asses we kick." (A few expletives were deleted from these quotes.) After this a silent cold war existed for the rest of our basic training.

During Vietnam the Army required so many troops that it was forced to relax its standards and the Army decided to allow the drafting of illiterate and "marginally retarded" working-class boys. This program was sometimes called "McNamara's Hundred Thousand" after Defense Secretary Robert McNamara who issued the policy.

This policy inspired the movie *Forrest Gump*. In the Army it was sometimes known as the U.S. 67 Program and the draftees were referred to as 67s. It was called this because it initially took place in 1967 and the Army in its infinite insensitivity used 67 as the first two numbers of these draftee's serial numbers so that their officers would know which soldiers had these limitations. However since most officers thought we were all retarded, it didn't seem to make much difference.

Ironically, while the U.S. Government and the Army allowed middle-class and leisure-class student deferments and had decided not to use the reserves at a time of severe wartime manpower shortages, the U.S. Government determined that these poor pathetic 67s were not as valuable as the middle-class and leisure-class boys and were therefore expendable. And despite their disabilities and disadvantages the 67s were chosen for combat, even if it meant that many were ill-equipped to defend themselves or their fellow soldiers.

I went through basic training with a 67. He cried every night for a week to go home to his "Mama." He couldn't learn the basic Army requirements, so we all had to cover up for him. One of the things he couldn't do despite threats and coaching was to use a rifle. He was terribly afraid of the weapon and could not fire it properly. He kept his eyes closed when firing his rifle despite the bodily threats from the drill sergeant. He caused several close calls on the firing range. In one live fire exercise, I was almost one of his casualties. Despite this the Captain told the drill sergeant that either the 67 qualified with the rifle and graduated from basic training or the drill sergeant would get the privilege of being reduced in rank and would be with the 67 as he repeated basic training.

I qualified as an excellent marksman with the rifle. On qualification day, the drill sergeant ordered me to shoot and qualify for the 67. When I protested, he told me that he would see to it that I repeated basic training with the 67 if I didn't qualify for him.

He then ordered me to change field jackets with him. He said: "All the range sergeants look at is the name on the jacket; they don't know one of you dumb cock suckers from another. And remember, just barely qualify him, I don't want you to make it too suspicious."

I did as ordered and it still weighs on my conscience that this mentally challenged man very likely went to Vietnam without the ability to fire a rifle.

The lives of military officers, made up of upper class "sirs" and "ma'ams," are considerably better than those of the working-class enlisted personnel. One of the major differences is that the officers are not property like the enlisted men. They are referred to as "Officers and Gentlemen" or "Officers and Ladies." Unlike the enlisted they are not indentured for fixed periods of time and are free to "resign their commissions" at any time. The officers enjoy much better pay, better duty, better food, and usually private quarters. While the enlisted have low pay, much worse duty, sometimes outright disgusting food, (anyone who has ever eaten the old C rations or K rations can testify to this) and generally live in crowded group quarters, although the non-commissioned officers (NCOs) enjoy slightly better things when they obtain the rank of sergeant. Officers also enjoy private clubs and entertainment and travel privileges not given to enlisted men.

The Christmas of 1967, I was 19 and I given leave to go home to my parents because it was expected that I would be sent overseas to Vietnam very shortly. At the time we traveled "military standby" on commercial airlines at about half the going rate, but we only got on a flight if there were vacant seats. During the Christmas season it was particularly difficult to get a seat on a plane and the officers are seated before enlisted men, even those who have waited much longer. However after seven hours, I finally moved up the list and I got aboard a flight headed for home, but before the door closed I was informed by the stewardess that an officer had just come to the gate and asked to take the seat of any enlisted man aboard and I was the only one. I asked her if she was making me give up my seat and she smiled and said the airline doesn't have any policy requiring you to give up your seat. I then asked if the officer could come onboard if I didn't give up my seat, and she smiled again and said it was airline policy that no one could come aboard without a confirmed seat. So I refused. The stewardess came back a few minutes later and said "I am sorry, but the officer is requesting your name, rank and duty post so that he can take appropriate action." Despite the fact that my last name was clearly on my uniform I told her that I was "Private Smith" and my next duty station is "Vietnam." She laughed and informed the fuming officer left standing at the gate as we took off. I was in the clear, but to be safe I dodged the Military Police when I arrived at my hometown terminal.

If caught, I could have been court-martialed for this offense, but I didn't feel that his rank should cause my parents to be without their child for Christmas or that my Christmas be destroyed in favor of his Christmas. I also admit to a bit of *schadenfreude*, because I still relish the thought of him fuming at the gate as I took off.

Army officers are generally college educated. They come from either West Point or a host of military academies and ROTC (Reserve Officer Training Corps) programs, or in some cases Officer Candidate School (OCS). During Vietnam there was such a large troop buildup that there was a shortage of officers since many of the upper-class boys were getting deferments or joining the reserves. It was complicated by the fact that the average life expectancy of a second lieutenant once in combat in Vietnam was very short, and the war was killing the leisure and upper middle-class West Point graduates who were serving. Some were even killed by their own men in what became known as "fragging."

In order to reduce the number of West Point graduate deaths the Army opened the door to working-class boys to become combat officers to be killed in their stead. They were offered this privilege only if they tested high in both intelligence and leadership.

Despite being kept awake all night in the rain the night before I took these tests I did very well in both and was recruited to go to OCS to become an Army officer after basic training and advanced infantry training. The catch was that you had to volunteer to be infantry which all but guaranteed that you would be going to a Vietnam combat unit, but since I was almost assured of going to Vietnam anyway, I agreed.

I was sold a false bill of goods. OCS, I was told, was just like college. It wasn't. It was much more like a very bad and on-going fraternity hazing with infantry training thrown in for good measure and it lasted for about six months. And what they didn't tell me before I agreed to attend was that I would have to serve an additional year in the Army if I accepted their commission as a second lieutenant at the end of OCS. I was not very enchanted with the program after I discovered this, and at the age of eighteen this extra year seemed a very long time.

I also found it amusing that the Army was entrusting this command position to me at the age of eighteen. As I told one of my friends, "Only the Army would put children in charge of adults in a life and death situation." However what I didn't know at the time was that in Vietnam it was mostly children, poor children. The average age of the combat troops in Vietnam was nineteen.

I also found out that in order to graduate from OCS that I would be discharged as an enlisted man a day before accepting a commission as an Army officer. I also knew that I could refuse the commission as an officer. In other words I was being discharged and if I refused my Commission the next day I would be free to go home.

Unfortunately I wasn't the only draftee with this great idea. I was informed after a about three months into OCS that in a class before me someone had figured this out and had refused their commission after being discharged, so the Department of Defense changed the rules. After the rule change a candidate could still turn down their commission and be discharged, but the Department of Defense would then immediately issue a new directive "redrafting" that individual to serve an additional two years as an enlisted man.

Shortly after receiving this news I resigned from OCS. It was a voluntary program. I chose to serve my remaining year in the Army as an enlisted man. At the time I was the Executive Officer of my OCS Company, a position given to me because of my leadership rating compared with my other classmates, so the Army didn't take too kindly to my resignation. Usually a candidate resigning or asked to leave OCS was entitled to keep their rank. However I was reduced in rank from what was the equivalent rank of sergeant (E5) to private for the very vague reason of "lack of training," despite the fact I had a whole year of the best Army infantry training in the world, and that my military occupation specialty, Long Range Recon Patrol Leader, required the rank of sergeant or above. I was then sent to a "holding company" made up of folks getting out of the stockade (Army prison) and then to a unit on post to await my shipment overseas to a combat unit in Vietnam.

However, not that long after my resignation from OCS, the North Koreans took the U.S.S. *Pueblo* prisoner in international waters and my orders were changed to Korea, by the Department of Defense, because they needed infantry trained personnel with secret security clearances to protect remote missile bases in South Korea. Most infantrymen don't have secret clearances, but I had the secret clearance because of my attending OCS. It was a bit of good luck.

If the officer's culture was that of the leisure or upper middle class, the culture of the enlisted men is most definitely working class. There is fatalism and an acceptance of the role of being second class among the working-class enlisted men that mirrors their working-class civilian life. Most soldiers believe they are getting what they deserve and that they are second class. The language of the enlisted Army is very informal and the use of those Celtic four-letter words is prolific. "Swearing" is imbedded in almost every sentence uttered. The enlisted ranks are anti-intellectual and the officers are frequently called "college boys" behind their backs. And the NCOs frequently use the phrase, "Don't call me 'sir,' I work for a living."

I continued my reading while in the Army, but because of this I was considered something of an odd duck by my enlisted friends. After people in my unit found out that I had planned on going to college after the Army a few began to refer to me derisively as "the Professor." As in: "How should I know? Why don't you ask the professor?"

The first time that two friends and I got a three day pass to Seoul, Korea, I took them to Duk Su Palace, the markets at Westgate, and the Korean National Museum. After that day they said I was boring and left me to spend the rest of their time at the bowling alley on the large American base to bowl, drink beer and eat hamburgers, and to go to the base movie theater. They said I had "gone too native."

However I did become a favorite of the Koreans attached to the United States Army. (The Army called them KATUSAs.) Ironically, all Korean men are required to serve in their armed forces regardless of class, but many of the upper-class Koreans use their influence to get their sons attached to the less harsh American Army.

The KATUSAs were unaccustomed to an American who wanted to learn about their country and they took the opportunity to show me the beauty of their culture, language and the cuisine of their country. It was an educational opportunity to which a poor working-class boy would have otherwise never been exposed. I still have a fondness for Korea.

It also became clear to me that these upper-class Koreans also quietly thought most Americans were crude barbarians. I learned they called Americans "the horse faces" behind our backs because of our comparatively longer, more narrow faces than the average very round Korean faces. It turned out that the Koreans were as biased about their ethnicity and culture as Americans were about theirs.

I received an Armed Forces Expeditionary Medal for my service in Korea. I am proud of my military service, although I admit it was not service I particularly enjoyed, but I am still very grateful for the G.I. Bill and my opportunity to go to college after my service.

On a wall in my home that my children call "the war wall" there are pictures and other mementos of my family's military service. It contains: the papers certifying my Great-great grandfather's service in the Civil War, and pictures of my great grandfather in the Spanish American War, my great uncle and wife's grandfather serving in World War I, my uncle who was killed as a tail gunner, my father-in-law, and my other uncle in World War II, me and my previously mentioned best friend serving during Vietnam, my nephew who served in the Persian Gulf War and my daughter who served in the Air Force during Bosnia. It is always the working class who serve.

Before his death, Senator Barry Goldwater, who was also an Air Force General, angered Christian conservatives by stating that everyone had the right to serve their country, and that included gays. He said, "You don't have to be straight to shoot straight."

When the Clinton administration proposed to allow gays to serve in the military the Christian conservatives were incensed. The Reverend Jerry Falwell threatened that it would destroy morale, cause an AIDS epidemic, and cost the taxpayers untold extra monies in military health care bills. Others lined up to say that gays couldn't be trusted and would be security threats because of their homosexuality. They also said it would tempt heterosexual members of the armed forces into the perverted gay lifestyle. And their final threat was that, with "Sodomites" in the military that God would no longer favor America and therefore not defend her during war.

The compromise that the Clinton administration put forward, "Don't Ask, And Don't Tell," was a spineless compromise that pleased no one.

CHAPTER 30. HEALTH AND THE WORKING CLASS

> America's health care system is second only to Japan, Canada, Sweden, Great Britain, and, well, all of Europe. But thank your lucky stars we don't live in Paraguay. — Homer Simpson, from the television show *The Simpsons*

A 2007–2008 medical study by Families USA stated that well over 86 million people in the United States were on public care while 46.3 million were without health insurance. This means that during the two year study period that one out of three Americans under the age of sixty-five had no health insurance. The working class has more health issues and less health care than the middle class and leisure class.

In March of 2008 the *New York Times* published an article summarizing a recent study by the Department of Health and Human Services which showed a significant gap in the life expectancy between the rich and poor, and that the gap has grown significantly over the past two decades. The gap shows that leisure-class Americans can expect on average to live at approximately four years longer than the poor working-class Americans. The researchers were quoted in the article saying that this gap also mirrored other studies showing the large and growing gap between the classes in infant mortality, heart disease, and in some cancers. The researchers said that the reasons for these gaps are that lower income people live in unsafe neighborhoods, sometimes lack food, eat unhealthy food, are exposed to more toxins and hazardous chemicals, have more hazardous employment, and that they have much less or no access to health insurance and health care, particularly preventative health care.

Contrary to popular belief, most of these 46.3 million without health insurance also do not have access to Medicare or Medicaid or other health programs offered to the poor.

The Kaiser Family Foundation reported that from 2001 to 2008 health premiums had risen 78 percent while wages rose only 19 percent. They also reported that the average family health insurance policy costs over $12,000 per year, and that even in the rapidly disappearing employer paid medical insurance programs the average worker is paying a quarter or more of their health insurance out of their pockets. Employers are struggling to pay these costs and many are laying increased costs on their employees or choosing to not provide any health care benefits.

In 2007 Reuters reported a GAO study that found that between 2001 and 2006 that employee health care coverage, with employers that have fewer than 200 employees, declined by more than eight percent with only sixty percent of all these companies now providing any employee health care coverage, and those who still provide coverage have asked their employees to pay more for this privilege. Many employers have also used their employee's health insurance costs as a bargaining tool to avoid giving them wage increases.

The GAO reported that medical coverage has declined the most for low wage workers who can least afford to pay for health care or out of pocket expenses, and for unhealthy workers with serious medical problems.

The health insurance industry plays Russian roulette with people's lives. People with previous health conditions that were not reported to their providers frequently lose their coverage, even when they are not aware of these previous conditions and could not have reported the condition. People who become sick are denied further coverage or are given limits on their coverage that will not provide for their health conditions. Because insurance policies are so technical most people don't know what kind of coverage they have or what kind of coverage they need.

Some employers, including the world's largest employer, Walt-Mart, have a policy of referring low wage workers to state and federal health care programs and may even devote personnel to assist employees in obtaining this coverage and in filling out their government applications, thereby using the taxpayer funded government safety net as their employee health care provider. Wal-Mart in particular has been greatly criticized for using the public coffers as its health care plan in many states.

In 2007 in the wake of growing public criticism, Wal-Mart and their long time critic and adversary, the Service Employees International Union (SEIU), surprised the nation by forming the Better Health Care Together, an alliance of unions and business to promote universal health care as the solution. In addition to these two giants, the Communication Workers of America, AT&T, Intel Corp., Kelly Services Inc., Embarq Corp., Maersk Line, Manpower Inc., and R.R. Donnelly and Sons have all joined the alliance. Three think tanks, the Center for American Progress, the Howard H. Baker Jr. Center for Public Policy, and the Committee for Economic Development have also joined. "We agree that America's health care system needs to be fixed and it needs to be fixed by 2012." said Walt-Mart Chief Executive H. Lee Scott at a recent Alliance event.

This movement was started jointly by big business and working-class institutions like the two participating unions gives some hope that new solutions and possibly universal health care like that offered in other first world nations may become reality. But in the interim while Congress is mired in debate and partisanship health care gets worse for the working class.

In the post 2007 housing bubble burst and the economic crisis it is becoming worse daily with people losing jobs and with the average family health insurance premiums at $12,000 per year they are also losing their health insurance as well. Some have suggested that in the wake of the economic crisis that approximately half of all Americans are now either uninsured or severely under insured to the point that it is effecting their health.

Universal health care is the solution. Christian Conservatives and the Republicans and some so called "Blue Dog" conservative Democrats have rejected universal health care for a couple of reasons. They fear a reduced quality of medicine, and they fear unaffordable costs. Their arguments lack validity. Americans have the best doctors and medical facilities, but America also ranks lower in medical care than many first world nations. The sad truth is we now have both poor quality medical care and fast rising unaffordable health insurance and Medicare costs. Yet are we still refuse to change our health care system.

Most other first world nations already have universal health care and they spend much less than Americans spend on their current system. Much of Europe, Canada, Japan, and Australia have universal health care and all are spending much less for medical care than the United States. Their health care quality is excellent, and some would argue much better because everyone has preventative care. An example of this gap is that the infant mortality rate is much lower in all those countries than in the United States.

A few years ago a Kaiser Family Foundation study estimated that America could provide universal health care to everyone for about $48 billion. This is an increase of only 3% more than we are paying now in national health outlays!

CHAPTER 31. THE GEOGRAPHY OF CLASS

"To me it seems a dreadful indignity to have a soul controlled by geography."—
American philosopher George Santayana

Is there geography to class? Yes. Most of us know this intuitively, the ghetto being the most obvious example. Place does make a difference.

A few years ago *American Demographics Magazine*, the marketing periodical, surveyed middle-class and working-class people for their preferences according to whether they were rural or urban. It was an interesting study. But before we look at the results of this survey there is a myth that should be dispelled.

If you asked the average American what the poster child of poverty looks like, the majority would say it was an adult person of color in an inner city. This is wrong, it is the exact opposite. The poster child is: a child since there are by far more poor children than adults in poverty, and white, since the majority of the poor in America are whites, and rural since the majority of poor are also rural. Knowing this, now let us look at the *American Demographics* survey.

The survey looked at four things: the favorite leisure activity, the favorite television station, the favorite music, and the favorite magazine of these groups with the following results:

• Leisure activity: working-class rural people overwhelmingly preferred auto races. (Remember the Republican NASCAR events) working-class urban people preferred watching pro-wrestling. Middle-class rural people preferred either skiing or golf, depending on the season, and middle-class urbans preferred watching pro-football.

- Television Station: working-class rural preferred TBS, which is an Atlanta station which at that time aired a variety of shows that would appeal to white rural people, such as *The Dukes of Hazard*, while working-class urban preferred the Black Entertainment Network.

See any patterns? One of the reason why Americans think of person of color in an inner city when they think poor is because the largest group of the working-class poor that are the most visible are urban African-Americans. African-Americans are not the only low income group in urban America, but they are the largest, and they are also the most visible. The media which is comprised of mostly white middle-class and urban people greatly contributes to this stereotype of a society of poor Blacks in overwhelming numbers.

Rural poverty on the other hand is larger, but it is much more hidden. Not many people travel the unpaved rural roads to see the trailers and small houses that contain most of the nation's poor, other than the poor who live in them.

The preferred station of middle-class rural people is CNBC, which if you think about it also makes some sense. In rural areas there are few daily newspapers and financial news in particular isn't very useful when it is a few days to a week old. The middle-class urban prefer PBS.

Music: working-class rural people prefer country music again reflecting that the majority are white. While working-class urban prefers RAP probably reflecting that the majority are Black. And while I admit that other folks than white like country music and other folks than Black like Rap it is this majority that make these choices the dominate preference. Among middle-class rural the music preference is soft rock, and with middle-class urban it is Jazz and classic rock.

Magazine: The favorite magazine of the rural working class is *Woman's World*. The favorite magazine of the working class urban is either *JET* or *Ebony*, which again reflects the urban majority of working-class is Black. The middle-class rural prefers *Bon Appétit* and the preference of the middle-class urban is *Rolling Stone*.

The very interesting thing about this geography is that you could have predicted many of these preferences just by knowing the majority race of each class in each area.

Keep in mind that these are national generalizations and that within the nation there are also some regional differences. In the Southwest Latinos are in much greater numbers than African-Americans and are the largest group of working class in many Southwestern cities. In the cities of North Dakota, where there are few minorities, the working-class urban people are mostly white.

Is there geography to income? Yes there is. In looking at the 2000 Census the states with the highest median household incomes are: Maryland, Alaska, and

Minnesota, one state from the East, one state from the West and one state from the Midwest. Of the four regions of the United States only the South is absent from this list. Now look at the states with the three lowest median household incomes: West Virginia, Arkansas, and Mississippi, all in the South. Three of the four regions of the United States are very close in median household income, while the South lags considerably behind.

Is there a difference between rural and urban? Yes there is. In the 2000 Census the median household income of the United States as a whole was $42,409. The median household income of the central cities was $37,315 and the median income of rural households was $34,135. Just to give you an idea of the severe Southern income lag the median household income for the state of West Virginia was $30,072, more than $12,000 less than the national median and more than $4,000 less than the national rural median.

We have seen that the largest group of poor is white and rural, but how does race and gender factor into income? Keeping in mind the national median was $42,409, it was $52,285 for Asian-Americans, for Whites it was $46,900, for Latinos it was $33,103, for African-Americans it was $29,177, and for female headed households it was $28,590, and for senior households it was only $23,496.

Any surprises? It should be noted that the Asian households are highest because a large number of Asian households are communal and have inter-generational families which have households with multiple wage earners. In other words Dad, Mom, Grandpa, Grandma, sons and daughters and in-laws may all be brining income into the household. A large number of Asian businesses tend to be family operated and staffed as well.

The other surprises may be that Hispanics households earn more than African-Americans which may also be partially because like Asian-American households they tend to also be more communal and inter-generational households. The two lowest groups of women and the elderly should not be surprising. The median American household has 1.5 wage earners meaning a female headed household not only faces a gender gap in wages, but has 50% less wage earners than the median household. The elderly continue to be the poorest group and with company pensions becoming rare and the as pension savings have disappeared during the current economic crisis this group may be even much worse off going forward than they are today, which is frightening considering the large number of baby boomers that are about to retire.

Chapter 32. Income Distribution

In the United States, "One sex is devoted to dollar hunting, and the other to breeding dollar hunters."—J.S. Mill

Milt Friedman, the leader of the currently dominant conservative Monetarist school of economics, wrote that all professions are aristocratic and provide barriers for new people to enter and those professions such as doctors, lawyers and bankers become exclusive clubs that restricts membership and artificially inflates wages.

The Monetarist economist George Sigler, a lifelong friend of Friedman, agreed with Friedman on the exclusivity of the professions and theorized that most government regulation is designed to further this exclusivity. "Business wants regulation because it protects them from the risks of dynamic competition." He said.

What he didn't say was that business almost always controls their regulators. It is known by economists as the "Capture Theory" where due to the public's lack of knowledge and interest, regulators will eventually become captors of the lobbying efforts of the entities they regulate. This capturing was most apparent in the financial and banking industries during the recent mortgage meltdown and financial crisis. This failure of the public to know and care is frequently known by economists as "rational ignorance." Since it isn't likely, nor is it realistic, to expect that the public can know every regulated business, or that they have the time to care and do anything about these issues. The average citizen assumes the regulators and or the government is watching taking care of this. Unfortunately rational ignorance is what politicians rely upon to grant large undeserved rewards to the influential, which in total are usually unnoticeable when compared to the huge government budget. The dance of the politician is to award these large gifts to friends and supporters without these gifts becoming noticeable enough for a large segment of the voting public to become concerned.

It makes no difference if you are or are not a capitalist. The fact is that without a fair and regulated distribution of wealth capitalism will fail. By 2005 the richest one percent, the leisure class made over 19 percent of the nation's total income. It is their largest share since 1929. Much of this was because Republicans since Ronald Regan have drastically reduced the taxes of the wealthy, and in 2001 George W. Bush succeeded in cutting the Estate Tax from 55% to zero, assuring that wealth will be kept in the hands of a few families, like the Bush family who now control most of America's wealth.

The bottom 20% of the population made only 3.4 percent of the total national income, so it should not be surprising that and one in eight Americans lived in poverty in 2005, even before the economy suffered the recent collapse. Also in 2005 The U.S. Department of Housing and Urban Development reported to Congress that in a count taken on a single night in January there were 754,000 homeless people in the United States. A quarter of these homeless were children, and a quarter of the homeless adults were disabled. It should be repugnant to all Americans that during 2005, a time of economic prosperity, America allowed large numbers of children and the disabled to live homeless on the streets. HUD also acknowledged in their report that they didn't take into consideration a very large group of people who were also homeless but had found temporary shelter in the homes of friends or relatives.

Research done by Professor Mark Rank at the University of Wisconsin concluded that 58% of all Americans will spend at least one year in poverty. And a Luxembourg Income Study showed that of all the industrialized nations only Russia and Mexico spent less on anti-poverty programs than the United States.

Another significant indicator of poverty is the GINI Index or coefficient. The GINI is a statistical measurement used to measure the inequality of income and wealth distribution of countries. It is defined as a ratio. A low GINI coefficient indicates a more equal income or wealth distribution, while a high GINI coefficient indicates a more unequal distribution. Here are the GINI ratios according to the Economic Policy Institute in order of the most inequitable distribution of wealth to most equitable distribution: The United States was the inequitable 5.6, The United Kingdom 4.2, Japan 4.1, Canada 3.9, France 3.3, Germany 3.2, and Sweden 2.6. This means that in the United States the top 10% of the population, the leisure class has more than 5.6 times more money than the lowest 10% of Americans. The United States has the worst wealth distribution of the first world countries and equals that of many third world countries.

According to the Economic Policy Institute the income of the leisure class, the upper 1% of the population, has more than doubled in the past twenty-five years while the income of the lowest twenty percent has lost income during this same period. The average CEO of a large corporation now makes 531 times more than his employees. The top two cities for CEO pay are New York at $5.24 million and Minneapolis at $4.87 million.

According to Standard and Poor's, the former CEO of Oracle, Larry Ellison, made a whopping $740 million in annual compensation. Michael Eisner while at the Disney Corporation made $570 million for his annual compensation and John Reed of Citigroup made $288 million.

Larry Ellison's $740 million annual compensation would pay 14,800 families $50,000 per year. Does Larry Ellison work harder than 14,800 people? Is he smarter than 14,800 people? Is he better than 14,800 people? If not, then something has gone horribly wrong.

Is Larry Ellison's work that more valuable than those 14,800 people? Adam Smith, the darling of conservative Republicans and Milton Friedman and his school of monetarists, said, "Labor is the great cause of public opulence, which is always proportioned to the industry of the people, and not the quantity of gold and silver, as is foolishly imagined."

The system is broken. Economics is defined as "the science that deals with the material well-being of humankind." It is not about the material well-being of one or the few. When one person is obscenely, rich it means many people will be even more obscenely poor. This unreasonable high compensation has to be defined as anti-economics.

The gap between the rich and working class is widening rapidly at an alarming pace. Kevin Phillips in his book, *Bad Money*, reported a 2007 *Forbes* survey that showed that the twenty highest paid hedge fund managers averaged over $657 million in annual compensation in 2006. Just one of the salaries of these hedge fund managers would pay over 13,100 families $50,000 a year, all combined these twenty salaries would pay 262,000 families $50,000 a year. Have they justified their income? Recently it could be well argued that hedge fund managers have done much more harm than good to the economy.

In his book, *Wealth and Democracy*, Kevin Phillips showed that the richest thirty individuals and families had increased their wealth ten-fold from 1982 to 1999. He also showed that the average compensation of the ten highest paid corporate executives went from an average of $3.5 million dollars in 1981 to an annual compensation of over $154 million by 2000. During this same time frame, working-class wage earners lost wages when inflation was factored into their earnings. It suggests that the one's gain is the other's loss.

If money is finite, what this means is that a very few leisure-class people have enough wealth to spend over a thousand lifetimes, which is subsidized by millions of working-class families who will struggle for enough income for their basic needs. This is contradictory to good economics, if we understand it to be the science that deals with the material well-being of humankind.

E.J. Dionne, a *Washington Post* columnist, once wrote: "Republicans once preached compassion, but then went off to war. Democrats waged a war on poverty, but then lost some elections. They decided that the middle class is where it's at."

Government plays a strong role in perpetuating the classes and is also culpable for the unfair distribution of wealth and the favoring of the leisure class.

The fast food industry is an example. Eric Schlosser in his book, *Fast Food Nation*, points out that the largest group of minimum wage workers in the United States are fast food workers. He detailed the how the fast food industry that pays the miserly minimum wage to its workers also receives a tax credit from the federal government of up to $2,400 for each low income worker hired by their chains. It is called the Work Opportunity Tax Credit. It is supposedly given to the fast food industry to subsidize employee training.

In 1996 the U.S. Department of Labor investigation of this practice concluded that there was no actual training, the jobs were mostly part time without health and pension benefits and that at least 92% of the workers would be hired without the subsidy. Despite this report Congress renewed the subsidy. The fast food industry received $385 million the next year from the subsidy. Considering the only government requirement for this subsidy was that the worker be employed for four hundred hours, which is fifty days at a regular shift of eight hours, meant that the chains could get rid of a worker after a couple of months and receive a new subsidy. So what the subsidy actually did was to make it very financially attractive for the restaurants to rid themselves of their workers after a few months, which is a likely reason why turnover in these establishments is so high. In other words the government was giving an incentive to the companies to rid themselves of their low income workers after a few months.

In addition if you take the minimum wage at the time and apply it over several months it approximates the $2,400 subsidy. Since the restaurants are paying no benefits, the subsidy covers the entire labor cost of their employees if they turn over their staff on a regular basis. What it means is that the government pays for nearly the entire workforce of the fast food industry.

In Schlosser's *Fast Food Nation*, he quotes a *Houston Chronicle* interview with Bill Singer the chief lobbyist for the industry who defended the subsidy by saying that there was nothing wrong with the government subsidizing low-pay, no benefit, and short-term jobs for the poor. "They've got to crawl before they can walk." And crawl is what the government and the fast food industry expects these working-class workers to do.

Economics is nothing more than a system of distributing wealth and resources. The economic system dictates who will prosper and who will be poor. Since the American economy is a consumer economy with two-thirds or more coming from consumer spending, than this concentration of wealth to the leisure class greatly restricts the potential of the American economy. Bill Gates for example may be thousands of times richer than the average American consumer, but he isn't going to eat thousands of bowls of cereal each morning. He isn't going to buy thousands of televisions, refrigerators or autos. America's economy would be much better if these working-class workers had more income to spend and our wealth was distributed more equitably

CHAPTER 33. AMERICAN POVERTY

"Money is better than poverty if only for financial reasons." —Woody Allen

According to a mid 1990s United Nations Development Programme report the 358 richest people in the world have more combined assets than the total combined annual income of half of the people of earth. It is often argued that compared to other parts of the world that America, including Americans in poverty, are much better off than most. Because of these poverty comparisons, some on the political right and Christian conservatives have argued that most Americans in poverty are not really poor. They argue that although the American poor "may lack some basics" that because they have a cell phone or a television they are somehow better than those in the third world who also lack the basics but also lack a cell phone or a television. They argue this even though it is difficult to eat a television or even resell it for any money to get food, although the American poor frequently try to do so by using pawn shops, or pledging all their household goods as collateral for small loans.

Interestingly one of the few economists to address this question of relative poverty between nations was Karl Marx. Marx defined the threshold level that one needed to be out of poverty as "subsistence" and he said that obtaining subsistence is dependent upon contemporary culture and lifestyles. Therefore a western person who has a meager roof over their heads and a few possessions can still be in poverty even compared to a third world person living with nothing in a grass hut. He noted that the living requirements of an urban person may differ greatly and appear extravagant compared to the lifestyle of a rural person even in the same country, but both could be poor and lack enough to meet their basic needs.

According to the U.S. Census Bureau the poverty threshold for a family of four in the United States is $20,614 annually. However anyone with a reasonable idea of living expenses in America knows that a family of four couldn't meet the subsistence level on this amount. Most probably know that a family of four couldn't reach subsistence on $25,000 which according to the U.S. poverty standards would be more than an additional $1,000 per person above U.S. poverty threshold in a household of four.

So why does the United States use poverty thresholds that make no sense? They do it because of politics. A few years ago on the television show *The West Wing*, a show about the life of a fictitious president and his advisors, they dealt with the poverty threshold issue. The president's advisors decided to use a more realistic threshold. The problem was that if they applied the new threshold that the total population of poor in the United States would raise to over a third of the population, and it would appear that the poverty rate had doubled during their presidency, so in the end they left the threshold alone. There is much truth in art.

The Economic Policy Institute conducted a survey a few years ago to determine what the threshold should be. Based upon their surveys it showed that over seventy percent of families of four earning about $33,000 missed some rent payments, used the local emergency room for all their medical care, and worried about having enough food. Using this survey it could be argued that about $35,000 is the income level needed for a family of four to achieve subsistence in the United States which means about a third of all Americans were actually in poverty which may be now greater considering the current economic crisis.

It is also generally thought that welfare makes up this difference in the lives of the poor, but the reality is that we lack an adequate economic safety net in America. The welfare system has been systematically eroded since Ronald Regan's crusade against "welfare queens," and was reduced even further under Bill Clinton's poorly thought out Welfare to Work programs. Remembering that the Luxembourg Income Study showed that of all the industrialized nations only Russia and Mexico spent less on anti-poverty programs than the United States, this lack of effort demonstrates an utter lack of commitment to provide any safety net by America for her poor. Indeed it is another valid argument that America is deliberately making and preserving a slave class.

CHAPTER 34. THE MIDDLE CLASS AND THE MYTH OF UPWARD CLASS MOBILITY

> "The distinctions separating the social classes are false; in the last analysis they rest on force."—Albert Einstein

The great myth of America is that it is a middle-class country, while the reality is that almost two-thirds of Americans are working class. One of the reasons for this myth is that American institutions, including government, schools, business, and nonprofits, are middle-class institutions and function with a middle-class culture. The other reason is that almost all Americans inflate their own class status. Most Americans will tell you they are middle class, even if they haven't graduated from high school, make less than $24,000 per year, and live in a trailer park.

The irony is that where class is different not better, most Americans believe the higher you are in class, the better person you are. (Remember the test: Do you really thing Paris Hilton of the leisure class is better than you as a person?) The working class will pretend they are middle class and the middle class will pretend they are leisure class.

As you may recall the middle class is divided into two sub-classes, the lower middle-class and the upper middle class. The upper middle-class is about thirteen percent of Americans, who are relentlessly trying to be leisure class. They do this by emulating the habits and culture of the leisure class and aspire, if not for themselves, then for at least for their children, to become leisure class. They hire nannies or "au pairs," and send their children to the best private schools that will take them, regardless of cost, in the hopes that social connections will be made and the class status granted. They buy the best their money and credit can afford to prove they belong.

The editor and columnist, and PBS commentator David Brooks even tried to make a new upper class, educated elitists he called "Bobos" (for "Bourgeois Bohemians"). He defined this as a class that considers itself above the middle class with their "superior education." His book *"Bobos in Paradise, The New Upper Class and How They Got There"* was very well written and a fun read, but in the end what David Brooks described was too much like the upper middle class in culture and his new "upper class" had the same air of desperation as the upper middle class in attempting to show their equality or superiority to the leisure class. His true upper middle-class leanings and bias came out in the book when he described anti-intellectual neoconservatives like George Bush as "mostly lower middle-class kids."

His conclusion was "For Americans to become engaged once again in public life and proud of their institutions...They (the new educated upper class) have to assume a leadership role. They are the best-educated segment of society and among the most affluent.... They have the ability to go down in history as the class that led America into another golden age."

This pretentiousness is the essence of the upper middle class. Mostly where this "best educated segment of society" has led us to be what the economist Thorstein Veblen called "conspicuous consumption." Brooks acknowledges that his new upper class shares these upper middle-class consumer traits. In his book he pointed out that with "Bobos" it is "virtuous" to spend $25,000 on their bathroom, but "vulgar" to spend $15,000 on a wide screen television. Their culture can be seen for its pretentiousness and inequities by comparing this difficult upper middle-class economic decision to spend their lavish incomes on a either a wide screen television or an overly expensive toilet, compared to the everyday working-class household reality of trying to make their rent or house payment so they will have a bathroom.

One of the major contributors to American classism is that all classes and their traits are defined by the middle class, through their lens and biases. David Brooks' *Bobos in Paradise* is just one example.

Paul Fussel, a writer, editor and professor of English, in his book *Class*, decided to expand the five classes most sociologists recognize and proposed nine. In addition to the three classes and the subdivision of the working and middle-class, he added a new leisure class at the top — he called it the "top out-of-sight." He then divided the working class from the customary underclass and blue collar workers into five categories he called: "high proletarian, mid-proletarian, low proletarian, destitute, and the bottom out-of-sight." In his book Fussel reduces the working class to what he calls "proles" (short for proletariat) and those who are destitute. In support of an explanation of these types, his book has a cartoon with the following caption: "A high prole regarding a destitute with distain, but less for his poverty than for his style." The cartoon shows this "high prole" as a fat man in an ill-fitting suit, with a comically wide tie which is improperly tied. In other words, he is a slob. The "destitute" man is layered in what appears to be rags and carrying a bottle wrapped in a paper bag in which one is led to presume is some kind of cheap alcohol. The conclusion is that in the working class it is a contest of class between a slob and a drunk. Both cartoon characters are obvious middle-class stereotypes of the working class. Fussel apparently thinks that "mid-proles and lower proles fall some place in between drunks and slobs."

Another cartoon was just as revealing. Captioned "The prole automobile rear view," it shows an automobile with leopard skin upholstery, fuzzy dice hanging from the mirror, and three bumper stickers which say: "Klutz University," "USA: Love It or Leave It," and "Honk if You Love Jesus." It also had an STP sticker (think NASCAR) and a Playboy Bunny sticker.

This cartoon reveals quite a bit about middle-class perceptions of the working class as it shows someone with poor taste, an inferior education from "Klutz University," (Klutz is defined in the dictionary as a person who is stupid, foolish, or clumsy) as a Xenophobe, inordinately religious, but into Playboy if not pornography.

Other middle-class definitions of American class structure have included defining the three classes as "the highbrow, middle-brow, and lowbrow." The intent is clear. They are describing the three main classes as the bright, the average and the stupid.

In pointing out these generalizations and biases one is always in danger of being accused of starting a class war, which in America is considered extremely rude, if not taboo (for example, when the Republican Party has come under attack for fiscal policies that greatly favor the leisure class to the detriment of everyone else, they scream "unfair class warfare"). The truth is that America is one perpetual class war where the working class is constantly being beaten and then told to be grateful and to thank those delivering the beating.

American middle-class culture is the dominant culture because they are the managers and overseers of the leisure-class wealth and manpower. It also has a double meaning. Middle class can mean the class between the working class and the leisure class, or "middle class" meaning average or the norm. To see just how much our American institutions are governed by the middle class, all we have to do is look at what was once called the "Bible" for successful people.

In 1975, John T. Molloy wrote *Dress for Success*, which immediately became a business standard, suggesting how to get a promotion by learning how to dress and behave in the workplace. His book can be summed up in one quote: "Successful dress is really no more than achieving good taste and the look of the upper middle class."

The 2005 *New York Times* study *Class in America* showed that there is little or no upward class mobility in America. In fact, twentieth century America shows only one major exception. It happened after the Second World War when working-class men were given funding via the G.I. Bill to go to trade school or college in exchange for their service. That fueled the post war boom and allowed some working class to move into the lower middle class, but even this was not enough to make the majority of the American population middle class. But it was enough to make some major changes in the culture of the lower middle class. If, for example, you are confused as to whether you belong in the middle class or working class, it is very likely that your family benefited from this movement. The lower middle class, because of this brief period of upward mobility, now carries some cultural traits of both the working class and the middle class.

This upward mobility ended in the 1970s, when the Vietnam veterans used up their G.I. Bill funds to go to school, after which the government effectively ended the G.I. Bill education program. The *New York Times* study also shows that not only did this upward mobility end with that program, but since then a substantial number of people have been sliding out of the lower middle class back into the working class. In other words, we are progressively becoming even more a working-class nation. Recent economics studies and the GINI Coefficient show that US wealth is being concentrated even more into the leisure class and with this money transfer the working class and particularly the underclass are the fastest growing classes.

Middle-class wealth transfer from generation to generation is a growing concept among sociologists and economists. They point to the fact that the middle class has retained its moderate wealth and status generation to generation. And they believe it is because middle-class wealth is more about culture than actual money. It is more about the transfer of culture from parent to child, such as the middle-class traits of sacrificing and saving today for tomorrow's gains, and gaining an education to provide for tomorrow's achievements and luxury. Middle-class priorities are about possessions and the future, versus the working-class priority of people, and now, and dealing with crisis, so that the middle class is better positioned for business and finance and to be gatekeepers for the rich.

Middle-class children are entitled and have seen and replicated their parent's success, however modest, and they have been told from cradle onward that they may even do better than their parents by obtaining an education and following the rules. Meanwhile, working-class children are disenfranchised, and told that they can't achieve or if they somehow manage to succeed that someone will take it away from them using sayings like: "The rich get rich and the poor get poor." "The rich get the gold and the poor get the shaft." "The King is King and the rich are rich because god made them that way, and the poor are poor because god made them that way — and who are we to question god?"

Chapter 35. Anomie: The Price of Upward Mobility

"Every once in a while, I meet middle-class Americans who were once lower class. They come from inner cities and from West Texas trailer parks. They are successful now beyond their dreams, but bewildered by the loss and betrayal, becoming so different from their parents. If only America would hear their stories, we might, at last, acknowledge social class." —Sociologist Richard Rodriguez

Although it's rare, people do move up in class. As noted, in the post Second World War economic boom of the 1950s and early 1960s, the G.I. Bill enabled some people to move into the lower middle class. Since about 1973 and continuing today, the children of these class climbers are falling back into the working class.

What happened to these people as they rose in class was not what they expected. While they are seen by their working-class friends and families as successful, they are, in the words of Sociologist Richard Rodriguez, "bewildered by the loss and betrayal of becoming so different" from those friends and families. Most of these new middle-class folks found themselves apart from their former class society and somehow different and apart most from almost everyone they knew. Sometimes this happens because the new middle-class person is "embarrassed" by former lower-class friends and even family; but more frequently it is the lower-class family and friends that choose to distance themselves. They see these "social climbers" as "uppity." This word is related to "upwardly mobile"; it means to be snobbish or arrogant, and to inflate one's self-importance.

I experienced this in my own life. I was the first in my family to get a high school education and the first to graduate from college. Because of this I was able to get a professional job, and as much as I still consider myself a working-class person, I have been more frequently described by others as lower middle class. Considering my tastes and preferences, this class status, much to my chagrin, may be truer than I like to admit. In fact, the lower middle-class and the Blue collar working class share many of the same cultural traits, and during the later twentieth century the lower middle-class became a sort of mixing pot of middle-class and working-class cultures. As I previously stated, this was due to this one time surge of working class into the lower middle class in the 1950s and 60s.

In fact if, after reviewing your own class traits, you are still confused as to which class you are, you are likely lower middle class. Keep in mind that class inflation is widespread, with most of the blue collar working class referring to themselves as middle class, and most of the upper middle-class think or pretend to be leisure class. This is why people buy and flaunt things they may not be able to comfortably afford. It is part of our class culture of "keeping up with the Jones."

Beauty also tends to marry up in class. A beautiful girl has a good possibility of attracting a husband in a class above her, if the upper-class man's mother, family and friends don't interfere. It is usually a mother's function to make sure her children maintain or rise in class and not marry "beneath their status."

My experience with upward mobility was as Rodriguez described. I was "bewildered by the loss and betrayal of becoming so different from my family." Although I felt I hadn't changed, my family and friends saw this differently. The most obvious example was in the relationship with my father.

My Dad was a hard-nosed, hardworking, hard-drinking blue collar man. He was very proud of my education, but it was also the source of his biggest problem with me, his only son. He felt it made me different and he didn't like it.

It wasn't my attitude or anything I said. My father very strongly felt that I had somehow become better than he was and he greatly resented me for it.

If I made a mistake he would say, "Apparently they don't teach that to college boys."

If I was successful, it was because "You are a spoiled cake-eater with everything given to you." I strongly deny that I am a cake-eater. Keep in mind that some of the places I lived as a child were in the projects, en el barrio, an abandoned Navy hospital, and an unheated Minnesota cabin, and that I went to work at the age of twelve as a busboy and a dishwasher in a railroad depot dining room to help with my family's financial problems and that I was working fulltime while in high school for the same reason.

People who observed my Dad's treatment of me thought my Dad was just plain mean, but his treatment of me was out of character. He was a grumpy old man, but he wasn't judgmental with anyone but me. He doted on my wife and children, and on my sisters. And he would have given me anything I asked for if he had it. But his treatment of me was usually belittling, mocking, and rude to the point that my mother was afraid that one day I would stop speaking to him.

My Dad treated me this way because he thought I had become better than him, and he couldn't help himself despite my efforts to assure him I didn't feel that way, or even his own realization that his behavior toward me was inappropriate and miserable. A big part of this was my Dad's guilt. He couldn't look at my success without feeling that he was a failure and that I had succeeded where he hadn't.

My Dad was a very proud person. It was a pride borne from poverty, put-downs and hard work. Like many working-class men of his age, he didn't apologize to anyone. So even when he realized his behavior toward me was mean-spirited and unwarranted, there was no apology or any attempt at reconciliation; he would just forget it happened, and I was expected to do the same.

Toward the end of my Dad's life, he suffered from Alzheimer's disease. Before his mind left him, I went to visit him in the memory care center with my two sons and my oldest grandson. He idolized all three of them and I wanted them to see him a final time before he lost all lucidity.

He was particularly lucid that day. At the end, when we were saying our goodbyes, Dad turned to my sons and said, "Your Dad probably thinks I am a big asshole, and he has every right to think so." My father died shortly afterward. It was as close to an apology my father ever made.

While this class estrangement toward me was the strongest from my Dad, it wasn't something peculiar just to my father. I experienced this distance with other family members and friends, who were not as vocal or strident as my father, but in quiet ways also let me know I was no longer one of them. I remember how they reacted to the news of my first professional job working in management for a local government, which became known in my family as me "feeding at the government trough." I also remember one particular comment from a family member, "So I guess you are somebody important now." It was said more as a sad lament than as congratulations. A similar remark was made by friends when I graduated from college. "So what does a college degree make you?" And before I could answer he said, "Somebody important, no doubt." To which my other friends echoed in laughter, "No doubt!" again, more in sad lament than as congratulations. It was said as if I had left or was leaving.

This distance created between a person who has moved up in class and has left his family and friends behind is a barrier that causes the upwardly mobile person to be unacceptable as a member of their own class, and yet such individuals will likely never fully feel they belong in the new class they have attained.

I find myself in this no man's land. I don't feel like a middle-class person, nor do I want to be one, but I am no longer a working-class person, either. I don't have a cultural home. The best word to describe this is anomie. *Webster's Dictionary* defines anomie as "as state or condition of an individual or society characterized by a breakdown or absence of social norms and values, as in the case of uprooted people." Upward mobility equals up-rooted people, of that there is no doubt.

CHAPTER 36. EDUCATION, INTELLIGENCE AND MIDDLE-CLASS BIAS

> "Tell me and I will forget, show me and I may not remember, but involve me and I will understand." —A Native American Proverb

The working class believes education is only for the smart. It is not meant for the average person. This belief is partially due to our culture, where among other things, scholarships are awarded to "smart" people. The actuality is that scholarships usually go to people with good grades, which has much more to do with attitude, behavior, and class than it does with intelligence.

In fact the few that are awarded for intelligence are rigged to only certain intelligence. America is a very-left-brained country. That is to say that it has a bias for deductive reasoning skills. This is why math and sequential thinking play the major role in US intelligence scoring.

Very little inductive reasoning skills are measured in either US intelligence testing or the education system, yet inductive reasoning is as valid as deductive reasoning. Most people use both methods of reasoning every day. US intelligence tests also measure only a few intelligences very well, while many more not at all, and it is a composite of only these few measures that determines "intelligence" in the US. If you are a genius in the fields that are tested minimally or not at all, but below average in the few areas of the testing bias, you will be ranked as below normal intelligence. If on the other hand you are below average in all the multiple areas that are untested, but above in the few tested areas, you are declared smart. American educational testing is similar to the inappropriately named "idiot savant," who may be a genius in music but severely limited in other intelligence skills. Our educational system gives scholarships to many average and some below average well-behaved middle-class students rather than to the brightest students because our intelligence and school testing like the ACT and SAT only measure a very limited left-brained and middle-class skill set. This may very well explain why many studies show that intelligence has really very little to do with success.

So what does it mean to be left-brained or right-brained? In 1980 Marilyn Ferguson wrote a book called *The Aquarian Conspiracy*. Although it focused on principally culture or more precisely counter-culture, it brought about the first general acknowledgment that there was a different, but equally valid way of reasoning, it compared inductive versus deductive reasoning.

To understand how the two differ let us use learning the alphabet as an example. Let us say you are a scientist and you have never seen nor do you know how to use the English alphabet. Using deductive reasoning you would look at A, then B, then C and proceed all the way through the alphabet in order to reach its conclusion at Z, and only then would you know there are twenty-six letters, the sounds each make, and how they could be used to make words from the spoken language. It is a long process and you cannot skip any letters nor do you take them out of order to reach your conclusions. This is deductive reasoning.

However, a person using inductive reasoning need not take the letters in order. They don't even need every letter. You can give them the letter M, then W, then B, and after a certain number of letters depending upon both the degree of how right-brained, and how high the intelligence of the user is, they will arrive at the same conclusions as above. It will usually be a much quicker, and much more comprehensive or big picture conclusion, but it may also lack more precision and detail than the deductive method. Much of our subconscious reasoning uses the inductive method which allows us to form quick impressions and make snap decisions

Left-brained thinking is what we call the "scientific method." And it is the cultural preference of Western particularly American thought and concentrates on details. Right-brained thinking is big picture and frequently associated with Eastern philosophy, artists, visionaries, or sometimes mockingly derided by the left-brained deductive practitioners as "fortune telling." And it is the ability to take many seemingly unrelated thoughts or things and find their connections to larger more complex patterns. It is the ability to not only to see the forest instead of the trees, but also to see all of the uses and possibilities of that forest. While almost everyone can do both of these types of thinking we each have a strong preference for one, and we usually do not stray too much from our preferred type of thinking. The two ways of thinking, are like the classes, they are different than, not better than.

In testing for left and right-brained thinking preference, the scale most frequently used goes 0 to 24 to the left and 0 to 24 to the right with zero being the very unusual person that is comfortable and finds it easy doing either type of thinking, and 24 on either end of the scale as a person who finds it difficult to think in the other method. The average American will test at about 10 or more to the left and probably eighty percent or more of Americans are left-brained thinkers. In America, unlike the cultures of the Far East, it is very unusual to find anyone past 10 to the right, these people are thought of as weird or visionaries and are usually are artists in some form. But because of their ability to see the big picture, an incredible number of these are also leaders and frequently the heads of corporations.

In business terms, the classic left-brained thinker is more likely to be the CFO or the legal counsel of a corporation, while the classic right-brained thinker, who may be totally unsuited for these jobs, is much more likely to be their visionary CEO; in fact the two intelligence types complement each other very well.

So back to college testing; which thinking preference is tested? College and intelligence testing has a heavy reliance on math and sequence testing and is almost exclusively left-brained thinking. And all middle-class children, even the few right-brained students, are coached by their parents or given to tutors to pass these tests. They are taught to be left-brained and to do well on these tests. Working-class children are not.

What this should tell us is that we are not the meritocracy we think we are, and that we may be wasting generations of gifted people who because of class, income, and thinking preferences are left out of the system and condemned to the life of underpaying and unrewarding work. It could be particularly painful for the very bright or the creative right-brained thinkers that would become our leaders, writers and artists with the opportunity to go to college. This lack of opportunity to access higher education is also one of the reasons there isn't upward class mobility in America. I give myself and the hundreds of thousands of Working-class veterans who served during the Second World War and through Korea and Vietnam as examples as why the G.I. Bill was able to briefly provide upward mobility to the working class in America. It was the first and only time that the working class, went to college or technical school in as large of numbers as the upper classes and were thus allowed to improve their lot in life.

Another cultural difference that gives the middle class an advantage over the working class in education and in preparing their children for higher education is that the middle-class culture gives its top priority and primary focus to achievements such as getting bachelor, master's and doctorate degrees, and obtaining a profession that is limited to others. It is these achievements that define who the middle-class person "is."

A middle-class person, when asked who or what they are, will say: "I am a doctor," "lawyer," etc. or say, "I have a doctorate," "a masters" or "college degree." The working-class person is more likely to answer they are "have been married for twenty years," "a father of four" or a "grandfather," or to state their community by saying they are from a town or city or a certain part of a city, as in "I am from in Queens," instead of giving their occupation or educational history.

Unlike the middle class, who define themselves by their occupation, in the working class an individual is almost solely defined by individual circumstances and personality or charisma. This means that middle-class parents will view their child's success based upon these "accomplishments," while working-class parents will be more concerned with their child's "happiness" and their family status. Accomplishments trump happiness in middle-class households who have the cultural trait of sacrificing now for a better future, versus the fatalism and acceptance of limitations and the second-class status by the working class.

This is magnified by the working class fear/hate of authority and because of this working-class parents are much less likely to take an obvious or active role in their children's school. The middle-class school principals and teachers will misinterpret this outward lack of parent involvement between the middle-class and the working class. They assume that, because they are not taking active roles, working-class parents do not care about their children's education or well being, and therefore they favor the middle-class child as more worthy of their efforts. Parent teacher associations are middle-class institutions. These are some of the reasons are why middle-class children have a better experience and receive better grades in school from their like-minded middle-class teachers.

In summary because of their income, their sense of entitlement, and the testing system which is designed for their culture of achievement, means that the middle-class child of average intelligence will very likely go to college. While the working-class child of average intelligence, as well as the very intelligent working-class child will likely not. And since working-class children are at least two-thirds of our population what kind of national intellectual resources are Americans sacrificing and what kind of future is America sacrificing to uphold the empty privilege of class?

CHAPTER 37. THE GRAYING OF WORKING-CLASS AMERICA

> "When I was young, I thought that money was the most important thing in life;
> now that I am old, I know it is."—Oscar Wilde

The working class will have more problems due to America's aging population. As the Baby Boom generation, the majority of whom are working class, begins to retire, the growing demand for more resources for retirement income, housing and health services will have a profound effect on America. The United Nations and the Center for Strategic and International Studies estimate that the world's population ratio of working age people to retired people will decline from the current 9-to-1 to just 4-to-1 by 2050. It will cause a massive problem in the retirement and Social Security and Medicare systems in the United States. And although we have high unemployment rates as this is written, we will soon have a worker shortage that will threaten the United States and the world economy.

The working-class Baby Boomers are said to be the generation least financially prepared to retire. Most Boomers no longer have the company pensions that the previous generation had, nor have they saved much money for their retirement. This situation is made worse by the fact that their life expectancy will also rise significantly. If the for example average Boomer lives between eighty-five and ninety-five it will cause enormous strain on the financial system. It isn't likely that the Boomers will be able to retire for thirty, forty or fifty years and live comfortably on their Social Security. Likewise it isn't reasonable to expect that the younger working-class generations can pay for this as the working-class Baby Boomers paid for their parents, because they are much smaller in numbers.

A Baby Boomer that lives to ninety-five may be retired for almost as long as they worked if he retires at sixty-five.

The current social security tax structure will not support this. One way to correct this is to apply the Social Security tax to incomes above the $108,600 which are currently exempted. Contrary to popular thought, Social Security payments are a tax not a retirement investment. They are a tax that the working-class and middle-class people who make less than $108,600 have to pay, but a tax which the rich have been exempted. Correcting this tax inequity by extending it to the rich would solve most of the Social Security shortfall. However this raise has been unacceptable to the conservatives and the Republicans who protect the wealthy.

Unfortunately Medicare will continue to be a problem until the Congress creates a universal national health care system that provides a single payer system that includes both the young and the old alike as is the practice in other industrialized countries.

Affordable senior housing will be crucial as the working-class Boomers retire. Senior citizen housing is different than other housing. It is needed and it is different than other housing because of the unique needs and vulnerability of these older people. There are five different levels of care in senior housing based upon the needs of the residents and the types of services offered to the residents. It ranges from senior apartments with no services up to high service housing like nursing homes and memory care facilities. We will need to provide an adequate supply of all of these housing types to insure that the needs of the working-class elderly are taken care of, and this senior housing will most likely have to be subsidized to be affordable because of their meager retirement incomes.

CHAPTER 38. CLASS AND RACE

> "Class, race, sexuality, gender and all other categories by which we categorize
> and dismiss each other need to be excavated from the inside." —Dorothy Allison
> writer and poet

America is more classist than racist, but as much as Americans are intolerant of people of different classes, they are even more intolerant of people that they believe are of a lesser class and of a different race or ethnicity. Class and race or class and ethnicity are in combination much more potent in eliciting bias. A white racist is more willing to accept social contact with Dr. Huxtable and his wife, Claire, even though they are African-American, because they are middle class, and are doctor and attorney, versus the lesser desired social interaction with a poor working-class Fred Sanford the African-American junk dealer.

The Los Angeles riots touched off by the vicious beating of Rodney King by the police, which then caused another vicious beating by Blacks of a white truck driver, Reginald Denny, is viewed by Americans as a "race riot." Most Americans thought at the time and many still believe that this was a Black race riot. However the Webster Commission, named after former FBI Director William Webster who chaired the Commission at the behest of the President, found that the riot was much more complicated and was also more about class and economic inequality than it was about race.

The Los Angeles neighborhoods where the riot occurred traditionally had been Black neighborhoods. However by 1990 the Black business community had mostly been replaced by Korean-American business owners. These owners were mostly first and second generation Koreans who had been middle-class merchants and business people in Korea before coming to the United States. Because these middle-class Korean merchants were new immigrants, they couldn't afford to buy an existing business or start a new one in the very expensive middle-class areas of Los Angeles, so they began buying Black businesses in this poor working-class area at bargain prices.

At the same time this was happening, the Latino population, who were also poor and working-class, began migrating into these traditionally Black neighborhoods, and they too began replacing the Black residents. There was on-going serious conflict between the Latinos and Blacks, which sometimes led to violence. And by the time of the riots Latinos made up fifty-five percent of the population. The majority population of the area at the time of the riots was Latino.

On March 3, 1991, Rodney King was beaten by the Los Angeles Police. The beating was captured on video. It was shown by the media and showed a restrained and subdued King being beaten. The Los Angeles Black community was angered, as was much of the nation. On March 15, four LAPD officers were charged with excessive force.

The next day on March 16, 1991 a fifteen-year-old black girl was shot and killed by a Korean merchant while they struggled over the alleged shoplifting of a bottle of orange juice. This incident was also captured on the store's video tape and later shown in the media.

On July 9, 1991 an independent commission appointed by the Mayor found that a pattern of racism and the use of excessive force existed within the Los Angeles Police Department.

On October 11, 1991 the Korean merchant was convicted of voluntary manslaughter, but was sentenced to only five years probation, which again enraged the local Black community.

On April 29, 1992 the Rodney King beating trial ended with the acquittal of the four LAPD officers of almost all charges, and the community erupted in a riot that lasted for four days until May 2, 1992. When it ended fifty-five people were dead, about 10,000 mostly Korean businesses and buildings were looted and destroyed by arson. The estimated damage was placed at over one billion dollars.

But it wasn't just the Black community that rioted the larger majority Latino population also rioted and were the largest group of rioters. The majority of the victims of these riots were the Korean business owners and not whites as most of the nation believed. If it had been race then why would the Latinos, who were in conflict with the Blacks over neighborhood turf issues also riot over injustices to Blacks? And if the riot was a Black response to white racism why did the Blacks and Latinos victimize these middle-class Korean merchants?

They did it because it was a class and economic riot, and that is what the Webster Commission found.

In a 2002 *Christian Science Monitor* article called *L.A.'s Darkest Days* reporter Daniel B. Wood interviewed Najee Ali, a former gang member who was imprisoned for his crimes during the riot. While in prison he had a change of heart, converted to Islam and upon his parole from prison began working as a community organizer to rebuild the community he helped to destroy. He made national headlines at one point for his role in negotiating a truce between the rival gangs. He also helped to build new relationships between the Korean, Latino and Black communities.

In discussing the riots Najee Ali told Wood, "We realized that we had been fighting each other over our own neighborhoods, over gang turf and concrete blocks that none of us owned, instead of focusing on the real oppressor, which was the economic establishment that kept us from economic empowerment."

Does race play into these class conflicts? Yes, race and class are a powerful combination. A middle-class person will disapprove of the working class, and usually much more so if they are of a different race or ethnicity, and the working class will also show the more distain for a middle-class person of a different race or ethnicity.

What the Webster Commission found in the Rodney King Riot was that the poor working-class Latinos and Blacks despised the Koreans because they were more prosperous middle-class merchants. One of the more complicated and interesting dynamics of American class conflict is that of the working class and their relationships with new middle-class immigrants.

Many new immigrants coming to America were middle-class merchants or professionals in their homelands who come to America with a small amount of resources. And like the Korean merchants in Los Angeles, their resources will not allow them to start or purchase a business in a prosperous middle-class area so they go to poor working-class neighborhoods to get their start in America. Usually these are service type businesses such as grocery and convenience stores, restaurants, liquor stores, clothing shops, laundromats, carwashes, and motels. These service businesses have a high degree of visibility and interaction with the local population. They are not hidden, particularly when there are many of them concentrated in an area like the Koreans were in these Los Angeles neighborhoods. Frequently these new merchants are disliked and unwelcome by their new working-class neighbors who exhibit resentment at these "new people" or "foreigners" who they see as taking their businesses, their jobs, and their money. They are seen by the residents as "taking over" and gentrifying their neighborhoods.

Chapter 39. Gentrification

> "People of quality know everything without ever having learned anything."
> —Moliere

I went to a large national forum not that long ago where about six hundred local government officials, nonprofit and neighborhood development corporation staff met to discuss the gentrification of urban neighborhoods. The irony is that the forum quickly shifted to discussions on race as it frequently does when gentrification is discussed. The participants had missed the point of the forum. Gentrification and its consequences are about class and are not about race. Gentrification comes from the word gentry, which means upper class, and to gentrify and gentrification is to change a lower class area into a higher class area. Webster's New Universal Unabridged Dictionary definition of gentrification is as follows: "the buying and renovation of houses and stores in deteriorated urban neighborhoods by upper and middle-class families or individuals, thus improving property values, but often displacing low-income families."

It was this displacement by Koreans that the Black and Latino residents were feeling at the time of the Los Angeles riots and it was not just racial hatred. As stated, if this was about white racism, why would the beating of a Black man by White police officers cause Blacks to attack Koreans? And why would Latinos who were also having racial and ethnic conflict with the Black community be concerned with white police officers beating a Black man, and why did the Latinos attack the Koreans? The answer is they weren't motivated to riot by race; they were motivated because of gentrification and the potential displacement by the Korean middle-class merchants. Rodney King was merely a trigger to what happened. Even King was horrified by the results and said his famous line, "Can't we all just get along?"

Gentrification is a growing problem in urban America. But to understand gentrification you have to first understand the dynamics and history of American urbanization. It has been a puzzle to geographers and urbanists that in the rest of the world the wealth is concentrated in the large inner cities and the poor at the urban extremities, but in America it is the opposite. In urbanized America the poor live in the inner city and while the suburbs are the home of the wealthy and the middle class. Rural areas are primarily poor in America and the rest of the world.

Urbanists pondered if this was due to some fundamental cultural difference. However as it turns out it has to do with the relative young age of American cities at the time of America's industrialization.

Cities have a lifecycle, they are born, they mature, they grow old, and they decline, and then they are sometimes reborn. America's large cities are very young compared to those of most of the rest of the world and had just started to mature when industrialization took place. Industrialization happened in these cities and demanded large amounts of workers. You may recall that prior to this industrialization that America was considered a "nation of farmers" by the Europeans, and a large majority of Americans before industrialization lived in rural areas and worked in primarily agriculture and related jobs. Industrialization happened when these agricultural jobs were becoming fewer because of the mechanization of American farms. We needed far fewer workers to produce enough food and fiber for American consumption and for export. These workers were forced to migrate to the urban areas in massive numbers to look for work and for most it wasn't voluntary.

The very popular country song, *Detroit City*, by Bobby Bare captures this forced migration with the following lyrics:

"Last night I spent the night in Detroit City and I dreamed about those cotton fields back home. I dreamed about my mother, my father, my sisters and my brothers, and I dreamed about the girl who waits patiently for me. I want to go home. I want to go home. Oh, how I want to go home."

The working-class rural migrants went to the cities to find work, and for most it was an economic necessity and not a voluntary choice. These rural people viewed cities as places of overcrowding, sin and corruption. And rural areas, despite their large areas of poverty, declining schools with few resources, massive soil and water agricultural pollution, and poor housing, transportation and services, many Americans still view rural areas as places that have better quality of life. This is due to our cultural heritage of rural bias.

As these negative attitudes about cities persisted in American culture, and as Americans acquired enough money in the post- Second World War economic boom with their G.I. Bill educations, and as the automobile and road systems made it possible to live further from work, Americans began to leave the cities for the suburbs, leaving only the poorest behind. It is not by coincidence the first suburbs were often called "garden cities" capturing a rural-like openness they desired.

As American cities continued to go through their lifecycle and have matured, and then declined, and as some of them are now being reborn, Americans with money are migrating back into the city, mirroring cities in the rest of the world. Some of this urban migration is also because the rural bias has slowly dissipated because most Americans are now three or four generations off the farm.

As the dictionary definition of gentrification describes, these mostly upper middle-class and leisure-class migrants are buying and renovating houses and stores in deteriorated urban neighborhoods. And while city officials are enthused about the beautification and accompanying improved property values, they often overlook or are often uncaring about the displacement of working-class low-income families. There is a false assumption shared by many that this gentrification is somehow alleviating poverty and poor conditions, but the opposite is true. These displaced families more often than not end up in worse places and in even worse economic conditions.

Chapter 40. Self-Cleaning Ovens

> "We are in danger of making our cities places where business goes on but where life, in its real sense, is lost." — Vice President Hubert H. Humphrey

Sometime in the decade of the 1950s, banks developed the common strategy of "redlining." In 1960s Chicago bankers began referring to these areas as a "self-cleaning oven." A self-cleaning oven in urban terms refers to an area of decline where banks will turn up the economic "heat" by forbidding lending and refusing to provide other financial services to the poor in the area until they have "cooked out the dirt," which means making conditions so terrible that it will force out all the poor people that these bankers believed were responsible for causing the area's decline.

The more general term, redlining, came from banks mapping out their service area and outlining in red the areas where loan officers were forbidden to lend. The practice of redlining became such a major cause of poverty and ghetto creation in the United States that in 1977 Congress passed the Community Reinvestment Act (CRA) to make these bank practices illegal. The law was applied to banks, thrifts, and savings and loans, because they all redlined as a common practice. In this book I will refer to all these depository institutions as banks since many consumers and those in the industry do the same.

Banks and savings and loans have always denied redlining and discrimination, but as mounting evidence and court cases showed, redlining and discrimination existed in most poor working-class urban and in many working-class poor rural areas. This redlining forced the Congress to take action. In addition to class discrimination much of redlining was also racially motivated. There are mountains of data and several court cases that proved that banks and savings and loans habitually discriminate against blacks, Latinos, Asians, and Native Americans. Many studies have shown that a person of color with the same credit and circumstances as a white borrower, will receive less money than the white customer, or may receive no loan at all.

In 1977 Senator William Proxmire of Wisconsin authored the Community Reinvestment Act (CRA), which was passed by Congress. The landmark legislation outlawed redlining and strengthened laws against discrimination in lending by forcing the lenders to open their records and to show where and to whom they were lending. The law further provided that if they were not lending to all people and places in their market areas, the federal government could punish the lenders by not approving bank expansions, new branch openings, new services, or bank mergers and sales.

The law also provided a rating system for lenders which gave them an "Outstanding," "Satisfactory," or a "Needs to Improve" rating. These ratings were made public and anyone can walk into a bank and ask to see the bank's current and past ratings.

As a part of the CRA review, the law provides that person or community group could comment for the record about how good or bad the lender was doing in serving their community. The regulators were also directed to seek out these community opinions and take them into consideration when rating a bank or savings and loan.

The primary casualties of most bank discrimination and redlining in lending were the working-class people seeking home loans. An area can't grow or thrive if no one will give a loan to buy a home. So another law, the Home Mortgage Disclosure Act (HMDA) was passed by Congress. It forced all banks and savings and loans to report where and to whom home loans were made. If a lender was redlining in an area it would become apparent in their HMDA Report. If a bank were giving less money, or placing greater restrictions on people of color, or working-class people it would also be apparent in their HMDA report. These reports are also open to public scrutiny. It is a good law.

Unfortunately one of the most powerful lobbies in Congress is the banking industry including the savings and loans. When CRA and HMDA passed they immediately began a campaign to weaken these laws. The first weakening of CRA came when the bankers got Congress to agree to allow their regulators to be the enforcement agencies for CRA rather than creating a new agency. Where this may sound logical, it isn't.

The Federal Reserve Bank, the Federal Deposit Corporation, the Office of the Controller of the Currency and the Office of Thrift Supervision are charged with the responsibility of making sure banks and savings and loans remain safe and sound. That is their mission and nothing else is or will ever be as important. Since these regulators almost always error on the side of safety and soundness, all a bank has to do to get out of CRA obligations is to give an argument about safe lending practices.

Since many of these redlined neighborhoods had been starved for capital by the banks since the 1950s and 1960s, they really were very depressed by the time CRA was passed in the late 1970s. And the bankers began to argue, with some success, that maybe these places really were risky areas and that to lend in them would affect the soundness of the bank. They argued that they should do a very small amount of lending in these areas. This argument doesn't always work but it has been used successfully enough to weaken the intent of the CRA Act.

Using the regulators to enforce CRA is very much like using the tobacco companies to do health studies on smoker related health problems. The lenders and their regulators are one industry. The regulators are too close to be objective particularly if their primary mission is safety and soundness. The regulators also see CRA as a contradiction to their mission, though they will publicly deny this.

The law stated that these institutions must lend in their entire service areas including poor areas and forbid discrimination against working class and minority clients who if they could demonstrate good credit and the ability to repay their loans must receive a loan. The prevalence of racism in banking is also another reason why gentrification is often confused with racial discrimination.

The Community Reinvestment Act was applied to national banks, state banks, thrifts, and savings and loans and each is regulated by a different regulator. So the act gave enforcement to them all, the Federal Reserve Bank, the Federal Deposit Insurance Corporation, the Office of the Comptroller of the Currency, and the Office of Thrift Supervision, which has further watered down the intentions of the act. The National Credit Union Administration and the Credit Unions were the only financial regulator and lenders exempted from these regulations, because credit unions which are member owned cooperatives had no history of redlining.

And since each of the regulators regulates in a different way and with a different emphasis and "enthusiasm" for the regulations CRA has been very unevenly applied as are many other consumer financial regulations. And because the distinctions have blurred over time between national banks, state banks, thrifts and savings and loans, they are now all very much alike, and this sometimes allows these banks to creatively restructure their financial corporations to obtain the regulator they want. This also gives greater advantage to large banks in manipulating the system and to pick and choose regulators for their wholly owned subsidiaries and to gain a competitive advantage against the smaller rivals. Indeed it is frequently well argued that the regulators work for the banks and that it is the banks that regulate the regulators.

The regulators have become servants of those they regulate through what economists call "capture theory." Economists say that the capture of the regulatory agency occurs because groups or individuals with a high-stakes interest in the outcome of policy or regulatory decisions, in this case the banks, focus their many resources and energies in attempting to gain the policy outcomes they prefer from the regulators, while members of the public, who have only a small individual stakes in the outcome, and find the subject difficult to comprehend will ignore the industry altogether. In other words it isn't likely that a working-class person will show up at a regulatory agency hearing to give expert testimony about bank problems, practices and failures. The process is also incestuous since most regulators come from the banking community and many return there after their public service in the regulatory agency.

Many regulators are former bankers and many former regulators become bankers. For Example the former Vice President of the Minneapolis Federal Reserve Bank quit her job of fourteen years after congress passed the Gramm-Leach-Bliley Act which wiped away the laws that kept banks from investing in insurance and the stock market. She quit so she could cash in her expertise as a regulator in these areas as a consultant to the very banks she used to regulate on how to get around the regulators. Bankers and their regulators are interdependent and interchangeable.

The savings and loan debacle of the 1980s was caused in a large part because the regulators and their financial institutions were too close. The savings and loan industry crashed because they were lending on inflated real estate prices and made too many bad business decisions in "wealthy" areas. The Office of Thrift Supervision who was created to prevent this very occurrence looked the other way because the bank managers told them that they didn't understand the local real estate markets as well as the bankers did. The bankers were wrong and they failed. The OTS and the industry lobbyists then successfully lobbied to bail out these savings and loans and to save their industry. The American taxpayer got to pay for the mistakes of the Savings and Loans and their overly lenient regulator. It was a hint of much worse things to come.

One of the more interesting things about this crash was that it didn't involve any loans to low income working-class people. These loans were to wealthy people and businesses. This should be noted because in the next housing financial crisis, the financial failure would be wrongly blamed on working-class people who were mostly victims of predatory lending and not because of bank lending to the poor or because of CRA which conservatives insist was the cause.

In fact nonprofit lenders like the Neighborworks Network have successfully made home loans to the working class for many years. Their success is because they provide homebuyer education and fiscal literacy to their clients and then match them up with homes and loan products they can afford. The banks failed to do this education and to make sure buyers both rich and poor could afford the homes they were buying, which is part of the reason for the eventual financial crisis.

The penalties for not complying with the Community Reinvestment Act (CRA) can be severe and can include limiting the ability of a bank from expanding, or buying another entity, or opening new branches, or even being sold to another bank unless it also has an appropriate CRA rating. However these penalties are rarely enforced on the banks. The measurement of the bank's compliance with CRA is also very generous to the banks in that there are only three very general categories: "Outstanding," "Satisfactory," and "Needs to Improve." The first two categories don't require a bank to do anything, and the third requires a bank to show improvement over time or possibly face some of the penalties.

Larger banks also use CRA as a competitive tool against smaller banks. In any distressed area there are only a limited amount of low income working-class borrowers who have the income and credit to obtain and repay a mortgage or small business loans, and the larger institutions will try to attract all these borrowers to their institution to prevent a small bank from obtaining a good rating, this may happen particularly if the large bank is competing with the small bank to open a new branch in this or another area, or are in the process of trying to acquire an unwilling smaller bank.

Chapter 41. A Brief History of Banking and the Working Class, No Shoes, No Shirt, No Credit

"A bank is a place that will lend you money if you can prove you don't need it."
—Bob Hope

"A rich man is nothing but a poor man with money". —W.C. Fields

It has become the primary purpose of a bank to transfer the wealth from the working class to the middle class, and from the middle class to the leisure class. This is how banks actually function, the only argument left to be made is whether this is deliberate or by accident. I contend that it is deliberate if sometimes unconscious. Because of their preference for serving the rich, I would offer that almost all banks are bad, but that not all bankers are bad. This favoring of the wealthy is systemic to banking and is not necessarily caused by individual choices. Although there are some smaller community banks, particularly in rural areas that are much more democratic than their large counterparts, the history of American banking generally reflects the unwillingness of banks to serve the common people.

Banks have a long history of unwillingness to loan money and serve the average consumer. It costs as much or almost as much to make a small loan as a large one, and since bank fees and profits are mostly based upon the size of these amounts, banks want to make large loans and serve wealthy people who make large deposits. It is also true that maintaining very small deposits, both in savings and checking, can frequently cost more to maintain than what the bank receives in fees. So banks discourage small depositors by demanding minimum deposits, charging higher fees to small depositors or simply refusing this business outright.

In reaction to this, a new class of financial institution, the "Thrift" and Savings and Loans were created to fill this void. Soon the thrifts and the S & Ls figured out that it was more profitable to serve the wealthy than the common folk and they too began to practice the same discrimination as the banks.

Since many banks require minimum deposits for checking and savings accounts and charge fees, many low income consumers find they can't afford bank services. A person living paycheck to paycheck doesn't usually have the $200 or $300 to leave permanently unused in an account to meet the bank's minimum deposit for having either a checking or savings account. Even after CRA was passed banks began to simply close their branches in low income working-class areas to avoid giving service to low income people, because under CRA banks only have to serve those low income people in their stated market area. So many banks made sure their market areas didn't contain large numbers of working-class people. A vacuum was created that was filled by a variety of very expensive alternatives. Pawn shops, loan sharks and payday lenders fill this void. They are called fringe banking institutions. These fringe banking institutions include the Pay Day lenders, which is currently about a $40 billion business and have twice as many storefronts as there are Starbucks in America.

Daniel Leibsohn in the conclusion of his book *Analysis of Business Models and Financial Feasibility of Fringe Banking Institutions* wrote the following: "Low income people in the United States do not have access to the full range of financial services that middle and upper income households do. As a result of this inadequate access, these households tend to pay a very high percentage of their available income for interest and fees to obtain these services, compared to most other people in the country. These higher payments significantly affect their ability to move out of poverty and attain higher living standards."

Fringe banks give cash starved households payday loans, whereby the working-class borrower can borrow some or all of their next paycheck for a fee, which can cost 400 to 600 annual percent annually or more. The industry argues that the annual percentage rate (APR) isn't relevant because these are short term loans; however since they are usually revolving debt, because the family generally has to take out a new loan each payday to cover the costs of their previous loan APR is a very appropriate gauge of actual cost.

The fringe institutions are in it for the long term gains and charge enough to make as much money as possible and still keep their customers coming back to insure they will be permanently indebted to them. It is a concept borne of the "company store" mentality originally used on the sharecroppers. Once a working-class family borrows a payday loan, they will usually find they are short the next payday and the next, etc. They actually work for the fringe bank with a permanent percentage of their check automatically given to the fringe banker each month. The Center for Responsible Lending says that sixty percent of payday loan borrowers borrow 12 or more times per year. Payday lending is real economic slavery. Once a family gets in they have great difficulty getting out.

The fringe bankers take advantage of working-class people in other ways too. They cash paychecks and other personal checks for a percentage of the check. They offer low balance credit cards at exorbitantly high rates. They sell "rent to own" goods which usually after interest and payments triple or more the money that these items would normally cost, and they charge high fees for other services such as money orders and money transfers. And when the federal government quit issuing paper checks in favor of electronic balance transfers, low income veterans, low income pensioners, social security and welfare recipients who could not afford the minimum deposits at a bank or who had no bank in their area were all forced to use the fringe banks as their depositories and they automatically deduct a significant percentage from their government checks for this "service" each month making them even more poor.

The fringe banking industry has become wealthy and fat from the fees from working class. These families have no other options since the traditional banks have taken their services away by demanding minimum deposits or by closing branches in low income areas.

Eventually the traditional the bankers took notice of the fringe banking profits and they began to partner or take over these fringe bank enterprises. Some operations became financed by the bankers personally, but eventually some traditional banks themselves became the financiers of these fringe bank operations and sometimes the fringe banks became just a front for a bank to do this unsavory business. Some banks with high minimum deposits for checking and savings accounts also began to boldly offer check cashing services for a percentage or flat fee in their bank lobby to the poor, while their account holding middle-class and leisure-class customers paid no or very small fees. And in some cases banks began opening small branches in low income under served working-class neighborhoods. These branches offered no services except check cashing for fees and the banks were actually given credit in their CRA audits for this service! Today large banks like Wells Fargo and U.S. Bank are doing payday lending at their banks calling it "proactive overdraft protection," which is a fancy phrase with the same dire consequences to their working-class borrowers as the fringe payday lenders. Their argument for doing this is that it is a public service and that they are marginally cheaper than the fringe banks.

These same banks are also getting rich off the overdraft fees from their customers. They offer free checking to entice working-class customers who they know are on the financial edge. They allow them to write checks and will cover these checks even if the client has no money. In fact many advertise this as a service to attract these low income customers. The banks use computer programs that do not pay these customers' checks in the order they are written or in the order that they arrive at the bank, but instead deduct the largest check first so that if an overdraft occurs they can then hit the customer with a fee for each small check that is then "over drafted." For example: Let's say you write ten checks for various small amounts for money you have in your account, but later write a larger check for your rent which is slightly over your account balance. Instead of giving you one overdraft fee for this check the bank will pay this check first and then hit you with ten overdraft fees on the other ten checks. This is predatory lending of the worst sort.

The amazing thing is that the regulators who are given the duty of looking out for the consumers, (In this case it is the Office of the Comptroller of the Currency that regulates Wells Fargo and U.S. Bank) have turned a blind eye to these operations. But the O.C.C. isn't the only bank regulator to fail in their duty to the working-class consumers. The Federal Insurance Deposit Corporation that regulates state banks has also failed very spectacularly.

Many states have tried to prevent these predatory banking practices and they began to pass usury laws limiting the interest that fringe banks and others could charge on payday loans and other bank fees. But large national banks are immune from this legislation because they claim it is "an unfair state restriction on inter-state commerce." However even the state banks and the fringe bankers who are supposedly subject to state law have found a loophole thanks to a friendly federal regulator, the F.D.I.C., who instead of looking out for consumers and the working class allows what has become known as "charter borrowing." Banks are chartered by their regulators and charter borrowing allows a state bank or fringe bank to borrow the charter of an out of state bank for making the economic transaction in their name, thereby invoking the "unfair restriction to interstate commerce clause." So for example a bank in Delaware or South Dakota which doesn't have restrictive usury laws can sell its name for a small fee to allow the fringe bank to ignore their state's usury laws by claiming it is the out of state bank actually making the loan or charging the fee.

Predatory lending has become an epidemic. It involves loans and services that are overly expensive, unaffordable, and many times may even be loans that people don't really need and can't afford. In addition to pawnshops, check cashing and payday loans, predatory lending also includes car loans, credit cards, rent to own, advance tax refund loans, home mortgage loans and home equity loans as well as car title loans.

In America "buyers beware" is a central theme of our capitalist philosophy. It relies on the presumption that buyers will always inform themselves and shop around for the best price. It also presumes that consumers have choices and competition in selecting financial institutions and products, which as we have seen does not really exist for many working-class consumers. And anyone who has read a typical credit card contract or a mortgage document or for that matter almost any loan document with their pages of small print written in legalese that many attorneys find very difficult to follow, knows that financial decisions are more often made on trust of the institution and the lender with the borrowers believing that these experts are working on their behalf which unfortunately isn't usually true. The assumption that is lending is informed consent is completely false. The financial system is deliberately designed to confuse and confound the borrower, protect the lender and to generate for them the most fees. In fact many loan officers receive bonuses for this business and no one protects the consumer.

These attitudes are endemic in American business and not confined to just the banking industry. Kurt Eichenwald, the former New York Times reporter wrote *The Informant*, an award winning book about a food price fixing scandal that eventually cost Archer Daniel Midlands (ADM) over a billion dollars in fines. He reported in the book that the ADM corporate executive's motto was "the competitors are our friends and the clients are our enemies." This scandal involved dozens of large food corporations who conspired to illegally inflate food prices, which took over thirty grand juries to uncover the truth. At one point when confronted about the illegal activities and the company's denial, the CEO of ADM at that time said arrogantly and smugly to the FBI, "We know when we are lying." It is how business is conducted in America. Unfortunately in banking and as in food prices most of the victims are usually the defenseless working class.

Predatory lending has become an accepted practice in banking. This acceptance of predatory lending was the primary reason America had a housing bubble so large that when it burst it crippled the world economy. In fact there is history to creating a housing bubble and allowing increased predatory lending by banks so the lenders can steal the equity from people's homes. It is condoned predatory mortgage lending and we will explore the consequences of this later.

Recognizing that the current regulators have failed to watch out for working-class consumers and are much more concerned with the safety and soundness and profits of their financial institutions, and recognizing that this conflict will never be solved in favor of the consumer by our current regulators, the Obama Administration is attempting to create a new agency which will have the single mission of regulating consumer protection on all financial institutions. It is currently being vehemently fought by the self- interested financial institutions and their existing regulators who fear the loss of their authority, and by their allies the Christian conservatives and their Republican Party. However even if this proposed agency overcomes this stiff opposition and is created, the new agency is still not proposed to have the power to put interest rate and fee limitations on the financial industry's predatory financial products.

Chapter 42. The Credit Union Movement

> "No institution — except the church — does more good for people than credit unions."—Congressman Wright Patman, the former Chair of the House Banking Committee

At the beginning of the twentieth century Congress saw that banks and thrifts did not serve the needs of the working class, so they allowed the creation of something different to serve people of what they called, "small means." This new financial corporation would be in the form of nonprofit cooperatives that would be member owned democratic institutions, where each member had equal say in policies and equal access to service regardless of the size of their wealth or the size of their deposits. These democratic financial institutions are called credit unions.

Banks, including thrifts, and savings and loans hate credit unions for the obvious reason. Regardless of income, why would you put your money in a bank so they can make profit from the use of your money, if you could own your own bank and keep any profits yourself? A credit union member makes the profits from their own money. As the member owned and governed financial institutions make money, the money made above their operating costs are paid back to the members in the form of higher interests on their investments, lower interest charges on their loans, or sometimes as a dividend paid out to all members equally. It is usually a combination of these things.

In addition to the cooperative profit sharing that results in lower fees and higher returns, another factor making credit unions less expensive and more lucrative for their members is that many, although not all credit unions, keep very moderate overheads and lack the big CEO and management salaries paid by the banks.

To say that banks can be grandiose with their senior staff and facilities is not an overstatement. A number of years ago I was invited to discuss a secondary market proposal for small business loans with a senior vice president of a large national bank. He wanted to meet at his office for a breakfast meeting and said we would meet in the dining room on the appointed morning. The dining room, I was surprised to learn, was his personal private dining room with a mahogany table and chairs for at least a dozen people. He even had his own private wait staff. He asked what I would like for breakfast and he said, "Order anything you want; I also have my own chef." There were paintings on the wall worth much more than my annual salary. The meal was served on fine china, the glasses were crystal and I am sure the utensils were silver as was the coffee service. He lived like a king on the money of his borrowers and depositors, such as my working-class father-in law and mother-in-law who banked there. The phrase "Pretentious, moi?" came to mind.

Since the creation of credit unions, banks have lobbied Congress to limit credit unions. The most debilitating requirement they achieved was to limit credit unions to very narrow fields of membership. In other words unlike banks where anyone can choose to use their service, only certain people are allowed to join credit unions.

There are three main types of credit unions. The most common type are the employment based credit unions. These credit unions include institutions such as: The Plumbers Credit Union, the Teachers Credit Union, the Postal Credit Union, the State Employees Credit Union, etc. Only those specific workers and their family members are allowed to be members. It is interesting to note that Congress created an employee credit union to serve members of Congress and their families.

The second most common type of credit unions are fraternal and include some associations, and many faith-based institutions such as: The First Baptist Church Credit Union, the Knights of Columbus Credit Union, etc.

The third type is the geographic based credit union which is mostly used in poor rural areas that are lacking appropriate financial institutions. These would include: The Upper Red River Valley Credit Union, the Tri-County Credit Union, and others defined as having members from a usually small geographic area. Many of these types of small credit unions serve people like farm workers. However there are also some geographic credit unions in urban areas.

There are both Federal and State credit unions, but all are regulated by the National Credit Union Administration. Credit unions were exempted from CRA because they were created "to serve people of small means" and have no history of redlining. In fact they are the best providers of financial services for low and moderate income people.

The largest credit union is Navy Federal Credit Union which was created to serve all members of the armed forces and their families. It was created because banks also refused to serve members of the armed forces whose incomes were deemed too low and who are required to relocate too often for most banks comfort, military members and their families were in the words of bankers "unreliable risks."

One of the other reasons that credit unions are not subject to CRA is that in the past they have been very active in reaching out to underserved populations and creating institutions like Navy Federal. They also have been instrumental in getting existing credit unions to reach out beyond their membership group to serve sub-groups of low income people.

In 1974 a group of credit unions that served low income working-class people created their own federation, the National Federation of Community Development Credit Unions, to serve low income and underserved working-class people. Although they received small amount of money from the Carter Administration they were funded primarily by foundation grants and other charitable donations along with their meager membership dues from their institutions. The Federation and their low income institutions languished for twelve years under the Reagan and Bush Administrations with little support. Under the Clinton Administration the Federation and their institutions became eligible for the new Community Development Financial Institutions funds through the Department of the Treasury which has increased their funding.

About this time the NCUA came under criticism by the banks for being exempted from CRA and not having to serve low income working-class people. In response to this in 1996 the NCUA held a national conference in Chicago called, "Serving the Underserved" to encourage mainstream credit unions to partner, start or support low income community development credit unions. They also began to provide more funding to the existing community development financial institutions.

However even with this increased funding support for these institutions is not as good as it should be. Having credit unions under CRA is one area where I may agree with the banks. It believe it would be an excellent idea for main stream and the large credit unions to have to comply with CRA, because to do so it would necessitate the expansion of all credit unions by widening their fields of membership, and would lead to the eventual end of membership limits on credit unions allowing them to compete on equal footing with the banks for customers as they should be allowed to do. If we want free markets then we should give the credit unions the right to compete for bank customers. It would encourage better service from banks whose customers would finally have alternative choices.

When the National Credit Union Administration created the special designation, the Community Development Credit Union, to serve these underserved people they have allowed the designation to be used to charter a new credit union, to add to or change the mission of an existing credit union, or to grant the designation a bank that is willing to do this service. There are special funds available for these institutions, although these too have been in very short supply.

Chapter 43. A Sad Story

In 1995, an urban nonprofit lending corporation in a large mid-western city decided to start a community development credit union for the underserved people of the city. The nonprofit was in the business of making mortgage loans and home improvement loans to low income working-class people in the city and two working-class first ring suburbs. Their clientele included mostly non-English speaking people including many Latinos, Southeast Asians including Hmong, Lao, Vietnamese, and Cambodian, and some Russian speaking people.

Many of these non-English speaking people did not have a bank, since most could not speak English and the banks didn't speak their language, but the nonprofit, through its staff, board and volunteer translators spoke all these languages and had their loan literature printed in these languages as well as English.

Part of the process to charter a credit union is to show need, and you do this by getting a sufficient number of people to pledge they will become members. In a short period of time, as the proposed credit union and its potential benefits became known, more and more of the community came forward to complain that they were underserved by the banks and wanted to pledge as members. The largest of these groups were the Hmong and Latinos, followed by the senior citizens of the city who lived in the large multi-storied senior citizen high rises in the city. The nonprofit decided they would charter a geographic credit union and offer it to all residents of the city and the two suburbs. The nonprofit was able to raise about 5,000 pledged members of which about half were non-English speaking. This was more than sufficient to convince the NCUA of its viability.

The nonprofit and its supporters received endorsements for the credit union from the Mayors of the city and the two suburbs, from their Congressman, their two U.S. Senators, and the Governor. The largest employment credit unions in the state pledged startup financial support, and technical support for this new credit union. Other credit union and foundation support was also obtained. The financing and the technical support need to start was in place. A solid business plan was developed through the help of a national organization and their donation of the work of a financial expert who helped the nonprofit organization develop and write the business plan.

The banks were very worried about this new entity and its growing popularity and quickly moved to kill it. Unfortunately, one of the charter requirements of the sponsoring nonprofit lender was that they were required to have bank representatives on their board of directors. The bankers quietly took over the board, particularly the executive committee and key board positions and were unopposed in this by the working-class members of the board who were intimidated by the bankers and their expertise. Just before the charter was to be submitted to the NCUA for approval, the Executive Committee controlled by the bankers held an emergency meeting while the nonprofit Executive Director was out of the state on vacation. They declared a state of emergency allowing the committee controlled by the bankers to act instead of the full board. Despite the strong business plan and the financing and technical assistance by the credit unions, they declared that the credit union was an economic threat to the nonprofit's well-being. They dismissed the Executive Director who was out of town at the time and who was leading the credit union effort on behalf of the low income community. In twenty-four hours the Committee destroyed all the paper and computer records of the credit union, and went into the vaults to obtain and destroy the computer tape back-ups of these documents. By the time they had finished, there wasn't a page left of the tens of thousands of documents and the four years of hard work that had gone into creating the credit union. And when the large Hmong organization that was supporting the credit union efforts complained, the banks with the foundations they controlled ended the funding of the Hmong organization and shut them down as a warning to all others. The Committee also refused to have a full board meeting of the nonprofit until months had passed, the Executive Director had moved on and their actions were irreversible.

In the aftermath it is hard to understand why the banks would oppose this credit union. These were people that clearly were not served by these banks and people the banks really didn't want to serve because they were the smallest of depositors. So why did this happen?

One senior bank official admitted privately, "It (the credit union) was a public relations nightmare for us and seemed to demonstrate in a very public way that we do not serve these people."

Chapter 44. Nonprofits and the Community Economic Development Movement

"There is nothing more difficult to plan, more doubtful of success, more dangerous to manage than the creation of a new system. The innovator has the enmity of all who profit by the preservation of the old system and only lukewarm defenders by those who would gain by the new system. —*Machiavelli*

From our nation's founding there have been community efforts to improve the community and assist the poor. In the nineteenth century there were settlement houses and organizations like the Salvation Army began to appear, and the Credit Union movement began. But by the middle of the twentieth century with Lyndon Johnson's War on Poverty and when America's central cities began their decline these efforts took on a new meaning, a new urgency, and developed into what can now be described as the Community Economic Development Movement.

Community Action was the first of these to make a significant impact. Community Action Agencies at one time called Community Action Programs, CAPS, were started in every region of the country and funded by the federal government out of the new Office of Economic Opportunity which was headed by President Kennedy's brother-in-law Sergeant Shriver.

Community Action was instrumental in starting an impressive array of social programs and organizations, including Head Start, VISTA, the Job Corps, Upward Bound, Foster Grandparents, the National Center on Poverty Law, Legal Aid and other legal services to the poor, Indian and Migrant Opportunities and Neighborhood Health Services including family planning clinics.

Community Action was different than other programs in that it was governed by the working-class people who were also its clients. Each local agency had its own board made up of the people who used its services. The many innovations were a direct result of this participation by the working-class and came from their wants and needs and their experiences. They knew what was needed and what would work for them.

In his book *The Promised Land*, Nicholas Lemann documents some of the unfortunate problems that changed Community Action. Some of these new boards lacked the financial acumen to manage their finances; consequently some were victimized by mismanagement and theft. But perhaps the most infamous problems were in Chicago where Community Action was greatly disliked by Mayor Richard Daley primarily because he couldn't control the organization and its new funds. Daley insisted that Community Action and other federal anti-poverty funds be managed by local officials like himself, but was told by Shriver and the feds that it was more important to have the input of the poor themselves. Daley's response was "Why the hell ask them? If they knew anything they wouldn't be poor."

Daley attempted to block the program and prevent its progress. The Office of Economic Opportunity Officials in Chicago constantly complained to Shriver about Mayor Daley, but he was too powerful for Washington to rein in. Daley had also killed a federal Department of Health Education and Welfare program given to Dr. Martin Luther King to operate a much needed literacy program in Chicago because like Community Action it wasn't under Daley's authority.

Unfortunately Shriver allowed and even promoted the Community Action job training program in Chicago to become dominated by two local gangs, the charismatic Jeff Fort and the Blackstone Rangers, and David Barksdale of the Disciples. Shriver was convinced by the Woodlawn Organization, a Chicago non-profit, that they could rehabilitate these men and their gangs to work for good purposes in Chicago's gang controlled Black neighborhoods. Shriver agreed and gave them a grant of $927,000 to operate for a year. Shriver was confident that the rehabilitation of the gangs and their leaders would demonstrate the power of Community Action Programs. He was wrong.

Unfortunately the gangs spent more time recruiting and fighting each other, and because of this only seventy-six of the eight hundred applicants in the job program ever received proper training and were placed in jobs. Jeff Fort of the Rangers and his second in command were also convicted of murder. And one of Barkdale's Disciples was convicted of shooting two participants in the program that he suspected were members of Fort's Blackstone Rangers, killing one of the men. In addition two Rangers were charged with raping a participant. Later in prison, Fort converted to Islam and changed his gang's name to the El Rukins and the gang became drug dealers in the 1980s.

Shriver (a leisure-class person) and the Woodlawn Institute (managed by an upper middle-class staff) mistakenly assumed that there was little difference between these gang members and other working-class people. Lacking any real knowledge of the working class, Shriver believed that the Chicago gangs were the legitimate leaders of this class, and his mistake cost Community Action a large part of its future. Daley and other local government leaders used the much publicized and infamous Chicago incidents to insist on local government control, which they achieved. They insisted and received regulations that provided for one third of all Community Action boards were to be appointed by local government, and another third would be appointed from business and community leaders, and only a third of their boards would now be made up from the working-class beneficiaries. The working class is no longer in charge of their destiny because they are outnumbered two to one by the middle-class and local politicians on their boards.

It is interesting to note that all the previously mentioned Community Action innovations like Head Start, VISTA, the Job Corps, Foster Grandparents, Legal Aid and other legal services to the poor, including family planning clinics, etc. were innovations that were created while Community Action was governed solely by the working class, and that very few social innovations have been made by Community Action since. Community Action became middle-class organizations and with these new middleclass dominated boards Community Action agencies changed to become social service providers modeled after their county government counterparts. These agencies have become bureaucracies more concerned with process and procedures than with the service and benefits to low and moderate income working-class people. They have also suffered perpetual budget cuts as succeeding waves of Republican administrations since Richard Nixon have tried to put Community Action and their programs out of existence and placed greater and greater bureaucracy and regulations on these agencies.

Another community development movement came from the Saul Alinsky's concepts of community organizing and from the settlement and neighborhood houses of the early twentieth century. It became known primarily as "neighborhood revitalization" based upon the Alinsky quote, "Think globally and act locally." It is interesting to note that President Barak Obama began his public career as a community organizer in the Saul Alinsky mold in Chicago.

Distressed working-class urban neighborhoods and small towns began organizing their communities to provide local impetus to improve the overall community and their micro-economy. It is now referred to as either "community development" or even more appropriately "community economic development."

The most common form these organizations are the nonprofit community development corporations (CDCs). These nonprofit corporations are allowed under Section 501 (c) (3) of the U.S. Tax Code as are most charities. It is interesting to note that credit unions and other cooperatives are nonprofits and are provided for under Section 501 (c) (4) of the code. The principal difference being that the first is a charity and can take charitable donations in which the donor can take a tax deduction, while the cooperatives are nonprofits, but not charities.

These nonprofit corporations operated at first totally independent but have gradually formed local, state and eventually national associations. Today there are tens of thousands of these nonprofit development corporations in a complex web of associations some related and some not. The movement is still not united or well organized. And since they are not unified they fail to become a significant enough lobby to counteract the conservatives, the U.S. Chamber of Commerce and big business lobbies who frequently oppose them at the local, state and federal levels.

Some of this disunity comes from the fact that these independent local corporations frequently have very different focuses. While all are concerned with service to their predominately working-class communities their emphasis may differ vastly. While some have a wide mission of community development and multiple programs for a specific geographic area, many other community development nonprofits will have a specific focus like crime watch, family services, children or youth, seniors, small business development, jobs, housing or education. Others will even target specific groups of people like the disabled, or racial, ethnic and linguistic groups. The federal government is also responsible for much of this disunity by creating and funding separate and frequently competing national associations for many of these disparate groups.

Banks and the many charitable foundation boards that bankers also sit on as board members, have also come to dominate many of these nonprofits by sitting on their board of directors and giving operating as well as program dollars to these nonprofits. The banks and their foundations have often caused tension between the working class communities and the nonprofits operating on their behalf. Operating dollars fund the salaries of the directors and staff of the nonprofits. Their salaries are therefore sometimes tied strongly to their bank board members and their foundations. In the poor neighborhoods of America these nonprofit staffs may sometimes put their livelihoods and the bank and foundation's interests above the community good have a name; they are called by the residents of these poor neighborhoods "poverty pimps." In many cases where these suspicions aren't justified some communities may still believe that the nonprofit and charity staffs are more interested in earning a living or advancing others interests than doing the community's work, particularly if these staffs are middle-class people. These suspicions are the reason why many of these nonprofits have a rocky relationship with the working-class neighborhoods that they serve.

Some of this working-class angst is the fear of government and authority. The federal government has a long history of creating nonprofits called Government Sponsored Enterprises (GSEs). The most famous of these are the three housing mortgage finance giants the Federal National Mortgage Association (Fannie Mae), the Federal Home Loan Mortgage Corporation (Freddie Mac) and under HUD the Government National Mortgage Association (Ginnie Mae). There is now almost a hundred year history of GSEs. The first GSE created was the Farm Credit System created in 1916 to help farmers and the second GSE created was the Federal Home Loan Bank, created in 1932. Sallie Mae was created to provide college education loans in 1972.

The largest most influential national community economic development nonprofits are also GSEs. The federal government created Enterprise, the Local Initiatives Support Corporation (LISC) and the Neighborhood Reinvestment Corporation, now called Neighborworks.

Arguably the most significant of these three is the Neighborhood Reinvestment Corporation (NRC) created in 1978 to help implement the Community Reinvestment Act (CRA) and to help and encourage the banks to reinvest in these working-class communities. NRC was created to foster the partnership of local community development corporations and the banks to do this community development lending. NRC has since changed their name to Neighborworks. Neighborworks grants these local nonprofit corporations a charter with conditions and provides funding, training and technical support to them. The charter conditions are identical to that required by Community Action agencies, these local corporation boards have to be made up of bankers, local government officials and lastly working-class people.

Unfortunately also like Community Action these corporations are usually dominated by the local government and bankers which frequently justifies the working-class angst. Unlike Community Action with its own federal funding, it is usually the bankers and local governments who provide the primary financial support to Neighborworks organizations. Although there are some outstanding exceptions, Neighborworks organizations are too often middle-class organizations.

As the implementers of CRA, Neighborworks nonprofit organizations and a handful are primarily small business lenders. Some Neighborworks organizations are small operations offering only housing (homeownership) counseling, but many are fair sized mortgage lenders, and some like the Chicago Neighborhood Housing Services are very large lenders.

One of the distinctions that make Neighborworks standout from LISC and Enterprise and from other national organizations is their National Training Institutes, which are open to all nonprofits, government officials, and bankers. These trainings institutes are funded by the federal government and from the tuition and fees from the attendees. There are four or five per year and they are a week long and have multiple classes that are two or three days in duration in ten general categories such as, Homeownership, Affordable Housing, Community Economic Development, Community Building and Organizing, Management and Leadership, etc. and have special courses, workshops and forums on current topics and practices. The participants can choose from many courses depending upon their own needs. The Institutes are offered at different sites across the country and have been attended by as many as two thousand people per event. It is truly a unique mobile school.

The innovator of this unique school was Gary Askerooth, a Minnesotan of a working-class background who left his job as a college instructor at the University of Minnesota Duluth to become the Executive Director of a nonprofit Neighborworks corporation in St. Paul, Minnesota. He later realized the vital need for community development training and left the local corporation to work for Neighborworks nationally and serve as the first director of the National Training Institutes.

The National Training Institute was developed because of a lack of community economic development training offered by colleges and universities. While universities and colleges offered courses and sometimes degrees in sociology, urban planning, micro-economics, finance, or sometimes even housing or community organizing, there was no specific program to serve the needs of these underserved working-class communities. In the 1990s this began to change. A group of Boston community development professionals developed a graduate degree program in community economic development. They formed a school and funds were obtained from the federal government and foundations.

Early on they realized that in order to achieve their mission that a certain amount of independence was needed to assure that the mission would not come second to a University's mission. Although there were some large and prestigious schools initially interested, the school chose Southern New Hampshire University for its home, and this small University promised and assured the school complete autonomy and independence to assure its mission, and made the school its show piece. It is now known as the National Graduate School for Community

Economic Development at Southern New Hampshire University, and it has campuses on the west coast and overseas in Africa and Asia, but it is headquartered at Southern New Hampshire University. The school offers a Masters degree in specific areas of community economic development and a Doctorate degree and most of its students are non-traditional in that they are older and have usually been working more than ten years in the field of community economic development. In fact admission to the school would be very difficult to obtain for a traditional graduate student with a few years or no working experience. The average degree graduate is in their late thirties or forties and some candidates are well into their sixties.

Not surprisingly the School and the National Training Institutes are partners and many of the National Training Institute faculty are also adjunct faculty at the National School for Community Economic Development, and courses at the National Training Institutes maybe used toward graduate credits at the School. The School also serves international students and as previously noted has overseas campuses. It also operates the International Micro-Lending Institute and a few other special programs. The School is also partnered with the Peace Corps. However recently the school has suffered from financial cut-backs and some of their key staff has left.

In addition to mortgage lending and home improvement loans many Community Development Corporations also do small business lending. Unfortunately unlike affordable housing loans there isn't a good secondary market available for small loans except for a fairly moderate national non-profit that operates out of Minneapolis called the Community Reinvestment Fund.

Recently the Obama Administration has used the American Recovery and Reinvestment Act to begin a secondary market guarantee for Small Business Administration (SBA) Loans with first mortgages on commercial property. While this will help it falls short of providing a secondary market that will stimulate small business activity.

Small business lending is another area where CDCs are doing the work that is ignored by conventional financial institutions. Most banks even with SBA guarantees are reluctant to make many small business loans. Incredibly credit cards are the number one financing mechanism for small business in America.

Many banks also prohibit their branches from lending to restaurants. And restaurants are the number one business in poor working-class communities, and the usually first startup business of new immigrants, ethnic minorities and working-class entrepreneurs.

While all CDCs have done a significant amount of good, they have never tapped their full potential, and as previously mentioned most of the organizations are predominately controlled by middle-class Board members and middle-class institutions such as foundations, banks, and local governments. Gentrification is one of the worst consequences of middle-class influence in community economic development.

CHAPTER 45. MORE MIDDLE-CLASS BIAS, NEW URBANISM, AND MORE
GENTRIFICATION

"We of the sinking middle class may sink without further struggles into the
working class where we belong, and probably when we get there it will not be
so dreadful as we feared, for, after all, we have nothing to lose." —George Orwell

You may recall earlier that gentrification was defined by *Webster's New Universal Unabridged Dictionary* as follows: "the buying and renovation of houses and
stores in deteriorated urban neighborhoods by upper and middle-class families
or individuals, thus improving property values, but often displacing low-income
families." Gentrification is the most prevalent consequence of middle-class bias
in community economic development. Because local governments obtain most of
their revenues and their power from property taxes, property values and the tax
base are a very important element in all their considerations. And the best way to
raise property values and taxes is to gentrify existing properties.

Banks, as we have seen, have very little appetite for lending to the working
class or in working-class areas, so the federal government passed the CRA legislation to get them to do it. However banks are more willing to lend in a distressed
area if the local government assures the bank that the area "is turning around,"
which in both their languages means gentrification.

In 1973 a group of well-meaning middle-class Chicago investors and activists
decided that they would cure urban poverty by setting up a financial institution
that would "lend people out of poverty." Their story has been well chronicled in
the book *Community Capitalism* by Richard P. Taub. Their original intention was
to form a credit union to facilitate this. However as they prepared to undertake

this venture a bank charter in the distressed South Shore community became available at a bargain price. So they obtained the bank and mobilized investors and began to lend the community out of poverty.

The South Shore Community was transformed and South Shore Bank, known today as ShoreBank became the model for urban revitalization. Today ShoreBank has many branches and serves communities all over the country. They were the inspiration for the Community Development Financial Institutions Program (CDFI) which is a program within the U.S. Treasury and now a large supplier of funds for community economic development. The multi-million dollar New Market Tax Credit program is part of the CDFI program, along with a large financial and technical assistance program for banks, credit unions and nonprofit lenders. They also have a special program for Native Americans.

Unfortunately ShoreBank actually failed in the South Shore community of Chicago. Opposite of their mission they failed to lend people out of poverty and in fact failed to make many loans to the poor people of the community. What happened in South Shore was that middle-class individuals and investors saw an opportunity to buy property at ghetto prices from a lender who was giving very favorable terms. And since the bank was a permanent institution in this community it assured these investors that in a short time it would become gentrified and a middle-class community. It was a safe bet for the investor and inexpensive bet with a possible huge upside. South Shore is the poster child for gentrification.

The federal government in their review of the "successful" results of ShoreBank in the community, decided to recreate these "successes" nationwide and they created CDFI to do this.

The problem with the South Shore project was that the poor Black working-class population was not lent out of poverty. Instead they were forced out of their neighborhood by middle-class investors and new middle class residents. Very few of the original residents who were the intended beneficiaries were able to take advantage of this community renovation. Subsequent studies showed that most of the working-class population of South Shore was forced into adjoining and even more decayed areas and into worse poverty. These studies concluded that the lives of a majority of poor South Shore residents became much worse as a result of the South Shore project.

While it was a success for the middle class, and the city of Chicago who greatly improved their tax values in the area, and a huge financial success for ShoreBank, it was a dismal failure for the working-class residents. And despite this failure the federal government has made it a national model and began a multi-million dollar program to replicate the results.

In partial recognition to this destruction of the working class in community revitalization programs and to make them more eco-friendly, a movement to create "mixed-income" communities began. It was called New Urbanism, or sometimes more accurately called "Neo-Classical."

New Urbanism is supposed to be a rebirth of nineteenth century commercial urban avenues, by constructing a high quality and high amenity developments, and by providing for very compact and high density developments to combat urban sprawl. These new urban developments will provide the first floor and sometimes second floors as retail and office space, and the second, third and fourth floors as residential units of apartments or condos. The idea was to recreate a nostalgic downtowns of the past, while "going green" by providing areas more compact and suitable for pedestrian and mass transit, with plenty of parks and community space. It was also seen as a sort of social experiment, a place where community would be stronger because residents of all incomes would walk to work, eat, shop together, and would therefore know and love their neighbors. These communities were proposed to be "mixed-income" and provide for upper middle-class and middle-class residences, as well as rent and cost subsidized housing for low income working class and elderly residences. The low income and elderly units would need to be cost subsidized because developing these high amenity communities are very expensive despite their rhetoric that their compactness and the use of less land will make them more cost-effective, which has proven in most cases to be untrue.

Despite the subsidized units New Urbanism fails to attract low income working-class residents. Why? Because they are middle class and more frequently upper middle-class communities and have a middle-class culture where working-class people will not feel either at home or welcome despite the opportunity to rub shoulders with the middle class while shopping, eating and working with their middle-class neighbors.

All you have to do is look at the typical retail units in these developments to understand just how much it is a middle class, if not upper middle-class community. A New Urban neighborhood not far from my home contains the following establishments that are typical of the New Urbanist genre: a fine wine shop, a high end coffee shop, an expensive custom bicycle shop, a high end bistro, a cigar bar, a gourmet kitchen and spice shop, a day spa, a book store, a high priced restaurant, a furrier, a sushi café, a jewelry store, a custom order computer and electronics store, and a host of high priced clothing stores. You may be able to imagine why a working-class person would find it difficult to call this home, especially since they couldn't afford to patronize any of these shops.

Most "low-income" inhabitants of the subsidized housing in these communities come from what one of my college professors called "the voluntary poor." They are mostly middle-class young people who forgo fulltime work after high school to work in mostly low paying service industry jobs while in college and for a short period of time after college work at these low paying jobs before they find their careers. These are typically the residents of the subsidized units in New Urban communities. They are middle-class children who have not yet realized their adult middle-class wages. There are also some middle-class retirees who now have less income and who may also qualify as 'low-income." As a social experiment to improve the lot of low income people these New Urban communities have failed.

Since the whole atmosphere of a New Urban community is to recapture the feel of a nineteenth century middle-class urban area, it is probably fitting that one of the first of the New Urban communities, Celebration, Florida, was developed by the Disney Corporation, the same folks that brought us, "Frontierland," "Fantasyland" and similar make-believe places.

A few years ago Jim Carrey starred in a movie entitled, *The Truman Show*. It was a satire about New Urbanism and modern middle-class life and was filmed at one of the first New Urban communities of Seaside, Florida. The plot of the movie was that the Truman's life was a television show and his community was actually a television stage where everyone knew it was a television stage except poor Truman who thought his life and his hometown were real.

There is one particularly very funny scene in the movie when Truman is slowly discovering the truth about his fraudulent life, where he rushes into a building only to discover that it is a façade and a television stage prop with no interior, which is what some critics and sociologists think of New Urban communities. I would suggest you watch or re-watch the *Truman Show* keeping in mind that it is a very good satire on New Urbanism, which makes this funny movie even much funnier.

CHAPTER 46. TRANSPORTATION AND CLASS

Even transportation systems are associated with class. Buses and mass transit in general are associated with the working class. Convenience aside, is it should not be a puzzle as to why we have trouble getting middle-class Americans to give up their cars in favor of mass transit. Much of this resistance to mass transit is because it is for "the masses." The middle-class sees mass transit as a step down in class. Most of this class concern is at the subconscious level. When studying mass transit in the Twin Cities, I asked an upper middle-class older woman who was having trouble driving why she didn't take the bus, since there was a convenient bus stop right in front of her home? Her reply was: "The busses are filled with rowdy poor people and drunks." I am not sure how she knew this since she admitted that she had never taken the bus.

The automobile is considered middle class. A working class joke about the car and the bus highlight the class distinctions when it comes to transportation. It goes something like this: Two men are standing on the corner talking about a third man who has come back to his working-class neighborhood after being away for a number of years. He came back in a new car worth about fifty thousand dollars to show the old neighborhood that he has done well. The one man on the corner observing him says to the other, "Well he sure thinks he is a big deal now that he is riding around in a fifty thousand dollar car. We should tell him he ain't nothing, since we ride in a three hundred thousand dollar chauffeured bus to work every day."

In the airplane, "first class" is for the middle and upper middle class, while having your own jet is associated with the leisure class.

One of the transportation systems that clearly marks a difference in classes are the electronic transportation systems. Computers, cell phones and the variety of electronic communication devices are also transportations systems, which move ideas, information and make the need for physical transportation much less. In many cases work can now be accomplished remotely from any location even from home. This is known as telecommuting.

According to Jala International and the *American Demographics Magazine*, the number of American telecommuters in 2000 was just under twenty million. They also predict that the number of telecommuters by 2025 will grow to about fifty million, and as telecommuting and nontraditional hours of work, consulting, and contracting for work become a larger part of the economy it will make some interesting changes in our settlement and transportation systems.

The working class is also at a disadvantage and frequently lack good access to the internet and the electronic equipment they need to be competitive in the new electronic workplace. The difference between the "haves" and the "have nots" are quickly becoming their access to the world of electronics.

Chapter 47. In the Hood

> "Years ago I recognized my kinship with all living things, and I made up my mind that I was not one bit better than the meanest on the earth. I said then and I say now, that while there is a lower class, I am in it; while there is a criminal element, I am of it; while there is a soul in prison, I am not free."—Eugene V. Debbs

A community is defined as people with common interests living in a defined area. A citizen is defined as a member of community who is responsible for and gives allegiance to that community, and is therefore entitled to protection and benefits from the community. As communities became larger and cities and urbanization began to occur, there was a need to define subsets or smaller groups that express and share common interests. A neighborhood is a subset of community. Neighbor comes from two Old English words, "neigh" meaning nearby, and "gebur" meaning dweller. A neighbor was a "nearby-dweller," a person who would also presumably share your common interests.

By the mid sixteenth century the word "neighborly," meaning friendly or amicable, was coined, and neighborhoods came to mean places of friendly nearby dwellers that shared common concerns and they were almost always of the same class.

Today neighborhoods are much more complex. They are found in a wide variety of places, located in urban, suburban, small towns and in rural areas. Neighborhoods gather around many different common interests, like employment types, race, ethnicity, religion, culture, and sometimes they form for reasons of sexual preference like the Castro District of San Francisco. They are usually also restricted by class.

There are now new electronic neighborhoods using computers and electronic devices to link people over great distances based upon their common interests. A "neighborhood" is no longer limited to geography as it has been in the past. It now is expanded to include a "nearby-dweller" whose lifestyle, experience and preferences are similar to our own wherever they are located.

So how does the economy in a poor neighborhood, a ghetto or a barrio work? There is an assumption that there is no money in poor neighborhoods. This is untrue. An impoverished working-class neighborhood doesn't have the plentiful resources of a middle-class American neighborhood, but it does have some wealth. What poor neighborhoods lack is the ability to keep their wealth and generate new wealth from it. In the average middle-class community a dollar is spent about seven and a half times before leaving the community. In a poor neighborhood a dollar is spent once with no regeneration in the neighborhood.

In a middle-class neighborhood a dollar from a paycheck or a retirement check will be spent in the local super market, who will pay their employees, who will spend it at the local hardware store, who will pay their employee who will save it at the local bank, who will lend it to a person who is buying a home, or a car, or starting a business. This circulation of funds will happen on average seven and a half times before the dollar leaves the community.

In the poor neighborhood a dollar is spent only once or twice. It is spent for rent to an absentee landlord that doesn't live in the neighborhood and on services outside the neighborhood. In poor communities a dollar is spent and it never generates wealth in the neighborhood where it originates. It cannot be spent in the super market, because super market chains shun poor neighborhoods worse than banks. In fact many business chains, besides the banks such as large grocery chains shun poor neighborhoods.

In 1974 I conducted a study while at the University of Minnesota which showed that grocery store chains base their prices according to the number of households with access to automobiles. In other words, since it is extremely hard to shop for groceries using public transportation, neighborhoods that have a high percentage of their households without access to automobiles usually pay much higher grocery prices than a neighborhood that has access to automobiles and could therefore go elsewhere to shop if prices are too high. Since mostly the elderly and many poor families lack automobiles, this means that poorest families will pay much higher food prices than middle-class and leisure-class families.

To verify this study go into any poor neighborhood grocery and get the price of a gallon of milk, a pound of hamburger, a loaf of bread and about ten or twelve other commonly used and inexpensive food items and check these prices against a super market in an affluent neighborhood. The poor almost always pay more, usually quite a bit more.

One of the most frequent super market alibis for these higher charges in poor neighborhoods is that they have to pay greater losses in theft and shoplifting. This alibi was deflated a number of years ago when it was found that the most frequent grocery store shoplifter was the middle-class suburban housewife and middle-class teens. These shoplifters weren't stealing to feed their families, but were taking, cosmetics, spices and other expensive luxury items.

If they can charge more for their goods then why do grocery stores disdain locating in poor neighborhoods? The answer is in luxury items. The mark up on common foods like milk, bread, hamburger, etc., even when bilking poor working-class people with higher food prices, are still not a enough to make up the profit the stores make on luxury items such as whole bean gourmet coffee, spices, imported foods and beverages, cut flowers, and deli goods. These are not items that will be bought in any quantity in poor neighborhoods. Grocery stores can make profits in working-class neighborhoods, but not as much profit as they can in middle-class and leisure-class places with high end goods. It is a matter of the highest possible return on the store's investment.

The intentional shunning of poor neighborhoods is a form of relining, and the redlining by grocery stores has been subject of federal and local legislative concerns for years. In 1993 the Minneapolis City Council asked the state legislature and their members of congress to take action outlawing grocery store redlining. The Grocery industry promised to comply voluntarily. However their voluntary efforts have not located stores or reduced prices in many working-class neighborhoods.

Over time banks found a way to avoid CRA requirements. Banks figured out how to manipulate their service areas to exclude working-class neighborhoods and found out that if they don't have a branch in a poor neighborhood, they will not be pressured by their regulators under CRA. In fact they have manipulated their market area by closing many branches in poor working-class areas. Because of this CRA may have actually hurt some working-class neighborhoods by removing their financial institutions.

The regulators are supposed to prevent this exodus of banks from poor neighborhoods. However since the first responsibility to the banks are safety and soundness, they have sometimes been persuaded by the banks to close some branches in very poor neighborhoods causing further neighborhood decline. Despite and in some cases because of CRA there has been a steady exodus of banks out of poor and working-class neighborhoods for the past twenty years.

I was at a financial conference in Cleveland in the mid 1990s and was given a tour of a large Black working-class blue collar neighborhood. The houses were well kept, there was little evidence of crime, and I was told that most families were active in the Baptist churches that appeared frequently on the street corners. There were still some of small businesses in the area. People in the neighborhoods didn't have a lot of money, but they had some. They were working families with at least one living wage, or at least two people working in a household whose combined earnings provided a living wage.

After touring the area for an hour or more, I noticed that we hadn't seen a bank in the entire area, and I asked, "Where do people bank?"

The leader of the tour laughed and said, "That is what we wanted to show you, there are no banks in the entire area. You have to go way downtown to find a bank. Many folks particularly the elderly have to get on a bus and transfer to another bus to get downtown. Even if you have a car but work during the day you still can't get there on a week day before they close, unless you work downtown."

"So what do people do?" I asked. My answer was at the next stop on the tour. It was a small credit union that until recently had been run out of the basements of the Baptist Church. We pulled up to what we were told was the last bank in their area that had left so as to not have to serve the area under CRA requirements. The bank was a large national chain and they cried safety and soundness to their regulators and were then allowed to close the branch.

However the neighborhood and the church credit union raised a stink to the regulators and for their complaints they were given the branch bank building for a sum of one dollar and the bank was forced to deposit a hundred thousand dollars into the credit union at a very low interest rate. The bank still saw this as preferable to serving this working-class community.

Most neighborhoods aren't as organized or as fortunate. This credit union was the only financial institution available for literally thousands of Black working-class families in this section of Cleveland.

Just like the grocery stores, banks can be profitable in poor areas, but they can make much more profit, can get a larger return on their investment and have much fewer CRA obligations when they are located in middle-class and leisure-class neighborhoods. It is a major flaw in the CRA Act.

In this service vacuum are a variety of expensive alternatives like the fringe banks that take advantage of working-class communities. The financial institution of most poor neighborhoods as we have seen are the pay day lenders, the check cashing stores and the pawn shops. The grocery stores have been replaced by the small high priced convenience stores, or "inconvenience stores" as they are called in some neighborhoods.

Very few middle-class and wealthy people pay for the privilege of cashing their checks, but many poor and working-class families have no choice. The check cashing stores charge whatever they like unless they are limited by state law. Check cashing stores also offer no savings, no checking accounts, no safe deposit boxes, and do no mortgage loans or a small business loans.

Paychecks in these neighborhoods are frequently converted to cash, which provides easy targets for thieves and burglars. It is not uncommon for the elderly and others to be robbed of their money on the way home from cashing their monthly checks. There are also the loan sharks in the illegal underground economy who prey on the poor where a default will get you beaten or even killed. And there are the rent to own shops charging astonishingly high costs on needed household items and amenities such as televisions, computers and cell phones. There are also fencing operations buying and selling stolen goods.

Almost all poor neighborhoods have an illegal underground cash economy. The economy offers loans, drugs, gambling, cheap stolen goods and prostitution. It takes in big money and "employs" many people. Many people who cannot find work in the mainstream economy are forced to the underground economy for survival.

If your only choices of occupations are flipping burgers for minimum wage, or making a good income in the underground economy, it isn't much of a choice. If you are the oldest child in a family headed by a single parent working at minimum wage, and you get offered a job by a gang to be a lookout on your corner for their local drug trade at a five hundred a week in cash, it is pretty difficult to turn that down for minimum wage even if it is available. Gangs frequently develop a hold on a community through this underground economy. The gangs also provide social opportunities, offer their members respect and status, provide personal and family protection in these frightened communities, and also offer a chance for advancement. For many poor children they see the Latin Kings, the Crips, the Bloods, or the Asian Dragons as their only real opportunity. They join even knowing that too many people will get hurt by their business, and that they may go to jail, or be killed or hurt in gang violence, but these drawbacks frequently become secondary to poor children and their family's immediate financial and safety needs.

In addition to the fringe bankers and lenders there are also some specialty lenders who will loan money at high interest rates for people able and willing to put up car titles, or all their household possessions as collateral, so that if you default they take everything you own such as your furniture, clothes, and household goods.

There are other scavengers that also prey on poor neighborhoods. There are debt consolidation companies, predatory legal advisors, and schemes such as the "work at home," "start a business," and get rich quick schemes, along with slum the lords who suck the money and wealth out of poor working-class neighborhoods. The poor are victims of crime much more than the middle-class or the leisure class. Most violent crime in America is committed on the poor underclass.

The check cashing business and payday lending has also become so profitable in underclass neighborhoods that many banks are also getting into the business. Banks have become so wise to the profits of check cashing that they, like the check cashing stores, are starting to charge "non-depositors" fees for check cashing services. There are now some banks that are opening small branches that are basically check cashing stores in very low income neighborhoods, and their regulators are giving them CRA credit for doing it! They supposedly offer all banking services, but with their high fees and deposit requirements the services remain unaffordable to the underclass except for check cashing, which they do for a fee.

I interviewed the customers of one of these new check cashing bank branches that supposedly offered "full bank services." After asking about a checking and savings account the working-class customers were told that if they wanted an account they had to go to the main bank downtown because they were out of forms, but that they could cash their checks today for a fee. This branch was always "out of forms" according to the people I interviewed.

I have interviewed many bankers thinking about operating check cashing for a fee services. I have only had one banker from a small bank who said, "I looked at it and the profit potential was amazing. I decided against it because I didn't feel morally comfortable doing it, but I don't know how long I can hold to that decision when my bank competitors are doing it and my board of directors are getting concerned about all that lost revenue."

New Jersey is one of only eleven states that regulate check cashers. But In the early and mid 1990s New Jersey illegal check cashing became so rampant that the New Jersey Check Cashers Association began complaining to state banking officials. Unfortunately the state took no action. Afterward Glenn Obssuth, the association's president, complained to the local press, "They aren't interested. They send back letters saying, 'Thank you, but we are very understaffed.' And nothing ever comes of it."

The local press investigated and found illegal check cashers operating openly without concern. The local press reported that one of the illegal check cashing operations was owned by the former chairman of the city police commission.

New Jersey lost almost nineteen percent of their branch banks in their six largest cities in the ten years between 1985 and 1995. These cities contain a fifth of the state's population. The majority of those bank closings were in low income working-class neighborhoods and where a majority of the working class were also non-white. Check cashing stores legal or not were the only option for these poor residents.

Discrimination against minorities and the redlining of poor and working-class neighborhoods is also done by the insurance industry. They particularly discriminate in homeowners and renters insurance. In one court case, Nationwide Insurance Company was forced to make an out of court settlement of seventeen and a half million dollars to a Virginia fair housing group for their discrimination against the poor. They agreed to stop redlining and agreed to improve service to minority and inner-city customers. The settlement came one day before the Virginia Supreme Court was to hear the case.

Congress has discussed a type of CRA for the insurance industry, but they have taken little action because like the health insurance industry and the bankers they have a powerful lobby that seems to buy the votes of Congress. Unfortunately the Nationwide settlement shows that industry self-compliance is not working. Homeowner or renters insurance is still unavailable or is much more expensive in poor and working-class neighborhoods.

In addition to homeowner and renter insurance problems, working-class families are usually required to get mortgage insurance when purchasing a home, particularly in poor areas. This insurance is usually required when a homebuyer has a down payment less than twenty percent of the purchase price of the home. This mortgage insurance is provided by buyers so that banks will not lose money in the case of foreclosure. Mortgage insurance can add a couple of hundred dollars per month or more on a payment for an inexpensive house, it rises depending on the amount borrowed. It is interesting to note that for many middle-class buyers, banks will give them a personal loan, sometimes in the form of a second mortgage for the twenty percent down payment, thereby saving the middle-class buyer from mortgage insurance and this high monthly payment. Banks rarely offer this personal loan to working-class buyers. Unfortunately the only time banks lent working-class loans to avoid mortgage insurance was on overpriced housing and predatory loans leading up to the housing bubble.

CHAPTER 48. HOUSING, MORTGAGE LENDING AND SECONDARY MARKETS

"Money often costs too much."— Ralph Waldo Emerson

As we have seen from their history, banks have never been too eager about making mortgages to average people until the regulators encouraged and allowed them to become predatory. And today we are forced to deal with their overzealous predatory actions and the laze faire of their regulators that have resulted in the housing bubble and the subsequent world-wide financial crisis.

Before the housing bubble, one of the reasons for the banks reluctance to make mortgages was practical. As a bank if you make a thirty year home loan from your deposits you would have to wait a very long time to get repaid and to see any profit from them, in addition not many depositors would leave deposits in banks for thirty years so that Banks could make these loans. Therefore banks were reluctant to make many mortgage loans. So the federal government in order to stimulate mortgage lending (In banker's language it is called their "appetite.") created the GSEs Fannie Mae, Freddie Mac and Ginnie Mae to buy these mortgages from the banks thereby quickly returning their funds and profit. The GSEs then packaged these mortgages to be sold to long term investors. They are called secondary markets. Banks that have a "seller/service" relationship with these GSEs and no longer have a need to keep these loans and in most cases they are not even responsible for any sold loans that go bad. It is called selling without recourse. A bank will sell a mortgage loan and get their money back and a part of the profit, while giving part of the profit to the secondary market and their eventual long term investors in exchange for this sale. Banks also keep the origination fees which can be substantial. Unfortunately sales to the secondary markets recently became a more complex and dangerous business when these markets and Wall Street began securitizing these mortgages into mortgage backed securities, collateralized debt obligations, and asset backed securities, and into financial derivatives and began selling them all over the world, which created a new financial demand which inflated the housing bubble even more and encouraged more predatory lending.

The banks became eager lenders and began making riskier loans because they no longer had responsibility or recourse, they had origination fees and they could also make additional profits by charging many other costs of the loans to the borrower and charging a slight profit to the secondary market to manage these loans during the life of the loan. They could even sell the management of the loans called "servicing rights" to another entity for more immediate profit. While the profits on an individual loan usually are very modest, with loan origination and servicing software a financial institution can manage a large number of these loans with very few people and very inexpensively, and with a high volume of loans and their origination fees they can make a lot of money for little cost, but volume is the key. This ability to sell without recourse making immediate profit, along with the profits that can be made off high volume servicing and fees, coupled with the new and growing demand for these new securitized debts and derivatives was one of the causes of wide-spread predatory lending and the mortgage and housing bubble crisis, but we are getting ahead of ourselves.

Fannie Mae, Freddie Mac, and Ginnie Mae are the largest secondary markets and are federally sponsored, but there are other secondary markets that function similar to these three giants. In fact the federal government even created Neighborhood Housing Services of America (NHSA), a small secondary market to serve the special needs of the low income mortgage providers of the Neighborworks organizations.

Chapter 49. Manipulation and Madness: The Housing Bubble and Financial Crisis

> "We're now in the 'middle innings' of the current economic expansion, and the next economic recession is not yet in sight." — David Seiders, Chief Economist, National Association of Home Builders, Jan 2006
>
> "There is no national housing market, so there can't be a national house-price bubble." — Michael Youngblood, Managing Director, Friedman Billings Ramsey & Co

Since the current financial crisis began the working class has been rolled around like marbles from hole to hole in a giant Chinese checker game. In terms of job and home losses they have been the largest group of victims, and they have had their ranks enlarged with former members of the lower middle-class and some upper middle-class who were victims of this national scam. The housing bubble burst of 2007and the financial crisis of 2008, were predictable and preventable. Many of us involved in the affordable housing industry knew there was a housing price bubble as early as 1998 and by 2005 many of us were frightened and warning of the potential consequences. Housing bubbles are caused by one of two things: too many houses causing an oversupply, or housing that is overpriced for the average buyer. Either of these can cause a housing bubble, but both can be catastrophic and they generally don't occur on a nationwide scale.

The Housing Bubble was simple mathematics, it occurred when the national median house price rose to $220,000 in 2005 while the median household income at the time was under $45,000. Since a mortgage lender cannot financially qualify a family with this median income to buy the median priced home, it meant that the average person could not afford the average house. It was very simple, prices were too high. Depending on the interest rates, a $45,000 income would at the time have qualified most buyers for home of about $170,000 or less.

Even in this era of unprecedented low interest rates the banking and finance industry had to make housing loans affordable for the average consumer by using short term "exotic" remedies such as interest only adjustable rate mortgages, reversed amortization loans, and loans using forty or fifty year mortgage terms in order to put these unqualified buyers into these overpriced homes. These are loans that are never successful over a period of time and are only successful in a market where prices continue to rise. The thinking at the time was that the buyers could always sell if necessary for a much higher price since it was argued that prices were still escalating rapidly and would never go down. They also argued that these buyers could if necessary refinance at a later date as the home price increased or when their household income increased. Unfortunately for these homebuyers none of these things happened and something had to give.

Couple this with the fact that America also has many more houses than households causing a huge oversupply, and it meant that we were in an unprecedented national housing bubble.

Economists like Robert Shiller of Yale and the namesake of the Case-Shiller Home Price Index, and Kevin Phillips the former Nixon Administration economist and the author of *Wealth and Democracy* and many other books on economics, warned early on about the housing and financial bubble and the potential consequences, but they were dismissed by the banking and real estate interests, and ignored by the government and the regulators. Most notably they were ignored by former Federal Reserve Chairman Alan Greenspan, the person who could have prevented this catastrophe.

Chapter 50. Greed, Stupidity, and Arrogance

> "I think it happened because there was no oversight of a very, very big, dynamic, growing market. Market participants don't look out for the public interest. Traditionally, government has had to protect the public interest by overseeing the marketplace and keeping the extreme behavior under some check."—Brooksley Born the former Chair of the Commodities Futures Trading Commission

Alan Greenspan didn't believe in government regulation of the financial institutions so it is with some irony that this man became the longest serving Chair of the Federal Reserve Bank and the nation's top financial regulator. He is a conservative Republican and considers the Russian born laissez-faire capitalist and libertarian writer and philosopher Ayn Rand his mentor. Rand is the author of *The Fountainhead* and *Atlas Shrugged*. She was against government regulation and almost anything limiting free market capitalism. Greenspan was so enamored with Rand that he even had her stand beside him when he was sworn in as the Chair of the Council of Economic Advisors in 1974. Like his mentor Greenspan disliked and abhorred regulation of the capital markets.

There is also a history with Greenspan and financial and housing bubbles and it relates to a little known and extremely powerful entity called the Plunge Protection Team (PPT). It is formally named the President's Working Group on Financial Markets.

The Plunge Protection Team was created by Executive Order of President Reagan and enacted on March 18, 1988. The Team was established explicitly in response to events of the stock market crash of October 19, 1987 called, "Black Monday." The PPT was given the enormous power to respond to financial crisis by co-opting and using and manipulating the private sector institutions to protect the financial markets and maintain investor confidence. The team is comprised of The Secretary of the Treasury, the Chairman of the Federal Reserve, The Chairman of the Security Exchange Commission, and the Chairman of the Commodities Futures Trading Commission, and although the Treasury Secretary is the Chair of the PPT, the most influential and decisive member and the implementer of its actions is the Fed Chair. Greenspan served as its implementer from its creation in 1988 until his resignation just before the housing bubble burst and the financial collapse of the world economy.

Although the actions of the PPT are very secret, it is widely thought that in response to Black Monday the PPT bought stock futures through the banks to prop up the market and prevent a further decline and a more severe crash. Robert Heller, the former Federal Reserve Board Member gave credence to this when he stated in the *Wall Street Journal*, "Instead of flooding the entire economy with liquidity, thereby increasing the danger of inflation, the Fed could support the stock market directly by buying market averages in the futures market thereby stabilizing the market as a whole."

In March of 2002, an article in *The Financial Times* quoted an anonymous federal official who said that the Fed using the authority of the PPT could "buy anything to pump money into the system." He said that these Fed purchases using the finance sector as a cover and as their agent could also buy "state and local debt, real estate, gold mines, (or) any asset."

The ability to buy real estate is an interesting option. Did Greenspan use the PPT to manipulate the financial and real estate markets in response to the tech stock bubble burst of 2002? Did Greenspan deliberately manipulate the markets and inflate the housing and real estate market to shore up the failing economy, and to cover the massive financial fraud at the three mortgage giants, and to stimulate consumer spending because consumer spending is at least two-thirds of the American economy and by doing so could Greenspan save the Bush Tax cuts? Did Greenspan use working-class home equity as his piggy bank? It is quite possible, and Kevin Phillips and others have suspected and alluded to this. A look at Greenspan's history would tend to support these suspicions.

Even before Greenspan became Chairman of the Federal Reserve Bank, he was fascinated with using real estate to stimulate the economy. In a paper on economics he had discussed how home equity borrowing had fueled consumer spending and pumped cash into the economy preventing further chaos in the mid 1970s financial turmoil. Greenspan was enamored with this idea. Greenspan believed he could use American's home equity as a potential future source for financial crisis management. Real estate equity he believed was like a giant piggy bank to induce consumer spending and grow the economy.

Some of this real estate manipulation most likely occurred at Greenspan's direction in 1988 when the PPT was created to deal with the Stock market crash of 1987. House prices were nationally inflated at this time and the subsequent housing price collapse that followed caused the nation to go through the first national housing bubble burst. This price collapse occurred from1988 through 1992. However Greenspan and the nation's financial managers apparently learned very little from this event. If these lessons had been learned we could have prevented the current crisis and prevented the massive loss of homes and jobs by the nation's working class.

The following are a sample of the results that the 1988-1992 bubble produced: In Los Angeles housing prices fell over twenty percent in value and took about ten years to recover. In Peoria, IL prices fell over fifteen percent and took over eight years to recover. In Detroit they fell over twelve percent and took six years to recover. In New Orleans they fell over nine percent and took seven years to recover. In New York City they fell over seven percent and took nine years to recover. And in Austin, Texas they fell almost twenty-six percent and took eight years to recover, but in other parts of Texas such as Houston the prices never recovered. While this may seem mild compared to the 2007 Bubble Burst it was a lesson not learned and a preview of bad things to come. Greenspan and the Fed were slow to learn. There were also other events that should have tipped off Greenspan and the other regulators of the consequences for their lack of regulatory oversight.

Brooksley Born was appointed as the Chair of the Commodities Futures Trading Commission (CFTC) in 1994 by Bill Clinton. She was an attorney who was also on President Clinton's shortlist as his Attorney General.

The CFTC is charged with the mission of regulating the futures markets and particularly to prevent fraud and manipulation. Born took her job seriously. After studying the new financial derivatives markets under her authority she became very concerned by the lack of any oversight of the largely unknown multi-trillion dollar market. She attempted to take action by creating regulations to provide oversight to prevent fraud and mismanagement. To her surprise she was met with fierce opposition by the Treasury Secretary Robert Rubin and Under Secretary Lawrence Summers who were being counseled by Greenspan to oppose her attempts at regulating the financial derivative markets. Initially the three men also persuaded the Chair of the Security Exchange Commission (SEC) Arthur Levitt to join in their concerns.

Since Born had the sole authority to regulate these markets she went ahead with her regulatory plans in 1998, but Greenspan, Rubin and Summers, and who were joined by Levitt, vehemently opposed her attempts in their testimony to Congress during their deliberations to create the new regulations. Congress sided with the four men over Born.

In a very short time Greenspan, Rubin, Summers and Levitt and the Congress were all proven wrong. Born's concerns came to pass. Long-Term capital Management (LTCM) a multi-billion dollar hedge fund trading in financial derivatives lost about $4.6 billion in a four month period following a financial crisis in Russia. LTMC would fold by early 2000, and although Born had been proven right Greenspan and the others incredibly insisted that regulation was still not in the best interests of the financial markets. They stubbornly refused to believe they were wrong.

In 1998 Greenspan cut interest rates to stimulate the economy which became one of the causes fueling the tech stock bubble of 2000 to 2002. These interest rate cuts also inflated a housing bubble in a market where housing prices were already too high and where there was already an oversupply of housing.

In July of 2003 in the wake of the tech stock bubble and what many suspect was Greenspan's and the PPT manipulation of the stock market after September 11, 2001, Greenspan cut the overnight bank interest rate to an unbelievable one percent and sent strong signals to the financial and banking communities that lending, particularly home loan and home equity lending, were strongly encouraged. Greenspan was going to use his working-class and lower middle-class "piggy bank." He wanted to use the American people's home equity to induce more consumer spending to shore up the economy. He knew Americans had billions of untapped wealth sitting as equity in their homes, and that many more Americans could be encouraged to buy new homes thereby creating new wealth by using the new securitized debt instruments and creating a demand for these products, so Greenspan sent signals to the financial community to take advantage of this situation. He also encouraged the use of the derivative markets to facilitate these investments.

President Bush lent his support by encouraging consumers to spend — to help their country. In the wake of September 11 and the tech stock bubble, it became, according to the President, "patriotic" to borrow and spend. Unfortunately, many of those in the working class and lower middle class who could not afford this spending went along anyway, partly because they were greatly encouraged by their President, and their borrowing was facilitated and urged by their trusted financial advisors and their banks.

Greenspan was going to stimulate the largest segment of the economy, consumer spending, into action. Greenspan gave the green light and mortgage debt in America went from about 4.9 billion dollars to about ten billion dollars, an increase in 102 percent in just six years. Greenspan allowed and promoted the use of risky new financial instruments, such as mortgage backed securities, collateralized debt obligations and asset backed securities coupled to the derivative markets to facilitate the financing of this unprecedented debt spending, and with his bias for regulation he turned an even more blind eye in making sure they were secure. He believed they could regulate themselves.

There is also some speculation that the financial institutions also received some assurances from Greenspan possibly in his role as the implementer of the PPT that the government would back some of these risks, which is why many have speculated that the financial institutions needed to be and were bailed out when these debts went bad. Greenspan resigned when he realized it was all going bad. It is apparent that Greenspan resigned when he did because he didn't want the financial mess he created accredited to his legacy.

During his bubble buildup, Greenspan had signaled to the lenders that the regulators were less concerned with regulating and more interested in stimulating lending, thus encouraging a wave of predatory lending the likes of which we haven't seen in modern times. After the bubble burst the FBI investigated over 800 cases of corporate mortgage fraud in 2007. In 2008 that number sky-rocketed to over 1200 cases as the housing crisis worsened.

This lack of regulatory oversight also encouraged the prolific use of "stated income loans" called by many in the trade, "liar loans." A liar loan is a loan made on the basis of the borrower providing a statement of annual income which isn't verified by the lender, which means a borrower can put down any amount they need to qualify for a home loan. And it appears they did. It also appears that this lying was frequently encouraged by their lenders telling borrowers not to worry because if they got in trouble they could likely sell their home for a higher amount and make a profit.

The *Washington Post* reported a study by the Mortgage Asset Research Institute showing that ninety percent of stated income loan borrowers had overstated their income and that sixty percent had overstated their income by more than fifty percent. It was apparent that many loan officers and mortgage brokers who were paid by commissions had deliberately looked the other way when these borrowers lied. In fact there are many cases in which the lenders told the borrowers exactly how much income to put on loan documents to get these loans, knowing full well that it was a lie and fraudulent. Many of these borrowers were low income working-class people who were duped into these arrangements by hungry predatory lenders seeking fees and commission who were assuring these customers that this was how the system worked. Frequently these predatory loan officers were under the direction of their institutions which encouraged these practices by giving the loan officers bonuses for volume and cared little about the borrower's ability to repay since they were selling the loans to the secondary markets.

CNN reported that in the 2003 there were about $60 billion in liar loans, but by 2006 that number had increased to $386 billion with a hundred million each in the last three quarters.

Three of the largest lenders of stated income loans were IndyMac Bancorp, Countrywide Financial and Washington Mutual. Because of these loans IndyMac failed in 2008 it was the fourth largest bank failure in United States history. The financially troubled Countrywide collapsed and was bought out by Bank of America at the urging of the regulators, and Washington Mutual in 2008 became the largest bank failure in United States history. By the spring of 2009 the F.D.I.C. reported that 46 U.S. banks had failed costing the American taxpayers well over $20 billion. It was money that would come out of the pockets of America's workers and principally the working class.

Greenspan also has a previous history with failed bank institutions and real estate lending. In 1984 before he became the Fed Chair, Greenspan was hired as a consultant by Charles Keating's infamous Lincoln Savings and Loan to intervene and assure the Federal Home Loan Bank of San Francisco that Lincoln Savings and Loan was financially sound so they could receive more money. Greenspan wrote of Lincoln at that time that Lincoln's management had succeeded "in a relatively short period of time in reviving an association that had become badly burdened by a large portfolio of long-term fixed-rate mortgages" and that they had "restored the association to a vibrant and healthy state, with a strong net worth position."

Despite Greenspan's glowing assessment of their financial condition, Lincoln Savings and Loan failed a short time later and cost the American taxpayer $3.4 billion. Ironically Lincoln's failure was because of their real estate lending, which Greenspan had specifically reviewed to give this glowing recommendation. Greenspan has a long history of giving more faith and credit to real estate investments than is warranted.

In the aftermath of his actions, in an interview with *CNBC* Greenspan said it was unfair to blame him for the housing bubble or the financial crisis and defended his policies and actions. "I have no regrets on any of the Federal Reserve policies that we initiated back then..." "Clearly, certain of our anticipations of what would happen as a consequence of those policies were off, but there was no way of avoiding that."

It was a lie. Greenspan is a slow learner or has other goals in mind, and because of this hundreds of thousands of working-class and lower middle-class people lost jobs, pensions and homes and the American and world economy went into crisis.

In 2007 Richard Moore, the State Treasurer of North Carolina, whose state pensions were threatened by severe stock losses in Countrywide, asked the Securities Exchange Commission (SEC) to review the actions of the former Countrywide CEO Angelo Mozilo. While Countrywide stock plummeted from $45 per share down to $4 in a year, and 12,000 Countrywide employees lost their jobs, and thousands of customers lost their homes to foreclosure, Mozilo made $138 million in what Moore claimed were questionable sales of Countrywide stock options. Moore said in his letter to the SEC that "Mozilo has been stuffing his pockets" at the expense of pensioners, employees and homebuyers. Moore accused Countrywide of "questionable loan practices."

The working class were the primary victims in the bubble burst and have also been unfairly blamed for this crisis. In an interesting footnote, during this unprecedented homebuyer frenzy, many families with children were still denied mortgages. According to the National Housing Conference while the nation was celebrating the fact that the homeownership rate had increased from 65 percent of all Americans in 1978, to 69 percent in 2005, the homeownership rate actually declined substantially for families with children from 70.5 percent in 1978 to only 55 percent in 2005. During this unprecedented housing boom and in the aftermath of the America's largest housing bubble burst, working-class families and their children became less likely to own a home.

The working class in the wake of the financial crisis are becoming more poor, and since they are a majority of the nation's population, and we are a consumer society with at least two thirds of our economy dependent upon their consumer spending, the economic supremacy of the United States may share their fate.

In 2009 Brooksley Born was awarded the John F. Kennedy Profiles in Courage Award for her vision and her attempts to regulate the financial markets and prevent the financial crisis. In October 2009 the *PBS* television documentary show *Frontline* presented a show called *The Warning* which documented Born's attempts to prevent economic crisis and fraud and how her efforts were vehemently opposed by Greenspan, Rubin and Lawrence Summers.

Perhaps the irony is that President Obama in 2009 appointed Lawrence Summers Director of the White House National Economic Council. It is Summers and Treasury Secretary Timothy Geithner, who was Under Secretary of Treasury for International Affairs under Rubin and who also claims Rubin and Summers as his mentors, who are now trying to clean up the financial crisis they all helped make.

In addition to opposing Born on trying to regulate the derivative industry, in 2008 Summers, as the then Harvard University President, came under fire in a *Vanity Fair* article where he was accused of losing approximately $1 billion of Harvard's money in financial derivatives. And now it is he and his mentee, Geithner, who are looking out for the future financial interests of America's working class.

In testimony before Congress in October 23, 2008, Greenspan admitted that he was "partially" wrong in opposing financial regulations and said, "Those of us who have looked to the self-interest of lending institutions to protect shareholder's equity, myself especially, are in a state of shocked disbelief." Referring to the free-market ideology, Greenspan stated, "I have found a flaw. I don't know how significant or permanent it is. But I have been very distressed by that fact." After months of refusing to accept blame, when pressed by Congressman Henry Waxman, Greenspan admitted fault in opposing regulation and acknowledged that the financial institutions had not protected their investments as well as he expected.

Greenspan had failed to protect the American people and had failed as the watchdog and regulator of America's treasure. In the financial crisis caused by him, his greatest victims are the American working class who lost their homes or their home equity, their pensions, their jobs, many lost their health insurance and they lost millions of dollars that could have been spent on their welfare. It is ironically they and their financial troubles who are blamed by some for this crisis and it is they and their families who will pay the highest price for Greenspan's failures.

Conclusion: The American Slave Class

> "The strongest bond of human sympathy outside the family relation should be one uniting working people of all nations" —Abraham Lincoln

> "Representative government means, chiefly, representation of business interests." Thorstein Veblen, The Theory of the leisure class

You can only have a king if you have many peasants. You can only have the super-rich if you have many who are poor. And these fundamentals are the basis of class. The primary purpose of democratic government and society is to provide for the welfare of the lead, not just their leaders; to provide for the masses, not just their masters.

In America economic slavery is systemic; it is part of the woven fabric of its history, religion and her institutions. America was founded on the backs of slaves and indentured servants. Since the abolition of Black slavery and a constitution that prohibits men from owning other men, the upper classes have struggled to find ways to support themselves on the backs of the working class, and they have successfully designed new systems to replace the old slave system. These systems have provided for unprecedented wealth for the leisure class at the expense of and because of the economic enslavement of the working class.

The new slave system of wage slaves has had a variety of forms some more egregious than others, but with the same devastating results upon the working class: a lack of upward mobility, low and unsupportable wages, a lack of opportunity including education, and a fatalistic culture supported by religion that has them believe that they, the working class, are getting what they deserve.

In the South slavery was replaced by share croppers and eventually by low wage factory and retail workers, who unlike their Northern counterparts, were not allowed to unionize and suffered low wages and received no benefits.

The South had always viewed the Civil War and its on-going struggle with the North as more of an economic and cultural clash rather than one just confined to slavery. Large Southern corporations such as Wal-Mart and Tyson Chicken began to dominate the American economic agenda with their Southern economic culture, and they have institutionalized their form of economic slavery nationwide. Even the President Clinton and Secretary of State Clinton, were cozy with and served on the boards of these two mega-corporations furthering their economic agendas.

The North and West were not immune from their own history of slave institutions. Sweat shops and migrant farm workers are also forms of economic slavery. The service sector with its fast food chains and the Targets, and now the Wal-Marts function as slave institutions with low wages, limited benefits, and they have now become the national economy. Working conditions, wages and benefits for the working class have deteriorated, and in the case of Wal-Mart there are even documented cases of many workers who are forced to work part of the time for free in violation of federal labor laws in order to keep their jobs. This is economic slavery. The working class is only allowed the freedom of choosing which corporate master to serve, but there is no real economic freedom because almost all offer low wages that are unsupportable, offer inadequate or no health insurance, and little or no retirement and other benefits, and give their workers no rights, no status, and no hope.

Slavery is an on-going American institution. It is endemic in American Christian culture and is now perceived to be a necessary part of Capitalism. The irony of the American democracy is that slavery in many forms has been the economic engine, and this perceived success provides the excuse for its continuance. But what is success if the working majority struggles? Is it success if the corporate bottom line is rich, but all of their workers are poor?

And while slavery has had the most devastating historic effects upon African Americans, the devastation isn't confined to them. The devastation has included white and Native American indentured servants, white and Black share croppers, Latino, Asian and white farm workers, and factory sweatshop workers. And it now includes today's service and retail workers.

Today's slave class includes almost all working-class people, and although people of color are impacted by greater percentages, the majority of the slave class is white, and poverty and its consequences claims people of all ethnicities and races.

And only when America recognizes these class problems and corrects these injustices will America's true cultural and economic potential be realized. America is a consumer society, with an economy that is two thirds or more dependent on consumer spending. The path to a grand economy lies in the realization that if the great American working class were given their fair share of the wealth, there would be more wealth for everyone including the middle class and leisure classes.

When the American working class is finally able to live life with the freedom of opportunity and choices, and to know that to follow the rules and laws of their rulers are acts of citizenship and charity and not a religious requirement or a forced duty, only then will America be rid of the legacy of economic slavery.

Bibliography

Analysis of Business Models and Financial Feasibility of Fringe Banking Institutions, by Daniel Liebsohn, Published 2005 The Community Economic Development Press.

The Aquarian Conspiracy, by Marilyn Ferguson, Published 1980 J.P. Tarcher Inc.

Community Capitalism, by Richard P. Taub, Published 1988 Harvard Business School Press.

The Acquisitive Society, by R.H. Tawney, Published 1920 Harcourt, Brace and Howe.

Bad Money, by Kevin Phillips, Published 2008 Viking Press.

Blink, by Malcom Gladwell, Published 2005 Little, Brown & Co.

Bobos in Paradise, by David Brooks, Published 2000 Simon & Schuster.

Class, by Paul Fussel, Published 1992 Simon & Schuster.

Domestic Revolutions: A Social History of American Family Life, by Susan Kellogg and Steven Mintz, Published 1988 by The Free Press.

Dress for Success, by John T. Molloy, Published 1975 Grand Central Publishing.

The End of Work, by Jeremy Rifkin, Published 1995 Putnam Publishing Group.

The Epic of America, by James Truslow Adams, Published 1941 Triangle Books.

Fast Food Nation, by Eric Schlosser, Published 2001 Houghton Mifflin Co.

The Feminine Mystique, by Betty Freidan, 1963 Dell Books.

The Founding of New England, by James Truslow Adams, Published 1921 Atlantic Monthly Press.

The General Theory of Employment Interest and Money, by John Maynard Keynes, Published 1935 Macmillan Cambridge University Press.

The Grapes of Wrath, by John Steinbeck, Published 1940 Viking Press.

The History of the United States of America, by George Bancroft, Published 1895 D. Appleton & Co.

The House of Bondage, by Wright Kauffman, Published 1910 Moffat, Yard & Co.

The Informant, by Kurt Eichenwald, Published 2000 Broadway Books.

Memorable Providences, by Reverend Cotton Mather, Printed 1689 and sold by Joseph Brunning.

Modern History, by Carlton J.H. Hayes and Parker Thomas Moon, Published 1928 Macmillan Co.

Nickel and Dimed, by Barbara Ehrenreich, Published 2001 Henry Holt & Co.

One Nation Underprivileged, by Mark Robert Rank, Published 2004 Oxford University Press.

Outliers, by Malcom Gladwell, Published 2008 Little, Brown & Co.

Inequality in the Age of Decline, by Paul Blumberg, Published 1980 Oxford University Press.

The Oxford History of the America People, by Samuel Eliot Morison, Published 1965 Oxford University Press.

The Principles of the Political Economy, by J.S. Mill Published, 1848 Longmans, Green & Company.

The Promised Land, by Nicholas Lemann, Published 1991 Alfred A. Knopf Inc.

Selections from Essays in Sociology, Max Weber as translated by H.H. Gerth and C. Wright Mills, Published 1946 Oxford University Press.

Social Darwinism in American Thought, by Richard Hofstadter, Published 1944 University of Pennsylvania Press.

The Theory of the Leisure Class, by Thorstein Veblen, Published 1912 Macmillan & Co.

Wealth and Democracy, by Kevin Phillips, Published 2002 Broadway Books.

The Wealth of Nations, by Adam Smith Published, 1776 Methuen & Company.

Webster's New Universal Unabridged Dictionary, Published 1996 Barnes & Noble Books.

Media Sources

American Demographics Magazine November 1, 2001 *Millennial Myths*.

——December 1, 2001 *Leisurely Occupations*

——August 1, 2001 The Zogby Polls, *Race and Politics*,

——December 2002 The Middle to Upper Class Middle Class. *The George Barna Group*

——March 1, 2003 *Religious Identity and Mobility*.

The Christian Science Monitor: April 29, 2002. L.A.'s Darkest Days by Daniel B. Wood.

—— July 15, 2002 *Police Incident Shows How LA Has Changed* by Daniel B. Wood.

CNBC: July 31, 2008 *Greenspan Interview*.

CNN: March 19, 2007 *Liar Loans: Mortgages Beyond Subprime* by Chris Isadore.

Nashville Business Journal: June 19, 2009 *Davis Hopes to Bring New Brand of Mortgage Firm* by Jeannie Naujeck.

The Financial Times: February 21, 2002 *Japan's Stock Buying Body*.

The Gallup Poll December 24, 2008 *The Complex Relationship between Religion and Purpose.* April 6, 2007 *Just Why Do American Attend Church?.*

The New York Times May 15-26, 2005 a series of Articles: *Class Matters*.

——February 27, 2009 *Scandinavian Non-believers* by Peter Steinfels.

——March 23, 2008 *Gap in Life Expectancy Widens for Nation* by Robert Pear.

Bibliography

Newsweek: December 8, 2003 An Abortion Foe's End.

PBS: June 17, 2003 POV: Flag Wars, by Linda Goode Bryant and Laura Poitras.

PBS: October 20, 2009 Frontline: The Warning.

Reuters: May 1, 2007 Fewer Employers Offer Health Benefits Study.

Standard & Poor's Annual Compensation Survey.

Time Magazine: September 18, 2006 Does God Want You to Be Rich?.

Vanity Fair: December 2009 Endless Summers by William D. Cohen.

The Wall Street Journal: October 27, 1989 Interview with Federal Reserve Governor Robert Heller.

The Washington Post: July 30, 2005 Lies Are Growing in Loan Process by Kenneth R. Harney.

Government and Nonprofit Research Entities and Publications

The Community Reinvestment Act of 1977, (12 U.S.C. 2901) Regulation BB (12 CFR 228).

Columbia University National Center for Children in Poverty: December 2009 Ten Important Questions About Child Poverty.

Economic Policy Institute: Online Downloads, Chapter 1. The State of Working America, February 6, 2007 Economic Opportunity and Poverty in America, July 24, 2001 One in Three Families with Three Children Can't Afford Basics....

Families USA: Press Release September 10, 2009.

JALA International, Telework and Telecommuting Frequently Asked Questions.

Kaiser Foundation: September 15, 2009 Family Health Premiums,

——September 11, 2007 Kaiser/ HRET Health Benefit Survey.

The Luxembourg Income Study and Anti-Poverty Program Comparisons.

The National Housing Conference, Center for Housing Policy: May 18, 2004, "Homeownership on the Decline Among America's families with Children."

The Pew Research Center January 24, 2003 Religion, Voting and the Campaign.

The United Nations Center for Strategic and International Studies.

The United Nations Development Programme: Annual Report Living Up to Commitments.

The U.S. Census.

The U.S. Department of Housing and Urban Development February 28, 2007 and July 9, 2008 Annual Homeless Assessment Report to Congress.

The Webster Commission, The City in Crisis. A Report by a Special Advisor to the Board of Police Commissioners on the Civil Disorder in Los Angeles, The Institute for Government and Public Affairs, UCLA, 1992.

Song Lyrics

Detroit City, 1963 Performed by Bobby Bare written by Danny Dill and Mel Tillis.